The Music of Lennox Berkeley

The Music of Lennox Berkeley

Peter Dickinson

THE BOYDELL PRESS

First published 1988

Second, revised, edition 2003
The Boydell Press, Woodbridge

ISBN 0 85115 936 2

The Boydell Press is an imprint of Boydell & Brewer Ltd
PO Box 9, Woodbridge, Suffolk IP12 3DF, UK
and of Boydell & Brewer Inc.
PO Box 41026, Rochester, NY 14604–4126, USA
website: www.boydell.co.uk

A catalogue record for this book is available
from the British Library

Library of Congress Cataloging-in-Publication Data
Dickinson, Peter.
The music of Lennox Berkeley / Peter Dickinson. 2nd rev. ed.
p. cm.
Includes bibliographical references (p.) and index.
ISBN 0851159362 (alk. paper)
1. Berkeley, Lennox, Sir, 1903 Criticism and interpretation. I. Title.
ML410.B4978 D43 2003
780′.92 dc21 2002152646

This publication is printed on acid-free paper

Typeset by Joshua Associates Ltd, Oxford
Printed in Great Britain by
St Edmundsbury Press Ltd, Bury St Edmunds, Suffolk

Contents

Foreword to the first edition vii
Foreword to the second, revised edition ix
Acknowledgements x
List of music examples xiii
List of plates xvii

1. The search for a style 1
2. Growing confidence 25
3. Maturity 43
4. The piano 63
5. Voices 87
6. Religious music 101
7. Grand opera 127
8. Operas comic and biblical 142
9. New directions 159
10. Final years 170

Appendix 1: List of works 201
Appendix 2: Writings by Berkeley 211
Appendix 3: Selected writings about Berkeley 213

Index to Berkeley's works 215
General index 217

Foreword to the first edition

I first came across Berkeley's music as a schoolboy in the music shop at Cambridge in the early 1950s: the Piano Sonata, the Five Short Pieces, the Preludes, the Mazurkas and more. I was captivated by the composer's ear for harmony, his melodic aim and his purely personal fantasy which combine to make his music unique. For more than thirty years I have followed his development work by work, and it has been a privilege to have been in touch with him and his family for most of that time. From Berkeley's sixtieth birthday onwards I have written regular tributes, interviews or studies of his work and I have also been involved in performances, broadcasts and recordings with my sister, Meriel. I have watched the music stand the test of time.

It is a fascinating experience to follow the development of a creative artist and to try to account for his individuality. The process involves unravelling the strands of personality and exploring both strengths and weaknesses. A good composer deserves no less. After gathering material for many years I am presenting it at a time when the composer's oeuvre is complete. After this prolonged study my admiration for both the man and his music is undiminished. If anything I am even more amazed that a personality with very human insecurities in his creative make-up could win through to the achievement of Berkeley's finest works, which I have consistently found to be on the highest level of British music in this century.

Some of his challenges have been those of his time and context. As so often, England was a discouraging environment for a young composer, so Berkeley escaped to Paris. He almost over-corrected under the extended tutelage of Nadia Boulanger but eventually returned to England and the influence of Britten. As a remedy this too was extreme because Britten was unique and Berkeley immediately understood. It is enormously to Berkeley's credit that he went on to find his own path through using Britten's dominance creatively. My quotations from Berkeley's letters to Britten reveal what he felt at the time – it must have been more intimidating than anyone realised. Other composers may now have been dwarfed by Britten – the survival of the fittest operates ruthlessly – but not Berkeley. His diffidence notwithstanding, his unassuming qualities both personally and artistically have shown a quiet strength and have nourished what I believe will turn out to be a lasting reputation. Somehow this achievement is the core of music, removed from egotism and self-promotion, and in the end this is what reaches musicians and audiences rather than the passing fashions of the moment. Surely this is what lies behind Mozart's G minor Quintet, which Berkeley, in a letter to Britten on 11 November 1940, called 'almost the greatest masterpiece in all music'. That understanding, allied with the spiritual purity of a composer who could say to a friend and colleague, as Berkeley did to Britten, that he liked his music better even than his own, makes for a rare temperament. Few composers have been as generous as that.

If a composer's music has communicated and has been found rewarding over many years, then nothing is lost by a critical approach. Scrutiny shows reasons for what one's instinct knew all along. It is in that spirit that I have chosen some works for examination out of a large output, not all of which could be considered. From this point of view the chamber music may have suffered since Berkeley's style was largely defined elsewhere. The works I have selected are there in their own right as well as landmarks in the composer's development. Berkeley's vintage years seem to me to be the 1940s and, to a slightly lesser degree, the 1950s. But the early music should not be as forgotten as it is, and that of the later 1960s is a remarkable move into new territory dependent neither on Britten nor anyone else. This music too, like later Stravinsky, is little known to the wider public. Its time will come.

Peter Dickinson,
London, 1988

Foreword to the second, revised edition

I am particularly grateful for the support which has made this second edition possible since the complete revision involved has allowed me to revise some judgements, to correct some imbalances and to add considerable extra material taken from interviews not long after the composer's death on 26 December 1989. *The Music of Lennox Berkeley* had a generous welcome from reviewers when it came out in 1988 and I have been able to remedy some omissions pointed out by old friends of the composer such as Winton Dean and the late Desmond Shawe-Taylor. I was also especially pleased to have been able to give the composer a copy of the book in the last months of his life and, in spite of his illness, I think he realised what it was.

The material from my interviews broadens the picture of Berkeley and supports the claims I have been making for his finest works for over forty years with evidence from performers, colleagues and pupils. I have retained and clarified my discussion of the actual music. Technical matters will not appeal to all readers, who can simply skip those pages, but such information shows that Berkeley bears detailed scrutiny as a way of accounting for what was already known through the experience of the music itself.

I have not provided a discography with this book. Some early recordings of Berkeley are disapppointing, others ought to have been reissued, and fortunately many new ones are emerging for the centenary in 2003. Any discography now would soon be out of date and reference can easily be made to current record catalogues. However, in the book itself I have referred to a number of recordings of importance as part of the career of individual works.

I hope that this revised and much extended version of *The Music of Lennox Berkeley* will direct many more performers and listeners to the music itself. That will be my reward – and theirs.

Peter Dickinson,
Aldeburgh, 2002

Acknowledgements

First edition (1988)

Many people have helped to make the first study of Berkeley's music possible. To begin with, the composer himself, who generously collaborated in interviews with me on many occasions over the years. The encouragement of Lady Berkeley has also been essential and I am grateful for permission to use quotations from unpublished letters. Donald Mitchell kindly read the typescript, made valuable suggestions, and provided the extracts from Britten's letters. The American researcher Joan Redding ingeniously brought to light published and unpublished Berkeley material from which this study has benefited.

I have had discussions or correspondence with many performers connected with Berkeley's music: these included Sir Peter Pears, Sir William Glock, Colin Horsley, John Francis and Mrs Mary Bernard, widow of the conductor Anthony Bernard. Tony Scotland gave me some details of Berkeley's family history. My unsuccessful efforts to trace Berkeley's early Auden songs at Oxford were aided by Sean Day-Lewis, Simon Heighes, and by Peter Ward Jones and his colleagues at the Bodleian Library. Other librarians who helped with details of Berkeley's early life were Mrs S. J. Davis at St George's School, Harpenden; M. J. Barrett at Gresham's School, Holt; R. Highfield at Merton College; and the staff at the BBC libraries.

I am grateful to the Britten-Pears Library, especially Rosamund Strode, for access to Britten manuscripts; to Boosey and Hawkes for access to files concerning Berkeley and permission to print extracts from works by Britten; and to Novellos. My overwhelming debt in the publishing field is of course to Berkeley's major publisher, Chester Music, and the staff there. Over many years my enquiries have been comprehensively dealt with, regardless of time and trouble.

I am pleased to have been able to quote from the film *Composers* about Sir Lennox and Michael Berkeley made for ATV Network Ltd, with Richie Stewart as director and J. B. J. Berrow as producer. I want to thank John Bishop for patiently nurturing this project as a result of our shared enthusiasm for the composer. Above all I thank my wife, Bridget, who read typescript and proofs and was a constant supporter of the book and its author at all stages.

Peter Dickinson,
London, 1988

Second, revised edition (2003)

In returning to Lennox Berkeley and his music to rewrite this book I am greatly indebted to Lady Berkeley for allowing me to consult family papers and to Tony Scotland for reading the typescript and most generously sharing his research with me. The opportunity to consult Lennox Berkeley's diaries and borrow original photographs from the family archives has been a great asset. I am also reminded of how much I owe the late Sheila MacCrindle, at Chester Music for many years, for her encouragement and enthusiasm. Further I valued the dedication of the late John Bishop whose catalogue, Thames Publishing, supported so many worthy causes which would never have reached publication without his determined interest.

This time I have benefited enormously from having been able to quote from detailed interviews given to me by Lady Berkeley, Michael Berkeley, Julian Bream, Colin Horsley, Sir John Manduell, Nicholas Maw, Malcolm Williamson and the late Basil Douglas, Desmond Shawe-Taylor and Norman del Mar. I gratefully acknowledge permission from the BBC to use material from my Radio 3 documentary 'Lennox Berkeley' broadcast on 31 August 1992, repeated on 13 September 1994, and produced by Arthur Johnson.

Since the first edition of this book came out, detailed research by Joan Redding and Stewart Craggs has made it possible to produce a more accurate list of works and some scores thought to have been lost have been found. Most of the manuscripts are now in the British Library. Another development has been the founding of the Lennox Berkeley Society by Kathleen Walker and Jim Nichol in 1999 – www.lennoxberkeley.org.uk – which has brought together enthusiasts for Berkeley's music, and its growing membership acts as a focus of interest and information.

Once again I thank James Rushton at Chester Music for permission to quote a large number of music examples. I am again grateful to the staff of the Britten-Pears Library, now directed by Jenny Doctor. The quotations from the letters of Benjamin Britten are copyright the Trustees of the Britten-Pears Foundation and may not be further reproduced without the written permission of the Trustees. Quotations from the letters of Lennox Berkeley to Benjamin Britten are reproduced courtesy of the Britten-Pears Library and the Lennox Berkeley Estate. Acknowledgements to music publishers are given in the list of music examples.

I am particularly fortunate to have had the experienced guidance of Nigel Fortune at the copy-editing stage and have much valued the interest and dedication of all the staff at Boydell and Brewer – initially Caroline Palmer and later Pru Harrison.

Grants towards this publication have been made equally by the Charlotte Bonham-Carter Trust and a private donor. Without this support it would not have been possible for this much enlarged and substantially rewritten edition to have appeared at all. Every attempt has been made to obtain the necessary permissions but if anything has been omitted this will be rectified at the next opportunity.

Peter Dickinson,
Aldeburgh, 2002

Music examples

All works are by Berkeley unless otherwise stated and these are copyright Chester Music and reproduced by permission. Other publishers are indicated.

1. Rondeau (*Three Early Songs*, No. 3), *Joyeux et animé* 6
2. Toccata for piano, *Vif* 7
3. *Tombeaux*, 'Le Tombeau du Sapho', *Très lent* 11
4. *Tombeaux*, 'Le Tombeau de Socrate', *Moderato* 11
5a. Suite for orchestra, Sinfonia, *Allegro moderato* 13
5b. Poulenc: Sonata for piano duet, Finale, *Très vite* 14
© J. & W. Chester, 1919
6. Suite for orchestra, Aria, figure 1 14
7. *Trois Poèmes de Vildrac*, No. 3 15
8. *Nelson*, Act II, figure 75 15
9. Ballet, *Java* 21
10. Ballet (untitled), *Andante* 22
11. Violin and Piano Sonata No. 2, Op. 1, *Andante* 25
12. Polka for two pianos, Op. 5 26
13. Polka for two pianos, 7 bars after figure 3 27
14. Walton: Polka from *Façade*, figure 2 27
© Oxford University Press 1951. Reproduced by permission
15. Three Pieces for piano, Op. 2, No. 2 28
16. *Jonah*, Op. 3, figure 106 31
17. *Jonah*, 4 bars after figure 128 32
18. Overture, Op. 8, *Allegro* 33
19. Britten: 'Night covers up the rigid land', *Andante con moto* 38
© The Britten Estate 1997
Text © W. H. Auden 1936, all rights reserved
Reproduced by permission of Boosey & Hawkes Music Publishers Ltd
20. Britten: 'Night covers up the rigid land', bar 39 38
Boosey and Hawkes
21. Berkeley: 'Night covers up the rigid land', last 11 bars 40
22. Britten: *Albert Herring*, Act I, scene 2, p. 133, line 2, bar 2 41
© Hawkes & Son (London) Ltd 1948
Text © Hawkes & Son (London) Ltd 1947
Reproduced by permission of Boosey & Hawkes Music Publishers Ltd
23. Serenade, Op. 12, *Vivace* 44
24. Serenade, *Andantino* 45
25. Serenade, *Lento* 46

26. Sonatina for recorder and piano, Op. 13, *Adagio* 51
27. Symphony No. 1, Op. 16, *Allegro moderato* 55
28. Symphony No. 1, *Allegro moderato*, bar 43 56
29. Symphony No. 1, *Allegretto* 56
30. Symphony No. 1, *Allegretto*, bar 70 57
31. Symphony No. 1, *Lento* 58
32. Symphony No. 1, *Allegro* 60
33. Six Preludes, Op. 23, No. 2 65
34a. Six Preludes, No. 3 67
34b. Six Preludes, No. 3, bar 31 68
35. Poulenc: *Trois Pièces*, No. 2, bar 25 69
© Heugel 1931. Reproduced by permission
36. Six Preludes, No. 4, *Allegretto* 70
37. Six Preludes, No. 6, *Andante* 71
38. Piano Sonata, Op. 20, *Moderato* 75
39. Piano Sonata, *Moderato* 75
40. Piano Sonata, *Adagio* 75
41. Piano Concerto, Op. 29, *Allegro moderato* 79
42. Piano Concerto, *Allegro moderato*, figure 10 80
43. Piano Concerto, *Allegro moderato*, figure 26 80
44. Piano Concerto, *Andante* 81
45. Piano Concerto, *Andante*, figure 4 82
46. Piano Concerto, *Vivace (Alla breve)* 83
47. Piano Concerto, *Vivace*, figure 4 83
48. *Five Housman Songs*, No. 5, *Andantino* 90
49. Britten: *Rejoice in the Lamb*, Op. 30, *Lento*, tenor solo 94
© Boosey & Co. Ltd 1943
Reproduced by permission of Boosey & Hawkes Music Publishers Ltd
50. *A Festival Anthem*, Op. 21, *Andantino*, treble solo 95
51. Britten: *Rejoice in the Lamb*, *Con brio* 96
© Boosey & Co. Ltd 1943
Reproduced by permission of Boosey & Hawkes Music Publishers Ltd
52. *A Festival Anthem*, figure 11 97
53. *A Festival Anthem*, figure 26 98
54. Britten: *Billy Budd*, Op. 50, Act I, scene 2, p. 185, bars 1–4 99
© Hawkes & Son Ltd 1951
Reproduced by permission of Boosey & Hawkes Music Publishers Ltd
55. *Four Poems of St Teresa of Avila*, Op. 27, No. 1, *Moderato* 103
56. Britten: *Sinfonia da Requiem*, Op. 20, 9 bars after figure 1 105
© Hawkes & Son Ltd 1942
Reproduced by permission of Boosey & Hawkes Music Publishers Ltd
57. *Four Poems of St Teresa of Avila*, No. 1, 3 bars before figure 2 105
58. *Four Poems of St Teresa of Avila*, No. 1, 5 bars before figure 3 106
59. *Four Poems of St Teresa of Avila*, No. 1, 2 bars before figure 6 107
60. *Four Poems of St Teresa of Avila*, No. 2, *Allegro* 108

61. *Four Poems of St Teresa of Avila*, No. 2, 2 bars before figure 8 109
62. *Four Poems of St Teresa of Avila*, No. 3, *Andante* 110
63. *Four Poems of St Teresa of Avila*, No. 3, figure 1 111
64. *Four Poems of St Teresa of Avila*, No. 3, 3 bars before figure 3 112
65. *Four Poems of St Teresa of Avila*, No. 4, *Allegro moderato* 113
66. *Four Poems of St Teresa of Avila*, No. 4, 2 bars before figure 5 114
67. *Stabat Mater*, Op. 28, I, figure 3 117
68. *Stabat Mater*, V, bar 3 119
69. *Stabat Mater*, VII, *Moderato* 119
70. *Stabat Mater*, IX, 5 bars after figure 37 119
71. *Stabat Mater*, X, figure 40 120
72. *Stabat Mater*, X, figure 44 121
73. *Stabat Mater*, X, 6 bars after figure 45 123
74. *Nelson*, Act I, figure 21 131
75. *Nelson*, Act 1, figure 22 132
76. *Nelson*, Act II, scene 1, opening 133
77. *Nelson*, Act II, scene 1, figure 1 133
78. *Nelson*, Act II, 7 bars after figure 22 134
79. *Nelson*, Act II, figure 61 135
80. *Nelson*, Act II, figure 75 136
81. *Nelson*, Act III, 2 bars before figure 62 137
82. *Nelson*, Act III, 6 bars after figure 79 138
83. *A Dinner Engagement*, Op. 45, figure 11 143
84. *A Dinner Engagement*, scene 1, figure 22 144
85. *A Dinner Engagement*, scene 1, figure 29 145
86. *A Dinner Engagement*, scene 2, figure 56 145
87. *A Dinner Engagement*, scene 2, figure 79 146
88. *A Dinner Engagement*, scene 2, figure 90 147
89. *A Dinner Engagement*, scene, 2, figure 107 148
90. *Ruth*, Op. 50, scene 1, opening 149
91. *Ruth*, scene 1, 3 bars after figure 2 150
92. *Ruth*, scene 1, figure 21 151
93. *Ruth*, scene 2, figure 8 152
94. *Ruth*, scene 2, 10 bars after figure 13 153
95. *Ruth*, scene 2, figure 23 153
96. *Ruth*, scene 3, figure 37 154
97. *Ruth*, scene 3, figure 38 155
98. *Ruth*, scene 3, figure 43 156
99. *Ruth*, scene 3, 2 bars after figure 49 156
100. *Ruth*, scene 3, figure 56 157
101. *Concertino*, Op. 49, Aria I 162
102. Violin Concerto, Op. 59, *Lento* 165
103. Sonatina for Oboe and Piano, Op. 61, *Molto moderato* 167
104. *Castaway*, Op. 69, 2 bars before figure 8 172
105. *Castaway*, 7 bars before figure 42 173

106. Symphony No. 3, Op. 74, *Allegro moderato* 175
107. Symphony No. 3, *Lento*, figure 14 176
108. Symphony No. 3, *Lento*, 1 bar after figure 16 178
109. Symphony No. 3, *Allegro*, figure 19 178
110. String Quartet No. 3, Op. 76, *Allegro vivace* 179
111. *Hail Holy Queen* 180
112. String Quartet No. 3, *Lento* 180
113. Britten: *Songs from the Chinese*, Op. 58, No. 3, *Very quick* 182
© Boosey & Co. Ltd 1959
Reproduced by permission of Boosey & Hawkes Music Publishers Ltd
114. *Chinese Songs*, Op. 78, No. 2, *Allegretto* 183
115. Guitar Concerto, Op. 88, *Andantino*, 5 bars after figure 1 187
116. Guitar Concerto, *Andantino*, 5 bars after figure 7 189
117. *Sonnet*, Op. 102, last 8 bars 192

Plates

The plates are placed between pages 78 and 79.

1. Lennox Berkeley in the twenties
2. Lennox Berkeley in the thirties
3. Benjamin Britten and Lennox Berkeley, 1938
   Photo: Howard Coster. Benjamin Britten and Lennox Berkeley, 1938. Copyright: National Portrait Gallery. Courtesy of the Britten-Pears Library, Aldeburgh
4. Lennox Berkeley in the forties
5. Freda Berkeley
   Copyright: Camilla Panufnik
6. Lennox Berkeley rehearsing the Violin Concerto with Yehudi Menuhin, Bath Abbey 1961
7. Lennox Berkeley with painter Derek Hill and singer Billy Patterson on a rowing trip to Iona
8. Deathbed scene from the 1954 Sadler's Wells production of *Nelson*
9. Scene from the English Opera Group's 1956 production of *Ruth*, with Una Hale, Anna Pollack and April Cantelo
10. Lennox and Freda Berkeley in Julian Bream's car
11. Lennox and Freda Berkeley
12. Dr Lennox Berkeley, Oxford 1970
13. Lennox Berkeley, Witold Lutoslawski and Peter Pears at the recording session for the *Ronsard Sonnets*, 1972
14. Lennox Berkeley with Nadia Boulanger, 1973
15. Lennox and Freda Berkeley with Desmond Shawe-Taylor, 1973
16. Peter Dickinson, Sir Lennox Berkeley, Alice Artzt and Lady Berkeley outside Keele University Chapel, 1975
17. Sir Lennox Berkeley
18. The Berkeley family, 1982

1. The search for a style

All composers have to find their own way towards a style, a personal technique designed to convey the results of their imagination through music to others. Ultimately their work will be measured by the highest standards. George Steiner has rather verbosely defined genius as 'the capacity to modulate an intensely personal, private, even pathological compulsion or angle of incidence into an intelligible enunciation or form in which numerous other human beings recognise something profoundly, necessarily their own'.[1] It is no wonder that the process of finding the right starting point and selecting the conditions for development can be hazardous, especially in times and places where the arts are barely taken seriously, or where temporary fashions intervene obstructively. Amongst British composers born in the first fifteen years of the last century, Walton and Britten were child prodigies, but Tippett and Berkeley started late and made little impact until their thirties. They were all affected by the uncertainties of the inter-war period in England and its parochial climate.

Walton matured under the aegis of a family of writers – the Sitwells; Britten derived much from his collaboration with W. H. Auden, a writer whose implied left-wing views were shared by Tippett. But ideas need supplementing by technique. When Tippett was studying strict counterpoint at the Royal College of Music with R. O. Morris, Berkeley was doing the same thing with Nadia Boulanger in Paris, and Britten learnt much from Frank Bridge and from working with films and radio. Whereas Tippett maintained his position as a pacifist right through the war in England, Auden left for America. Auden's influence probably affected Britten, also a pacifist, in his decision to go to America with Peter Pears in 1939, but they returned in 1942. In a letter to Britten written the day war broke out, 3 September 1939, Berkeley wrote: 'I've always been a pacifist at heart, how can one be anything else? But I think if there ever was a case where force has got to be used, this is it.' Britten resented these sentiments and maintained his idealistic views.[2] His sister, Beth Britten, remembered in 1986:

> Although Ben was fairly content in his life with Lennox Berkeley in Snape, he felt frustrated, and unable to make headway as a composer in this country. Many

[1] *The Times*, 28 August 1987.

[2] D. Mitchell and P. Reed, eds, *Letters from a Life: Selected Letters and Diaries of Benjamin Britten, Volume 2 1939–45*, London, 1991, p. 707.

> creative artists were also feeling the spread of Nazism and Fascism in Europe and the persecution of artists under those regimes. Many had already left for the new world, among them Wystan Auden and Christopher Isherwood, and Ben was very much influenced by these older men. Peter Pears was then a member of the BBC Singers, and he had already been twice to the States.[3]

Berkeley was a contemporary of Auden at Oxford and was almost certainly the first composer to set his poetry, probably in 1926. Berkeley and Britten met at the International Society for Contemporary Music Festival at Barcelona in 1936. Ten years older than Britten and still involved with the struggle to define his own musical personality, Berkeley immediately recognised Britten's natural brilliance. It was a case of hero worship and they became friends, a crucial influence which paved the way for Berkeley's maturity as a composer during the war years.

Lennox Randal (Francis) Berkeley was born at Sunningwell Plain, near Oxford, on 12 May 1903, into an aristocratic family.[4] His grandfather was George Lennox Rawdon (1827–88), who became Seventh Earl of Berkeley on the death of a cousin in 1882, but never took his seat in the Lords. He married Cécile, daughter of Edward Drummond, Comte de Melfort, a family of French and Scots origin. In the early nineteenth century a celebrated case failed to establish the right to succession of the first seven children of the Fifth Earl of Berkeley, who were born before his legally recognised marriage to Mary Cole.[5] In the late nineteenth century, history was repeated when Cécile was unable to obtain a divorce from her elderly first husband and the first two children were born before the marriage took place. Consequently the third son of the Seventh Earl came in to the title rather than the composer's father, Captain Hastings George FitzHardinge Berkeley RN (1855–1934). He, as the eldest son, would normally have inherited the title to which Lennox Berkeley, as his only son, would have succeeded. Or, as the composer's eldest son Michael remembered:

> I remember as a child going to the school library and looking in Anthony Sampson's *Anatomy of Britain* and finding out that the Berkeleys went back to before the Norman conquest. And then he went on to refer to my father saying, 'Had it not been for irregular behaviour amongst his forebears he would have been an Earl' – the Earl of Berkeley. I was very excited about this irregular behaviour and discovered that in fact the grandparents hadn't been able to get married – one of them had already been married – and so somebody was born the wrong side of the blanket. But it does pose a rather wonderful thought. Could he possibly have got on a horse and led a hunt and looked after a castle? I think probably not. I think one can honestly say that we have all been a great deal better served by his having been a composer.[6]

[3] B. Britten (Welford), *My Brother Benjamin*, Kensal Press, Bourne End, Buckinghamshire, 1986, p. 109.

[4] Berkeley took the name Francis when he became a Roman Catholic. His birth certificate has Sunningwell Plain rather than Boars Hill, which he always gave as his birthplace.

[5] H. Costley-White, *Mary Cole, Countess of Berkeley*, London, 1961. Bernard Falk, *The Berkeleys of Berkeley Square and some of their Kinsfolk*, London, 1944.

[6] Interview with author, 27 November 1990.

Berkeley's mother was Aline Carla Harris, daughter of Sir James Harris, the British consul for Monaco. This encouraged regular visits to France during the childhood of Lennox and his older sister Geraldine but before that Berkeley's paternal grandmother, Cécile Dowager Countess of Berkeley, had a villa in Nice and shared a house with her sister, Albine Baroness van Havre in Fontainebleau. From about 1920 Berkeley's parents settled in France, where they had met, and lived near Nice – finally at Villa Melfort at Cap Ferrat.

Berkeley kept a diary from the 1960s onwards but from time to time, within its pages, wondered why he bothered. In 1978 he felt the need to explain about his family:

> My parents led a very quiet and outwardly uneventful life. I have realised since that there was a reason for this. It was certainly far from being the case with my grandparents, since they eloped and went to live abroad, my grandmother being married at the time, in order to avoid living together openly in England . . . It was, I think, shortly after their flight from England that my father and his next brother were born, and a little later my grandmother obtained a divorce. I understand now why my father chose to live as unobtrusively as possible – he was very devoted to his mother and anxious that the family situation should not be known and her somewhat unconventional life frowned upon. This, I think, shows delicacy of feeling on his part and I have always admired him for it.[7]

Berkeley's grandmother died when he was a child but when he asked Sybil Jackson, his American cousin who was also his godmother, what she was like she said: 'she was gaiety itself!'

Apart from his naval career, Berkeley's father wrote three unusual books. *Wealth and Welfare: our Trade Policy and its Cost*; *Mysticism in Modern Mathematics*; and *Japanese Letters*, an imaginary correspondence between two Japanese gentlemen recording their impressions of Paris and London. Berkeley wished his father had written more but felt 'he was modest and retiring and probably undervalued himself' – obviously a family tradition!

In spite of the French connections, Lennox's early education was conventionally English. He attended Lynam's (later the Dragon School) at Oxford briefly as a dayboy since at that time his parents lived in north Oxford off the Woodstock Road. He had a bicycle but he remembered horse-drawn trams on the Banbury Road. Sybil Jackson, at the age of ninety-five, remembered him even before that:

> I can remember when he was only about three. I used to sing – Schubert and things – and I can remember him standing there absolutely motionless, watching and listening. It was the first time I noticed he was at all musical. He was a tiny little chap. He always asked, though, when I went to the house – would I sing?[8]

[7] L. Berkeley diary, August 1978.

[8] A. Wood, 'Lennox Berkeley, 70, hits the high point of his career', *Oxford Mail*, 3 August 1973.

From 1914 to 1918 Berkeley was a boarder at Gresham's School, Holt. Two years after he left Gresham's, Auden entered the school and ten years later Britten arrived: none of them overlapped at this stage. The writer John Pudney was a contemporary of Auden:

> In my time the school was neither consciously progressive nor in any sense dedicated to the arts. Indeed the headmaster divided his interest between God and physics. There was great emphasis on science, none whatever on classics or English. The lack of formal encouragement of the arts was healthy enough in that it went hand in hand with an atmosphere of live and let live. Nobody was lauded for artistic activities, nor was anyone decried. Most important of all, nobody had the arts thrust down their throats. Such people as Wystan Auden and Benjamin Britten, who were there during that particularly fruitful decade, came through unscathed.[9]

From the winter term of 1919 until the end of the following calendar year, Berkeley was at St George's School, Harpenden. It appears that the first performance of any music of his took place there – a work in a concert of cello and piano music on 26 June 1920. The future composer of profoundly felt religious works gained the Certificate in the Diocesan Scripture Examination in the Winter Term that year and – maybe with characteristic disengagement – spoke at the Debating Society on a motion 'That All is Vanity'. According to Peter Collis, 'Berkeley seconded the proposition, drawing attention to the pride of average persons, both in the political world and otherwise. He showed how vanity often leads to crime and concluded with the quotation from Ecclesiastes: "Vanity, vanity saith the preacher, vanity of vanities, all is vanity. What profit a man of all his labour which he taketh under the sun? One generation passeth away and another generation cometh". Sadly the motion was lost 10–22.'[10]

There is more information about Berkeley's university career. He went up to Merton College, Oxford, in October 1922 to read French, Old French and Philology and he rowed. He was cox of the Merton VIII in 1923, 1924 and finally in 1925, when the second Merton VIII, coxed by him, won the OUBC Clinker Fours by two lengths over Worcester. Academically, Berkeley scraped through with a Fourth in Modern Languages in 1926, which is slightly surprising since, as he admitted, he knew French anyway.

Amongst his earliest compositions to survive are the Three Songs to French texts: *D'un Vanneur de blé aux vents* (Joachim du Bellay); *Pastourelle* (XIIIth century anonymous); and *Rondeau* (Charles d'Orléans). These were completed by 1924, since the second one was performed at the Oxford University Musical Club and Union on 16 June, along with Berkeley's now lost setting of Keats' *La belle Dame sans merci*. Two further songs, performed on 4 December 1924, have

[9] J. Pudney, *Home and Away: an Autobiographical Gambit*, London, 1960, p. 49.

[10] Detail provided in 1987 by Mrs S. Davies, Librarian of St George's School, Harpenden, but supplemented by information provided by Peter Collis in the programme of a concert given at the school on 8 May 1993 by the Lea Singers with soloists and orchestra from the Guildhall School of Music and Drama under Collis.

not survived: *Sonette de Ronsard*, showing how far back Berkeley's connection with this poet went, and *Les Dimanches*. On 12 March 1925, *D'un Vanneur de blé* was performed at the OUMCU in another programme of members' compositions which opened with *Two Dances* for piano duet by Berkeley, now lost. *D'un Vanneur de blé*, for some time better known by its English title 'The Thresher', became Berkeley's first published work when it came out separately with Oxford University Press in 1927.[11] This song is dedicated to John Greenidge, who shared a flat with Berkeley in Paris for the first year or two. His father was an Oxford don and his portrait of Berkeley as a young man in Paris appears on the cover of *The Complete French Songs*.[12] Two other known songs of this period are lost. They were settings of poems by W. H. Auden sung by the poet C. Day Lewis, who recalls this uncomfortable occasion in his autobiography:

> Although Auden and I really preferred singing hymns together, he rightly thought that my repertoire should be enlarged . . . But his ambition for me o'erleapt itself when he persuaded Lennox Berkeley to let me sing three new songs of his at the Musical Union. I had no trouble over Berkeley's setting of *D'un Vanneur de blé*, which I still think one of the most musical pieces of song-writing produced during our period. But then came two rather unmelodious settings of poems by Wystan. I had kept fluffing when I practised them with Lennox Berkeley, nor was it all right on the day – I just managed to limp through the first, but in the second I broke down and had to start again, the song being received by the audience with a sustained burst of silence.[13]

In view of Berkeley's later sensitivity about his early works he probably withdrew these songs by losing them, which is much to be regretted since one of the poems seem to have disappeared too. He often admitted that whereas some composers burnt their scores others lost them – like him!

D'un Vanneur de blé combines Berkeley's French connections with his natural

[11] *Lennox Berkeley: The Complete French Songs for solo voice and piano* was published by Chester Music in 1992 in an edition by Roger Nichols. *D'un Vanneur* is printed in the original form as well as the revised, published edition. Only the latter should be used for performance.

[12] R. Nichols, ed., *Lennox Berkeley: The Complete French Songs*, Chester Music, 1992.

[13] C. Day Lewis, *The Buried Day*, London, 1960. On 3 July1977 Sean Day Lewis wrote to me: 'The only information I have about those Auden songs was given to me by Lennox Berkeley himself when I was researching for my biography on my father. The concert mentioned on page 186 of *The Buried Day* must have happened in 1926 when Berkeley and Day Lewis were both undergraduates. Apparently one of the two Auden songs was called *Trippers* and reflected on some people in a motor coach. Berkeley could not remember the other one and there is no trace of either work in any Day Lewis papers that I have seen.' In the first edition of this book in 1988 I thought that the poem about trippers must have been *Bank Holiday*, which appeared in *Oxford Outlook*, November 1926, pp. 242–4. However Katherine Bucknell thinks it must have been the unpublished *Trippers* itself, although this is only four lines. See *W. H. Auden: Juvenilia Poems 1922–1928*, ed., K. Bucknell, Princeton, 1994, pp. 119, 159. Auden edited *Oxford Poetry 1926*, published by Basil Blackwell, and inscribed a copy 'For Lennox with love from Wystan'.

musical lyricism. It is a strophic setting for medium voice, with the accompaniment considerably revised and improved for the first published version. Many details in the piano part of the original version are nondescript, although the tune, which is the same, flows beautifully. So does the melody of the neo-medieval *Pastourelle* which follows in the original set of three. Its parallel triads and bare octaves and fifths are in striking contrast to the Debussian harmony in the final *Rondeau*, where the surging vocal line combines to suggest the sensuality of a song like *Love's Philosophy* by Delius, whom Berkeley for some time admired:

Example 1. Rondeau (*Three Early Songs*, No. 3)

In *D'un Vanneur de blé* the English tradition is not far away, with chains of consecutive fifths, neo-baroque ornaments, and one chromatic progression redolent of Delius which was put in at the revision stage. Pointers to the future are the memorable tune but also the voice-leading of the piano part. Roger Nichols wonders if this reflected the influence of Nadia Boulanger.[14]

At Oxford, Berkeley studied the organ with W. H. Harris, then organist of New College and conductor of the Bach Choir, and attended concerts at the Holywell Music Room. One instrumental work which has survived from his Oxford years is his Toccata for piano dedicated to the composer's Merton

[14] R. Nichols, introduction to *Lennox Berkeley: The Complete French Songs*, Chester Music, 1992.

contemporary J. F. Waterhouse, who later became music critic of the *Birmingham Post* and was a capable pianist. It was written at Negron in late 1925 and the opening at once reflects the pace of the twenties, even the popping of champagne corks for the privileged. This was the Oxford of Berkeley's contemporaries such as the aesthete Harold Acton and Evelyn Waugh, who captured it unforgettably in *Brideshead Revisited.* At the time when Berkeley went up in 1922, Oxford was a hive of exaggerated pretension expressed through novelty in dress, elaborate hoaxes, eccentric clubs and wars between the aesthetes and the hearties. Homosexuality was fashionable, as Alan Pryce-Jones, Berkeley's future librettist, recalled: 'It was *chic* to be queer, rather as it was *chic* to know something about the twelve-tone scale and about Duchamp's "Nude descending a staircase".'[15]

Example 2. Toccata for piano

The Toccata is a virtuoso piece, unlikely to have been played by the composer himself, and is in very much the high spirits of Berkeley's Polka, in the same key, which was to launch him with his principal publisher, J. and W. Chester, in 1934. The figuration suggests Ravel, more obviously later on where the first movement of his Sonatine shows through, but the rondo form works well. A weakness is the tendency to use passage-work at high speed where the layout changes pattern unnecessarily from bar to bar, making it awkward to play. This applies to the sets of piano studies later on, and a few other pieces, but rarely to the Sonata.

[15] H. Carpenter, *The Brideshead Generation*, London, 1989, p. 81.

At Oxford Berkeley shared rooms with Vere Pilkington and afterwards a flat in London. Their two families were friends and used to meet in the south of France, where they attended a performance of Debussy's *Pelléas* at the Monte Carlo Opera in March 1925. Although Berkeley would always be closer to Ravel than Debussy, the performance must have been a landmark for him. So was the atmosphere of the early music revival at Oxford. Pilkington owned a harpsichord and Berkeley wrote pieces for him with Elizabethan titles such as *Mr. Pilkington's Toye* (1926), which is close to the style of Scarlatti, a short flourish *For Vere* (1927) in up-to-date Parisian bitonality, and finally his substantial five-movement Suite (1930).[16] Contemporary with the earliest songs is a March for piano, with parallel fifths out of Vaughan Williams, and a very elementary Minuet for two recorders.

At this stage at Oxford, Berkeley's musical training had hardly begun. Amongst the lost scores is the Introduction and Dance for small orchestra, which was played in a BBC concert at the New Chenil Galleries in London on 26 April 1926 by the London Chamber Orchestra conducted by Anthony Bernard. The composer heard his own scoring for the first time; Gordon Bryan called it a 'brief but effective little work';[17] but Berkeley withdrew it soon afterwards. With his orchestra, Bernard gave Berkeley valuable opportunities to hear his work at a crucial stage and gave first performances of seven pieces between 1926 and 1950: the Divertimento under his baton was the composer's first recorded work.[18]

In 1978 Berkeley remembered:

> I already wanted to compose music: I felt it was the one thing I could do, or stood a chance of getting anywhere with, but it was a bit difficult to know how to start . . . I got an introduction to Ravel, who was staying in London with some friends I knew. He was very kind to me and . . . it was he who advised me to go and work with Nadia Boulanger.[19]

He needed support since Mary Bernard recalls her husband telling her that Berkeley asked him, anxiously: 'Do you think I'm good enough to be a composer?'[20]

[16] A copy of the Three Pieces for piano, Op. 2, exists where the third piece is inscribed 'For Vere: souvenir de la côte d'Azure. Lennox.' Lisa Cox catalogue B/3 Winter/Spring 1993. Pilkington maintained his interest in music and became a member of the Royal Musical Association.

[17] G. Bryan, 'The Younger English Composers, Part V, Lennox Berkeley', *Monthly Musical Record* 59, June 1929, pp. 161–2. A shorter version of this article appeared in *Le Guide musical et théâtrical, supplément mensuel au guide du concert*, November 1928, p. 214. Gordon Bryan was the pianist with the Aeolian Players in a recital at Holywell Music Room, Oxford, on 1 November 1927 which included Berkeley's *Prelude, Intermezzo (Blues) and Finale* for flute, violin, viola and piano. Another blues link.

[18] Divertimento in B flat, Op. 18, recorded on two 78s by Decca, K1882–3.

[19] *Desert Island Discs*, with Roy Plomley, BBC Radio 4, 13 May 1978.

[20] Telephone conversation with Mrs Mary Bernard, who thought her late husband also had a role in suggesting Nadia Boulanger. See also Ewald Junge, *Anthony Bernard: a Life in Music*, Tunbridge Wells, 1992, p. 28, for a different version of how Berkeley went to Boulanger. The Berkeley scores in Bernard's possession were probably destroyed when his flat was bombed in 1942.

In 1972 Berkeley recalled that it was partly his admiration for Ravel's music that caused him to want to study in France.[21]

All the same, since he was never a particularly good performer, Berkeley must have remained uncertain about music as a career. In England in the nineteenth century, as Elgar found to his cost, there were obstacles to becoming a professional musician. The situation was far from new. Nicholas Temperley wrote of the English composer Henry Hugo Pierson (1815–73) who went to live abroad:

> To those of his own class, above all his father, a musician was not a gentleman; to those in the profession, a gentleman was not a musician. In Germany he found no difficulty in being both.[22]

In 1929 Gordon Bryan reported that Berkeley was 'out of sympathy with English musical life, in which he finds a regrettable lack of interest in the newer developments of art'.[23] So Berkeley must have enjoyed escaping British philistinism in France. He moved to Paris in the autumn of 1926, leaving a country that had been dominated for months by the General Strike. Harold Acton encapsulated the attractions of Paris in the twenties:

> Intellectually Paris was the capital of the world, and the judgement of Paris was final. The Entente Cordiale in the fine arts had never been stronger. Bloomsbury was only an extension of Montparnasse, and its prophet Clive Bell wrote in a language that was nearer French than English . . . English painters borrowed French eye-glasses for their landscapes, nudes and still lifes. Our standards were increasingly Gallic. In their exuberant moments T. S. Eliot wrote French verse about *L'Editeur du Spectateur*, Nancy Cunard about the Sitwells; and Aldous Huxley was so saturated by Laforge that he paraphrased him unconsciously in most of his prose poems. The best of our younger critics, Raymond Mortimer, Francis Birrell and Richard Aldington, were primarily concerned with the diffusion of French criteria in England.[24]

In one of his reports for the *Monthly Musical Record* five years later Berkeley gave some idea of the musical appeal of Paris:

> I say contemporary music in Paris and not contemporary French music because among the young composers in Paris (I mean those of outstanding merit) the French by no means predominate – and this fact is one of supreme importance in studying present-day tendencies. In the old days artists went to a certain place to study their art because there was a 'school' there. In Paris this is no longer the case. The French school seems to have died with Fauré; for it is obvious that the

[21] P. Dickinson, ed., *Twenty British Composers: the Feeney Trust Commissions*, London, 1975, pp. 23–9. Transcription of a BBC Radio 3 interview with Berkeley on 15 May 1972.

[22] N. Temperley, 'Henry Hugo Pierson, 1815–73', *Musical Times* 115, January 1974, p. 30.

[23] G. Bryan, 'The Younger English Composers: Part V, Lennox Berkeley', *Monthly Musical Record* 59, June 1929, pp. 161–2.

[24] H. Acton, *Memoirs of an Aesthete*, London, 1948, p. 149. The T. S. Eliot poem is *Le Directeur*. Berkeley dedicated his 1944 piano piece *Paysage* to Raymond Mortimer.

> so-called school of 'The Six' was composed of musicians of great talent but who beyond that had nothing whatever in common, or at all events not enough to create what is known as a school in art. It would be difficult to find in the same generation two composers more different than Honegger and Poulenc, for instance. Therefore those musicians who go to Paris to study go there rather to be in a centre (if not *the* centre) of modern art rather than to study any particular school of composition. It is difficult to say whether this state of affairs is a factor for good or ill in the development of contemporary music in general, but it is perhaps a pity for the French themselves, since the modern Russian and German masters seem to have taken possession of Paris and to have temporarily usurped their natural position.[25]

Berkeley went on to recognise the importance of teachers such as Boulanger, Koechlin, Dukas, Cortot and Philipp and to compliment the French on being 'excellent technicians and amazingly hard workers, thus creating the right atmosphere for anyone who wishes to study seriously . . . a place favourable to the formation and development of a young musician'.

One of the earliest of Berkeley's Parisian works to survive is the Petite Suite for Oboe and Cello (1927). The whole style is distinctly neo-baroque with Bach as a clear model. The Bourrée is for cello alone; the succeeding Aria for solo oboe; and the Suite ends with a Gigue. In January 1931, five years before he met Berkeley, Britten heard it and reported in his diary: 'v. Interesting suite of L. Berkeley'.[26] This student work resurfaced on BBC Radio 3 in 1988 and ten years later on CD.[27] *Tombeaux* (1926), five songs to poems by Jean Cocteau, shows far more personality. The cycle was originally for voice and piano but a version with orchestra was broadcast in 1929 and a live performance, described as the premiere, was given by Jeanne Dusseau with Anthony Bernard and his London Chamber Orchestra at the Aeolian Hall on 10 February 1931. However, there was an earlier performance of the version with piano when Berkeley himself accompanied Charles Sautelet at the Salle Gaveau in Paris on 1 June 1927.[28] So Berkeley must have liked the set well enough to score them, but not to retain the manuscripts, which disappeared for more than half a century.[29] The tombs evoked in the five poems are those of Sappho, Socrates, a rivulet, Narcissus and Don Juan. The model is the concentrated song-set of the type Poulenc and Milhaud were writing at this time, especially Poulenc's *Le Bestiaire* (1919). This bitonality in the first song is a new departure:

[25] L. Berkeley, 'Music in Paris', *Monthly Musical Record* 61, December 1931, p. 360.

[26] D. Mitchell and P. Reed, eds, *Letters from a Life: Selected Letters and Diaries of Benjamin Britten, Volume 1 1923–39*, London, 1991, p. 168.

[27] Endymion Ensemble on Dutton CDLX 7100 (1998). See also note 54 for details of BBC performance.

[28] M. Duchesneau, *L'Avant-garde musicale et ses socits, Paris 1876–1939*, 1997. Information kindly supplied by Allan Jones.

[29] The first modern performance was given by Meriel Dickinson and myself at the British Music Information Centre on 4 November 1987 in a short recital to mark the Centre's twentieth anniversary.

Example 3. 'Le Tombeau de Sapho'

Example 4. 'Le Tombeau de Socrate'

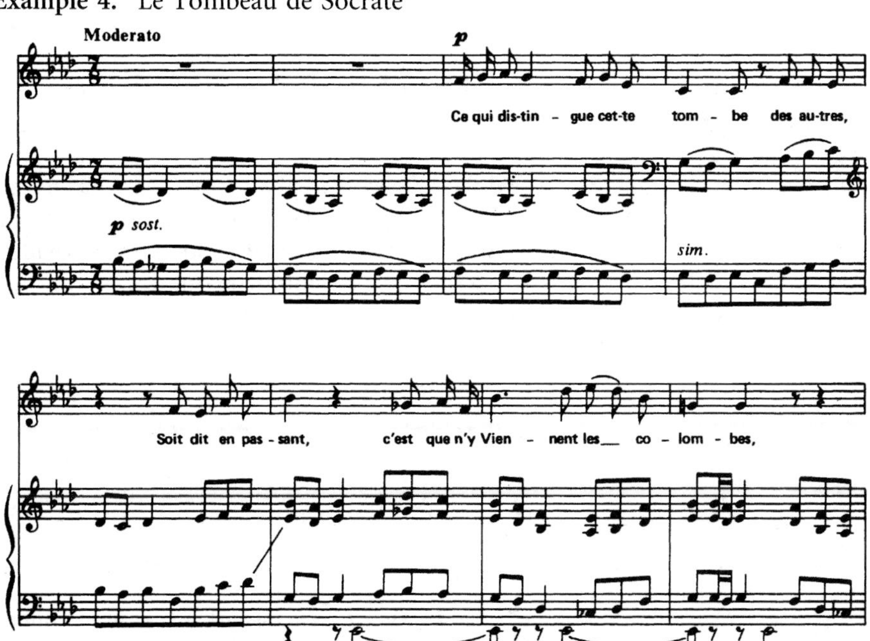

The constant in the first song is the ostinato pattern. The one in the next song, about Socrates, recalls Satie, who died the year before and whose *Socrate* was premiered in Paris only eight years earlier. But it also contains another obvious reminiscence of Vaughan Williams in parallel triads (see Example 4 on p. 11). The diatonic charm found in *D'un Vanneur de blé* returns in the F major of the third song; the fourth employs a gentle 3+2+3 metre; and finally Don Juan is dashingly Spanish via Ravel and prefigures Berkeley's close relationship with the guitar.

As a set *Tombeaux* shows a variety of styles, but each one is sharply focussed. Nothing is wasted. Almost immediately and instinctively Berkeley has absorbed the Parisian atmosphere of *Les six*. He soon made strides on a larger scale. Bernard performed a three-movement Concertino, now lost, at a private concert of the London Contemporary Music Centre and the British Music Society in London on 6 April 1927. This went well enough for further performances to follow, under Basil Cameron at the Harrogate Festival later that year and under the composer himself. The Concertino came to the notice of Walter Straram in Paris. In 1933 Berkeley acknowledged this conductor's role:

> The Straram orchestra is perhaps the best in Paris at the moment, and that which gives the greatest number of first performances. M. Straram has done more for young and unknown composers than any other conductor here. In almost every programme he finds room for one new work . . .[30]

Norman Demuth noted Straram's commitment to Albert Roussel in the week-long festival for his sixtieth birthday in 1929 and called his orchestra 'one of the best Paris ever had'.[31] Berkeley had reason to appreciate Straram's interest because it gave him the chance to write for large orchestra for the first time. His Suite (1927) has four movements – Sinfonia, Bourrée, Aria and Gigue. Even the titles indicate the continued neo-baroque orientation. In 1975, Berkeley recalled: 'Performances of Bach's B minor Mass and Passions must rank, for many of us, among our first great musical experiences.'[32] Regular rhythmic patterns are a feature of mature Berkeley too, based equally on neo-classical Stravinsky and Bach. The Suite went further than its Paris premiere under Straram at the Salle Pleyel on 16 February 1928: it was given at the Proms in London on 12 September 1929 with the Henry Wood Symphony Orchestra conducted by Berkeley.

The Times was perceptive:

> The first novelty was Lennox Berkeley's Suite of four movements. It had at least one rare and admirable quality: it was cheerful. In fact, it might almost earn for

[30] L. Berkeley, 'Music in Paris', *Monthly Musical Record* 63, June 1933, p. 112.
[31] N. Demuth, *Albert Roussel*, London, 1947.
[32] L. Berkeley, *Radio Times*, 16–22 August, 1975, p 32. Berkeley wrote brief notes in the *Radio Times* on each Prom for the entire season. On 19 July 1975 he noted in his diary that it 'took up a lot of time and proved difficult'.

itself the sub-title, Cheerful Nights at the Russian Ballet, for that was the kind of music it mostly was. The subject matter is pithy, the tempo animated, the orchestration clear and playful. Mr. Berkeley has not yet quite fully absorbed the influences that have gone to make his style, but this suite shows a definite advance towards a personal utterance upon his former suite for orchestra. It ensures for him a hearing of anything he writes in the future.[33]

The *Musical Times* (signed F.H.) made the same point:

A promising work was Constant Lambert's Music for Orchestra, good contrapuntal stuff, but not quite free from influences. Similarly, though still less independent, Lennox Berkeley's Suite of four numbers earned its composer a right to further hearings.[34]

The Times found the work cosmopolitan compared with Moeran – naturally enough – and there is the suggestion that continental influences could be a danger. Lord Berners, strongly affected by Diaghilev's Ballets Russes, suffered from this prejudice and so did Frank Bridge. It delayed acceptance of Berkeley as the conservative climate of the 1930s in England worsened with Stravinsky considered to be on the wrong track and the young Britten merely clever.

The opening Sinfonia from Berkeley's Suite has exactly the breezy flavour one might expect from the review in *The Times*, but it derives partly from the perkiness of the composers of *Les six*. Compare Berkeley's opening, using consecutive chords within the key, with a similar melody in the finale of Poulenc's Sonata for piano duet (1918):

Example 5a. Suite for Orchestra, Sinfonia

[33] *The Times*, 13 September 1929. The Suite for Orchestra was found in Goodwin and Tabb's hire library later handled by Novello. The full score is sketchy in parts. No 'former suite' has been traced: the writer probably meant the Concertino.

[34] *Musical Times*, 1 October 1929: possibly Frank Howes.

Example 5b. Poulenc: Sonata for piano duet, Finale

In the third of the four movements, the Aria, *lento sostenuto*, there is more than a suggestion of the mature Berkeley in creating a mood through a repeated chordal background:

Example 6. Suite for orchestra, Aria

The colour of the trombones, softly, and the celesta shows the kind of ear for texture and harmony which was to become an original fingerprint. How fortunate for Berkeley to have the chance of learning in public at this stage even if he rejected the results by ignoring the scores for the rest of his life!

His next large-scale piece was the Symphony for Strings (1930–31), played at the Queen's Hall under Bernard on 14 December 1931, but now lost. The Suite for Orchestra was discovered in 1987 but several early pieces described in Gordon Bryan's *Monthly Musical Record* article have disappeared. However, Bryan recalled Three Piano Pieces (1927) played by the Polish Chopin specialist Jan Smeterlin in London in 1929 which were rediscovered in the 1980s. A curt *Allegro moderato* is followed by an eloquent slow piece (no tempo marking) saturated with bluesy false-relations and then a brusque

Moderato makes an effective ending. The *Piece* (1929) for flute, clarinet and bassoon shows a neat, terse neo-classical technique without obvious personality – the same could be said about some early Britten. The *Trois Poèmes de Vildrac* (1929) are dedicated 'à Mademoiselle Nadia Boulanger en toute admiration et gratitude'. The opening of the last song in this set is worth quoting:

Example 7. *Trois Poèmes de Vildrac*, No. 3

The spacing may be Stravinskian, but the piano melody is almost exactly that of Nelson's aria at the end of Act II of Berkeley's grand opera *Nelson*:

Example 8. *Nelson*, Act II, figure 75

Berkeley's connection with probably the most influential composition teacher of the twentieth century now seems to have been inevitable. Nadia Boulanger (1887–1979) had a remarkable career, not least as a woman in a demanding professional world. She stopped composing herself after the premature death of her sister Lili in 1918, but concentrated on teaching both for institutions and privately and was active as a conductor, pianist and organist. Her impact on American composers was enormous at a crucial time of national self-discovery and her relationship with Berkeley can be compared to that with Copland. They both idolised Boulanger and this sometimes led to subservience. In 1972 Berkeley told me: 'I think that, as with all teachers who have great personality, one did try and write the kind of music she approved of, a bit.'[35]

In 1959 Berkeley looked back to his difficulties as a composer in the 1930s:

> I was thinking too much about technique, and Benjamin Britten helped me a lot then. He used to say: 'If you want to do that, do it: don't think all the time about whether Nadia Boulanger would approve.'[36]

[35] P. Dickinson, ed., *Twenty British Composers*.

[36] Special Correspondent, 'Mr. Lennox Berkeley on the Composer's Need to hear his own Works', *The Times*, 12 April 1959.

Her influence may have gone further than music when Berkeley became a Roman Catholic in 1928. Lady Berkeley confirmed that he took his Catholicism very seriously and went to Mass every Sunday and I asked her how far Boulanger was responsible for his Catholicism.

> **FB** It was certainly to do with Nadia because she was a very devout Catholic and up till her last days she went to Mass regularly . . . He was devoted to her and respected her enormously and was always bowled over by any performance she gave of the Fauré Requiem.
>
> **PD** Do you think she was a kind of mother figure to him?
>
> **FB** Not really: he was devoted to his own mother, whom he looked after as an invalid for the last years of her life. I think Nadia was very much the professor to him. But there was a great bond between them and I feel the religious thing played an enormous part there, binding them together.
>
> **PD** How French did Lennox seem?
>
> **FB** Very French. Whenever we went to France people always thought he was French because his French was so perfect. He always had a tremendous sympathy with French writers, French composers and he loved France, loved Paris.[37]

The critic Desmond Shawe-Taylor saw things a little differently:

> I think that slightly too much can be made of the French influence. Of course Nadia Boulanger was a tremendous influence, as she was on all those Americans who passed through her hands. It didn't stop them from being thoroughly American when they got home and I don't think it stopped Lennox from being thoroughly English. The French influence gave a kind of polish and style, an ease to what he had to say rather than taking over the subject matter.[38]

In 1931 Berkeley reported on Boulanger's methods for British readers in the *Monthly Musical Record*:

> . . . the chief points are: the study of the works of the great masters (chiefly for form and orchestration), the writing of musical exercises, and the submitting to her of compositions. With regard to the first point, her system is to lecture at the piano on some work or series of works which the pupils have analysed themselves. For instance, we have studied recently in class Beethoven's piano sonatas and string quartets, a large number of Bach cantatas, some early polyphonic music, Stravinsky's *Les Noces*, and works by Debussy and Ravel. The musical exercises are the ordinary series involved in the study of counterpoint and fugue. These have to be done with absolute correctness, and if wrong, have to be done again until they are right. It is, however, the advice given for actual composition that is the most valuable part of her teaching. Here the important thing to note is that she is very severe, but extremely impartial – that is to say, she is severe in condemnation of

[37] Interview with author, 28 January 1991. Berkeley particularly admired Julien Green: extracts from his writings were read by Tony Scotland at the Requiem Mass in memory of Sir Lennox Berkeley at Westminster Cathedral on 20 March 1990. Scotland said that in the last few years of his life Berkeley used to play the fourth of Poulenc's Nocturnes on the piano over and over again. It is entitled 'Bal fantome', was written in March 1934, and was inspired by a passage from Julien Green's novel *Le Visionnaire*.

[38] Interview with author, 28 November 1990.

> the least technical flaw or failing in unity of style, but impartial in that she admits any innovation that will come off. It does not matter what style you use as long as you use it consistently.[39]

Berkeley accepted Boulanger's discipline and commented in a 1973 BBC programme:

> It was quite obvious that I had very little technique and lacked facility in part-writing and all that kind of thing, which is why she thought it essential that I should do all these exercises . . . She was always writing . . . under places she'd underlined or put a cross for a mistake: 'Very musical, but forbidden'! I thought, really, that it's sad that it should be forbidden if it's very musical. But she was perfectly right because there's no point in undertaking a discipline unless you're prepared to abide by the rules.[40]

He was excused harmony because even at that stage Boulanger recognised that Berkeley had 'a natural ear for harmony that made it unnecessary'.

Berkeley was clearly a model pupil. The same might be said of Elliott Carter, in his early period, but not Virgil Thomson or Roy Harris. Copland – perhaps her greatest protégé – was very dependent upon Boulanger's approval well into the 1930s, although his Americanisms always gave him an element slightly outside her control. In 1924 Copland wrote to Boulanger about his Symphony for Organ and Orchestra: 'It goes without saying that any corrections you make I approve of a priori.'[41] Although Copland said this about a work which Boulanger was going to play herself, it indicates his attitude. Was her influence stifling and could Berkeley have reached maturity earlier if he had been less submissive? The music critic of *The Times* had no doubts: 'His training with Nadia Boulanger nearly wrecked his chances – or so many, though not all, of his admirers think – and it took him years to get over it and to find himself.'[42]

Even as late as his Seventieth Birthday Concert on 22 May 1973 at the Goldsmiths Hall in London, Berkeley had qualms about Boulanger. She was there and a programme of his music ended with a performance of the *Palm Court Waltz* for piano duet, which he played with me. He confessed to his diary: 'I was a little frightened about playing this frivolous extravaganza in front of Nadia but I think she took it in good part.'[43]

In response to Boulanger's death in 1979 Berkeley summed up her significance in his diary:

[39] L. Berkeley, 'Nadia Boulanger as Teacher', *Monthly Musical Record* 61, January 1931, p. 4. An opportunity to hear some of Nadia Boulanger's own music was provided by BBC Radio 3, 15–19 April 2002, when her sister Lili Boulanger (1893–1918) was Composer of the Week. Berkeley admired Lili Boulanger and wrote an article for the *Listener* on 21 November 1968 to mark the fiftieth anniversary of her untimely death.

[40] BBC Radio 3 feature, 'The Tender Tyrant', presented by Bernard Keefe in 1973.

[41] A. Copland and V. Perlis, *Copland 1900–1942*, London, 1984, p. 97.

[42] Our Music Critic, 'The Career of Mr. Lennox Berkeley', *The Times*, 19 October 1956.

[43] L. Berkeley diary, 11 June 1973.

> It is difficult to describe her or to account for the extraordinary influence she exercised on all who came in contact with her, particularly her pupils, beyond saying that in her, a brilliant intelligence and musical understanding was allied to goodness and warmth of heart. She had no positive method in her teaching other than insisting on a disciplinary training in academic counterpoint and fugue and the general acquiring of an excellent ear . . . She distrusted systems, and had no use for serialism at the time I was with her. She had a deep love of the great masters of the past and of the music of Stravinsky, though how she reconciled this latter admiration with his own conversion to serial technique in his later works I have never understood. Indeed there were many things about which I was unable to agree with her, but these are of no matter in comparison with the enormous debt I shall always owe her and the love and admiration I shall always feel.[44]

Two years later he gave a talk to the Franco-British Society on Boulanger and identified qualities which apply equally to Berkeley himself:

> I wanted to stress her utter disinterest in the sense of never seeking to gain by music – her wanting to be only the servant of music, and indeed putting her fabulous technique and understanding at its service with many remarkable results.[45]

Berkeley's formal studies took at least five years and he retained his contact with Paris right through the 1930s, later keeping a flat at 1 Cité Chaptal, Paris IX, next to Rue Ballu where Boulanger lived. The Parisian experience was not just through study with Boulanger but consisted of everything which went on there. Berkeley confided to his diary in 1981: 'I still love Paris very much and often wished we lived there, as indeed I once did. I've never got to love London though I've spent the greater part of my life there.'[46] Berkeley's response is documented from 1929 until 1934 when he wrote reports on music in Paris for the *Monthly Musical Record*, a total of eighteen articles. These reveal his sources and influences in contemporary events at a formative stage.[47]

He found Honegger's *Rugby* 'a masterpiece' and admired a performance of Stravinsky's Octet – 'perhaps Stravinsky's best work of that period'. Berkeley was present at the Parisian premiere of Walton's *Façade* in 1929 and admired 'the wit and colour of this delightful work'. Copland's technique he found 'outstandingly good': also Martinu's, some of whose chamber works he rather surprisingly thought could be called 'great music'. Poulenc, who became a lifelong friend, was not found at his best in the *Aubade*: 'Poulenc seems to have reached an uncomfortable stage, having lost something of the freshness and originality of his earlier works, and failed to find any more solid qualities with which to replace them.' Berkeley admired Honegger's Cello Concerto and regarded the Cantata by the seventeen-year-old Igor Markevitch as a justifiable sensation.

The Paris premiere of Stravinsky's *Symphony of Psalms* in 1931 had a great impact and Berkeley marvelled that 'the same composer can use a different style

[44] L. Berkeley diary, 29 October 1979.
[45] L. Berkeley diary, 17 March 1981.
[46] L. Berkeley diary, 1 April 1981.
[47] These articles, originally drawn to my attention by Joan Redding, make a fascinating series revealing both Berkeley and his French context.

for each work without ever losing his own individuality. I suppose this has never been done to such an extent before, and it is a fine thing to see an artist despise the success that is so easily obtained by repeating himself after one successful work, and boldly striking out afresh each time at the risk of being misunderstood by his late admirers.' In 1991 Malcolm Williamson rembered being at a meeting of the Catholic Musicians' Guild when the Viennese-born composer and musicologist Egon Wellesz was present. He was celebrated for his pioneering work on Byzantine chant and at this meeting he said that in his opinion the *Symphony of Psalms* was not genuinely Byzantine. Berkeley came out quite violently and said: 'Possibly not – but it's a masterpiece!'[48]

The centrality of Stravinsky to composers of Berkeley's generation – and to Boulanger's teaching – should not be forgotten. In 1973 Berkeley read Robert Craft's book on Stravinsky:

> It made me look back to the evening, so many years ago, when I was taken to dinner by Soulima at the Stravinsky flat, where the family was living in the Rue St Honoré, but I was so awestruck at finding myself in the company of the great man (I was still a student) that I remember little of what was said – I do remember though that he was kind (even making me play something I had written) very good-natured and elegant. This must have been about 1930.[49]

In 1978 Berkeley looked further back at the whole phenomenon:

> *Sacre* remains one of the most exciting works ever written but one can understand the dismay of the audience who heard it in 1913. How unlike what people imagine Stravinsky was as a man. I remember his good manners, his elegance – he was small but very well dressed – his courtesy to whoever he was with, though he held very definite opinions about everything and could be devastatingly critical of what he didn't like. I wonder how he will be rated in a hundred or even fifty years' time. That he was pre-eminent in his younger days is beyond question – *Firebird*, *Petroushka* and the *Rite of Spring* are acknowledged masterpieces, and some of the works of his neo-classical period such as the *Symphony of Psalmes*, *Duo concertant*, Two-Piano Sonata, and *Apollon musagète*, are outstanding, but what of the late works in serial technique? I find it impossible to love them as I do his earlier music – I suppose through my inability to come to terms with atonality.[50]

The status of late Stravinsky remains unsettled.

In his youth Berkeley preferred Ravel's earlier works to *Bolero* – 'a wonderful idea brilliantly executed . . . [but] one feels that such a method of composing is too arbitrary to lead anywhere, and its final paroxism so calculated that it can only thrill one once – however, it is better to be thrilled once than not at all'. But later his enthusiasm for *La Valse* was paramount:

> I can never quite explain why I like this piece so much. I think it must be its bitter-sweet quality, its moments of sentiment and charm, tinged with irony, which

[48] Interview with author, 22 February 1991.

[49] L. Berkeley diary, 5 January 1973. The book was probably *Stravinsky: the Chronicle of a Friendship*, New York/London, 1972.

[50] L. Berkeley diary, 12 December 1978.

> contrast with the more robust passages equally characteristic of the Viennese waltz – what Roland Manuel calls 'ses élans de volupté et sa pompe éclatante'. I suppose it's only a light piece, but nowhere except in *Daphnis and Chloé*, has Ravel's subtle ear for harmony or the virtuosity of his scoring been more evident.[51]

Milhaud he found 'patchy' and Honegger and Poulenc utterly different, adding to the richness of Parisian musical life which included many foreign elements too. As for the French people, 'their love of and interest in anything new (in which they differ so strikingly from the English) assures a fair hearing for the young composer'. And again they feel that 'art is a thing to be encouraged, and that it is in no way abnormal to be an artist'. That must have seemed different from England too.

Stravinsky continued to be a strong influence on Berkeley – he admired both the Violin Concerto and, as we have seen, the *Duo Concertant* for violin and piano, especially Eglogue II and the Gigue. This type of violin writing – and the double-stopping of *L'Histoire du soldat* – made an indelible impression, establishing the character of the instrument for Berkeley in most of his mature music. Finally these reports again draw attention to Martinu, admire Poulenc's *Le Bal masqué*, and worship Stravinsky. *Perséphone* was the outstanding work of 1934: 'It is music that has been ruthlessly stripped of every element that is not purely musical, and it is this austerity and restraint that many people find so disconcerting. There are no orchestral "effects" in this score, and one would listen in vain for those purple patches so dear to conductors (and to audiences).'[52] And in 1932, after the premiere of the Violin Concerto: '. . . most people consider the new concerto is a big work and think that Stravinsky is very much on the right lines in setting his face against all sensuous and sentimental appeals, in bringing music back to the sterner classical style, and in making for pure aesthetic feeling only'.[53]

Berkeley would have known that such views were not widely shared on the English side of the channel and may still have felt doubtful about his chances of establishing himself at home. Further compositions of this period, before he attached opus numbers, presumably belong to the early thirties and several of these he simply left with Nadia Boulanger and forgot about them until her executors returned them in 1979.[54] The Suite for flute, oboe, violin, viola and

[51] L. Berkeley diary, 4 February 1969.

[52] L. Berkeley, *Monthly Musical Record* 64, June 1934, p. 110.

[53] L. Berkeley, *Monthly Musical Record* 62, March–April 1932, p. 63.

[54] Some of this early music became known for the first time through four programmes I devised for BBC Radio 3 which were broadcast on the composer's eighty-fifth birthday on 12 May 1988, and the following three weeks.
Programme I: March (piano); Three Songs (*D'un Vanneur, Pastourelle, Rondeau*); Toccata (piano); *Tombeaux* (five Cocteau poems); Petite Suite (oboe and cello).
Programme II: *For Vere* (piano); *Trois Poèmes de Vildrac*; Piece (flute, clarinet and bassoon); Andante (Blues) from ballet, arranged for piano by Peter Dickinson; Violin and Piano Sonata No. 2, Op. 1.
Programme III: Three Pieces, Op. 5 (two pianos); *How Love came in* (song); Three Pieces (clarinet solo); Three Pieces, Op. 2 (piano).

cello (1930) continues baroque and earlier stylisations with more confidence; *La Poulette grise* (1931) is a sparkling setting for children's voices accompanied by trumpet and two pianos – the earliest of a series of works involving piano duo; and the lost Symphony for Strings (1931) apparently ended with a fugue. So does the Trio (1935) for flute, oboe and piano. *Three Pieces* for solo clarinet – an undated manuscript in Berkeley's writing of the middle to late 1930s – are thoroughly effective, no mere echo of Stravinsky's. They were not published until 1983 when Berkeley inscribed them to Thea King, who edited and performed them.

An untitled ballet score, written in Paris in May and June 1932, survives in manuscript. It borrows sections from the Suite, so may have been written to order in a hurry, and is at times close to Poulenc and Milhaud, especially with this *Java*, but is not mere juvenilia:

Example 9. Ballet, *Java*

Programme IV: Trio (flute, oboe and piano); Five Short Pieces, Op. 4 (piano); *Lay your sleeping head, my love* (song); *Night covers up the rigid land* (song); Three Impromptus, Op. 7 (piano).

Much of the score is in this jocular vein, which veers at times into a cross between Paris and the Berlin of Kurt Weill, whom Berkeley admired. There is an *Andante* which ought to have been called a blues:

Example 10. Ballet (untitled)

This suggests the influence of jazz or of Lambert, whose *The Rio Grande* (1927) made such an impact by using popular idioms in an extended piece as opposed to the short numbers of *Façade* and dances like *Bliss* (1923) and *The Rout Trot*

(1927) by Arthur Bliss. Berkeley would probably have heard *The Rio Grande* at the Queen's Hall on 14 December 1931, when it followed the first performance of his own Symphony for Strings. By March 1933, reviewing Weill's *Mahagonny* and *Der Jasager* for the *Monthly Musical Record*, Berkeley was still intrigued by the jazz connection: 'And yet the music is very far removed from ordinary jazz – it is simpler, more melodic, and much stronger in harmony: also there is something profoundly German about it, as there was in the same composer's music to the film *Die Dreigroschenoper*, which removes it still further from what one associates with the word jazz.'

The nearest parallel to the *Andante* in Berkeley's untitled ballet score is Lambert's *Elegiac Blues* (1927), written in memory of the black singer Florence Mills, or the blues in Ravel's Violin and Piano Sonata (1927). But there are two other works which show Berkeley involved in popular mannerisms. The Prelude, Intermezzo and Finale for flute, violin, viola and piano (1927) has a blues as its central movement, and the lost Sonatina for violin solo (1927) contained a tango.[55] There are many examples in Berkeley's later work where a false relation seems to have blues origins, as we shall see. It is difficult to be precise about such sources. Symphonic jazz was fashionable after Gershwin's *Rhapsody in Blue* (1924), and Ravel began *L'Enfant et les sortilèges* and the Violin and Piano Sonata before this – and continued with his own type of sublimated blues inflections in *Bolero* and the left-hand Piano Concerto.

It is possible that Berkeley's connection with jazz came through meeting Ravel in Paris, although jazz was everywhere. In 1975 he broadcast a tribute for the Ravel centenary:

> I only knew him in later life when he had shed certain affectations in evidence in younger days, and I find descriptions of him as an elegant dandy, rather unapproachable and given to sarcastic comment, not at all like the kindly middle-aged composer I knew. Unlike many great men, the more successful and famous he became, the less he would allow any trace of self-importance to show itself. I used to meet him sometimes after concerts when he would take me, generally with another student or young composer, to one of the big cafés in the St. Lazare district where he would talk with us about the music we'd heard. It strikes me now, though it didn't then, that he could so easily have spent the evening in better company both socially and intellectually, but I think he was bored by the world he had already conquered and preferred to be with young musicians, however humble. He was apt to prolong the evening by inviting us to accompany him to a night-club. It was in these establishments that one first heard the real virtuoso playing that has characterised good jazz ever since.[56]

In later life Berkeley became evasive when asked about any connections with popular music in his own works. He tried to discourage John Francis and the

[55] According to *Le Guide du concert*, 5 October 1928, the Sonatina for solo violin was written in 1927 and had three movements: Allegro moderato, Allegretto (Tango), Presto.

[56] L. Berkeley, 'Ravel', talk for BBC Radio 3, 3 March 1975.

Sylvan Trio from playing his Trio for flute, oboe and piano, written for them in 1935, and seemed embarrassed by the Latin American 3+2+3 rhythm of its slow movement. The *Andante*, from the ballet score, provides evidence that Berkeley's sources are wider than expected. The score includes a saxophone part complete with idiomatic smears. There were reputable jazz musicians in Paris from the mid-twenties whom Berkeley probably heard. These included Ray Ventura with his Collegians, Gregor and the Gregoriens, the trumpeter Philippe Brun who performed with both groups, and the guitarist Django Reinhardt. The best American bands were regularly in Paris. They did not, of course, get into Berkeley's reports for the *Monthly Musical Record*: but somehow jazz or its derivatives got absorbed as a subtle inflection in his musical idiom, but was rejected as anything more. It was nothing like the overt treatments of Lambert or the profound significance the blues came to have for Tippett. By comparison Berkeley brushed lightly against this world, more like Britten than Walton, who picked up rhythmic traits from jazz which remained throughout his career. But Britten's Piano Concerto (1938) originally had a jazzy slow movement, which the composer replaced, and there is nothing superficial about the blues in his operetta *Paul Bunyan* (1941). However, one is left wondering what Berkeley would have become if he had accepted a stronger injection of African American music or its derivations at this formative stage.

2. Growing confidence

Both Berkeley's ancestry and his training show through in his Opus 1, although he commented later that some people might think it odd that his Opus 1 should in fact be the Violin and Piano Sonata No. 2 (1933). The Violin and Piano Sonata No. 1 (1931) – discarded by implication – is often surprisingly effective, if self-consciously brittle, and Berkeley improved a similar three-movement approach in No. 2. Its commanding outer movements absorb the rhythmic dislocations of Stravinsky's *Duo concertant*, but the slow movement has more Berkeley character:

Example 11. Violin and Piano Sonata No. 2, Opus 1

The neo-baroque ornamentation – trills and rapid decorative figures – is profuse in the outer sections. But the melodic period which opens the A section in this A–B–A structure is striking: the two bars of piano introduction may be coldly Stravinskian but the melody is distinctly warmer, and its regular backing in piano chords is a fingerprint of maturity.

In April 1934, J. and W. Chester announced that the Violin and Piano Sonata No. 2 and the Polka for two pianos would inaugurate the connection of Lennox Berkeley with their catalogue. The Polka became a hit in this country and in the USA as the publisher's blurb explains:

> This brilliant composition achieved fame even before it could be published, having secured enormous success when featured in the programmes of those eminent duettists Ethel Bartlett and Rae Robertson, to whom it is aptly dedicated. The reasons are not hard to find, for the sparkling vitality of the work holds the hearer from start to finish.[1]

It ought not to be difficult to hold attention in such a short piece, however, especially one which refers back to the Paris of *Les six*. The backchat between the two pianos is missing in Berkeley's rarely played solo piano adaptation, which makes an interesting study since some details are quite different. In fact the Polka may be an arrangement anyway, since Alan Pryce-Jones, Berkeley's librettist for *Nelson*, connects it with a much earlier operatic project: 'Very little was written by either of us, and all that survives is a polka which, arranged for two pianos, made an amusing piece for Ethel Bartlett and Rae Robertson in the early 1930s.'[2] The opening is for Piano I on its own, which recalls the early Toccata:

Example 12. Polka for two pianos, Opus 5

[1] *The Chesterian*, April 1934, p. 149; see also pp. 114–15.
[2] A. Pryce Jones, 'Some Notes on the Text of *Nelson*', *Opera* 5, October 1954, pp. 595–8.

The central section in F major has a passage in dotted rhythm as a sly near-quotation, which shows English rather than French ancestry.

Example 13. Polka for two pianos

Example 14. Walton: Polka from *Façade*

In the first of his concert reports from Paris, which included *Façade*, Berkeley told the *Monthly Musical Record*: 'The wit and colour of this delightful work made an instant appeal to the audience; and the composer, who conducted, together with Miss Edith Sitwell and Mr. Constant Lambert who recited the poems, was warmly applauded.'[3] Berkeley may have felt that the Polka on its own was merely an encore piece, so he added two more movements – a Nocturne and a Capriccio – which were published as Three Pieces, Opus 5, in 1938. The atmospheric textures of the Nocturne are richly evocative, and the Capriccio in G minor – the same key as parts of Stravinsky's Capriccio for piano and orchestra – concludes an excellent set.

Opus 2 is another triptych: three piano pieces called Etude, Berceuse and Capriccio. Harriet Cohen saw the second and third pieces in 1934 and Berkeley wrote the first specially for her, to complete the group.[4] Berkeley met Harriet Cohen through Alan Searle, Somerset Maughan's companion, and dedicated the Berceuse to him. The opening melody is wonderfully poised and the echoes of Chopin later on in the central section must be deliberate, but at the beginning the bars of 7/8 ventilate the texture and there is even a blue note:

Example 15. Berceuse, Opus 2, No. 2

A major landmark from several points of view was Berkeley's oratorio *Jonah*, Opus 3. It occupied him from 1933 to 1935; by the time he had completed it, both his parents had died, and it became a memorial tribute. Bereavement cannot have helped at a time of uncertainty when the period of study in Paris was ending – and neither can the reviews of *Jonah*. Robin Hull later recalled that 'it was attacked with a wanton brutality of which English critics have seldom been guilty'. He went on: 'A study of *Jonah* from the perspective of today brings home the inadequacy of regarding this work as transitional . . . The sheer musicianship of the oratorio, the logic and lucidity of its construction, entitle its pages to the impartial hearing which they have

[3] L. Berkeley, *Monthly Musical Record* 59, June 1929, p. 174.
[4] H. Cohen, *A Bundle of Time*, London, 1969, p. 247.

never yet been granted.'[5] M. D. Calvocoressi introduced the first performance of *Jonah* in the *Radio Times* in a sympathetic and factual way:

> The music is essentially melodic. The composer has achieved an appropriate and effective melodic style, austere and yet flexible, which may owe something to the recitatives in Stravinsky's *Oedipus Rex*. The melodies proceed mainly in ample curves, with many ornaments of an archaic declamatory character. They lend themselves quite naturally to a contrapuntal treatment which is ingenious and never over-elaborate; and the bold but unostentatious harmonic scheme, in which modern dissonances and short cuts play a big part, fits perfectly.[6]

That is accurate comment, but Berkeley got into difficulties with the performance at the Leeds Festival, which he conducted himself the following year. *The Times* came straight out: 'Why the programme committee, having had the opportunity of hearing Lennox Berkeley's oratorio *Jonah* by wireless, should have supposed it could be anything but a failure passes understanding.'[7] Neville Cardus in the *Manchester Guardian* was more balanced: 'Mr. Berkeley's work suggests genius now and again: he sets his scene in flashes, or rather paragraphs, of instrumentation.' And finally: 'Another performance should be heard at once and under a conductor of genius. Tonight Mr. Berkeley conducted and, though he led his forces firmly along alien ways, the chances are that much was left inarticulate.'[8] *The Times* also castigated both the performance and Berkeley's conducting – a lesson he did not take to heart since he continued to conduct his own works in prominent performances and was later to make recordings.

In 1990 Basil Douglas, on the music staff of the BBC at the time, remembered the hostility with which *Jonah* was greeted. It is difficult to realise today that with *Jonah* Berkeley was regarded as an avant-garde composer who 'came under suspicion from the musical establishment'. It was the same kind of antagonism that Britten suffered. Douglas recalled that the performers did not like the work and that Berkeley's conducting was inadequate.[9] On the other hand, Berkeley wrote to his publisher after the BBC broadcast: 'I was very pleased with Friday's performance – I have received many appreciative letters and I still think that it is a work that might become popular.'[10]

But there was another observer at *Jonah* – Benjamin Britten, who must have seen Berkeley as in the front line of attack suffering from British philistinism. On 7 October 1937, Britten wrote from Leeds:

[5] R. Hull, 'The Style of Lennox Berkeley', *Chesterian* 24, April 1950, pp. 84–7.
[6] M. D. Calvocoressi, 'Oratorio in Modern Idiom', *Radio Times*, 12 June 1936.
[7] *The Times*, 9 October 1937.
[8] N. Cardus, *Manchester Guardian*, 10 October 1937.
[9] Interview with author, 28 November 1990.
[10] L. Berkeley, letter to Mr Chenery, 23 June 1936.

> On to Scarborough for tea, & back in time to hear Lennox's *Jonah* – which he conducts very well, & has a good show. It has some good things in it & is even more promising for the future.[11]

Before this Britten had heard the BBC broadcast of *Jonah* on 19 June 1936 and must have written to Berkeley then. On 23 June Berkeley replied:

> I can't tell you how pleased I was with your letter. It is the greatest encouragement to know that you appreciated *Jonah* – I am by no means satisfied with it but I think it is the right kind of music. I can't really say anything more about it now – I know it so well with all the rehearsals etc. that I can't look at it objectively. I was much pleased by your saying that it was emotionally dramatic rather than eventfully descriptive, because I feel that descriptive music is impossible now. In *Jonah* I have only put in just enough description to make a décor for the real business. The reverse process seems to me to end in complete nonsense – an orchestra composed entirely of wind machines.[12]

As late as 1950, when Britten was conducting his *Spring Symphony* in Leeds Town Hall, he told Berkeley: 'What nice memories I have of *Jonah* there.'[13]

In spite of this support from a colleague he had only recently met, *Jonah* must have felt like a failure. This impression would have been strengthened by the fact that it took place in Leeds only six years after Walton's *Belshazzar's Feast*, which has cast its shadow over *Jonah* in other ways too. How does Berkeley's first large-scale vocal work appear now, over sixty years later, after the opportunity of hearing the first London performance under Jonathan Rennert at St Michael's Cornhill on 31 March 1990? Firstly, it seems certain that only a very inadequate rendering could have turned the work into a disaster. There are reminiscences of Stravinsky, of course, but these are no more disfiguring than with other composers of Berkeley's generation. These can even look both ways, since there are arias in *Jonah*, such as No. 8, which suggest *The Rake's Progress*. Secondly, the different musical types used to propel and enhance the story of *Jonah* – arias, choruses, interludes and recitatives – are all convincing and well contrasted. The cohesion is often tighter than in Berkeley's later operas, and it builds well to the end. Thirdly, the work has special personal significance. Not only was *Jonah* in memory of Berkeley's parents: its religious context was one of increasing importance to the composer and his music. *Jonah* is rooted in the Bach Passions as well as in the *Symphony of Psalms*. The final tenor aria, No. 18, shows both derivations but is typical of Berkeley too:

[11] D. Mitchell and P. Reed, eds, *Letters from a Life: Selected Letters and Diaries of Benjamin Britten, Volume 1 1923–39*, London, 1991, p. 517.

[12] Copies of Berkeley's letters to Britten are held at the Britten-Pears Library.

[13] B. Britten, letter to Berkeley, 27 June 1950.

Example 16. ***Jonah*, Opus 3**

The final chorus adds a boys' choir, before such a sound became associated with Britten, and the last Alleluias are quiet, before a brief loud ending with the orchestra. The subtlety of the harmony is acute, bearing out Boulanger's confidence in Berkeley's ear (see Example 17 on p. 32). Edward Greenfield, in the *Guardian* noted:

> *Jonah* is divided into numbers, arias, choruses and recitatives, very much on the pattern of a Bach passion, and it was fascinating in the early choruses to note the way that this piece must have influenced Berkeley's close colleague at the time, Benjamin Britten, when he came to write his cantata *St. Nicolas.* The problem of the piece is that Berkeley failed to press ahead dramatically when he needed to, leaving one too regularly in an easy *andante*, with the biblical text stretched out too far. But one revels in much beautifuly crafted choral writing, and some of the richest sounds that even Berkeley conceived.[14]

Ultimately, Berkeley was unjustly treated over *Jonah*, which could be seen as a link between *Belshazzar's Feast* and Tippett's *A Child of our Time.* There are weaknesses in the conventional repetitions of the text, but the work as a whole shows what Berkeley's future would be as he gained in confidence. The results of this process were noted by Wilfrid Mellers in 1954: 'Berkeley's growth to maturity has been a growth in lyrical conviction: as lyricism has become the essence of his music, so he has translated his French idiom into English.'[15]

[14] E. Greenfield, *Guardian*, 3 April 1990.
[15] W. Mellers, 'The Music of Lennox Berkeley', *Listener*, 24 June 1954, p. 1113.

Example 17. *Jonah*

The translation of French training into English expression is a perceptive point, but it takes us too far ahead. Even before *Jonah* was performed, Berkeley had completed his String Quartet No. 1, Opus 6, and the Overture, Opus 8, which was given at the Proms in 1935 and was selected for the International Society for Contemporary Music Festival at Barcelona in April 1936. The Overture has a first subject sustained over an ostinato, but a quiet oboe theme later has a characteristic turn in its melodic contour:

Example 18. Overture, Opus 8

In 1972, Berkeley could – with characteristic modesty – remember nothing of his own Overture, which he later withdrew, but only the impact of the Berg Violin Concerto which, he said, 'rather cancelled out everything else'.[16] Not quite, however, since Benjamin Britten was the other British composer, represented by his Suite for Violin and Piano, Opus 6, which he played with Antonio Brosa. Britten, too, was enormously impressed by Berg's Violin Concerto, but for Berkeley this was a momentous meeting. Everything he had been struggling to acquire technically for over a decade Britten seemed to possess already:

> We met in Barcelona . . . It's important to me because we became very close friends and he had a great influence on me later . . . I was very interested in his career because he was already a superb technical musician and I could foresee what was coming.[17]

Meeting Britten may have confirmed Berkeley's dissatisfaction with his own larger works, so he withdrew both the Overture and *Jonah* and told me: 'I don't think I was really able to speak with my own voice, particularly in such a big-scale composition [as *Jonah*] . . . I'm not interested in them any more.'[18] That reaction in 1972 was typical of Berkeley's attitude to his early works, although the first performance of the Cello Concerto (1939), delayed until 1982, showed that he was not always right. Wilfrid Mellers, in 1954, was equally dismissive: 'The most successful of these early works are undoubtedly the least pretentious.'[19]

Among the least pretentious are the Five Short Pieces, Opus 4, for piano, which seem to be later than the opus number suggests. Each one of them articulates a different texture with absolute economy and balance: the set is a microcosm of Berkeley's technique at the time of *Jonah*, and works well with its rapid concluding piece in varied metres. Notice the connection between the rhythm of No. 3 and the central section of the Nocturne for two pianos – further examples of a typical Berkeley atmosphere created by a regular pulse. They are dedicated to José Raffalli, the Corsican friend who shared the flat in Paris with Berkeley and was later killed fighting in the French resistance. When

[16] P. Dickinson, ed., *Twenty British Composers*, London, 1975, p. 26.
[17] Ibid.
[18] Ibid.
[19] W. Mellers, 'The Music of Lennox Berkeley', *Listener*, 24 June 1954, p. 1113.

Berkeley went to stay with Britten in Newquay, Cornwall, in July 1937 they looked at each other's recent works – Britten's *Our Hunting Fathers*, which would be premiered at the Norwich Festival the following September, and Berkeley's *Jonah*, which Britten had heard on the radio a few weeks before, and the Five Short Pieces. Berkeley had brought with him the scores of Walton's First Symphony and Vaughan Williams' Fourth, which they found amateurish, pretentious and abominably scored.[20] They found they had much in common personally as well as musically and those five days were significant, as Britten confided to his diary:

> He is an awful dear – very intelligent and kind – & I am very attached to him, even after this short time. In spite of his avowed sexual weakness for young men of my age and form – he is considerate and open, & we have come to an agreement on that subject.[21]

This confirms Berkeley's sexual orientation until his marriage ten years later and shows his pre-eminent position amongst Britten's closest friends for at least a few months until Britten got to know Peter Pears and took a flat with him in London in March 1938. Later that year Berkeley admitted: 'When I've pulled myself together a bit I feel an awful fool to have let myself fall in love so violently – I really ought to know better at my age.'[22] However, they succeeded in maintaining a special friendship and Britten supported Berkeley above all other British composers.

Britten later met José Raffalli and realised his importance in Berkeley's life. So much so that only two months before he and Pears left for America he wrote rather confusingly to Berkeley in Paris:

> I am sure that you're feeling fine now that you're in Paris & with José & all those friends of yours. I was going to say that you are now where you really belong to cheer you up – but I'm not so sure about that – I think Snape is really your spiritual home – whatever it is physically!![23]

An unexplored influence on the lighter side of Berkeley at the time when he first met Britten may have been Jean Françaix. In a letter to Britten on 18 July 1936, Berkeley urged him to listen to the broadcast of Françaix' Concertino; on 28 December 1937 he reported on his visit to Françaix and then he accompanied him on his first visit to England on 6 February. An unusual Berkeley work, which lay forgotten in the Boulanger collection of manuscripts, was performed in London at the Queen's Hall on 24 November 1936 in a programme with the Oriana Madrigal Society Choir and the London Symphony Orchestra conducted by Boulanger. This included her beloved Fauré Requiem, and her old pupil's

[20] D. Mitchell and P. Reed, eds, *Letters from a Life: Selected Letters and Diaries of Benjamin Britten, Volume 1 1923–39*, London, 1991, p. 437.
[21] Ibid.
[22] L. Berkeley, undated letter from Rudge House, Painswick, Gloucestershire.
[23] B. Britten, letter to Berkeley, 1 January 1939.

work was *Deux Poèmes de Pindar*, settings for chorus and orchestra of the Ancient Greek lyric poet, dedicated to the influential patron the Princesse de Polignac. The harmonic language is more dissonant than in *Jonah* but the sombre choral writing is a new departure. An *Ode* for chorus (SATB), trumpet and strings, also from the Boulanger collection, shows the same stark qualities and may also date from the mid-1930s. Judging from the scores, both these works ought not to have been forgotten and they merit performance.

It was soon after they met at Barcelona that Berkeley and Britten started to plan their collaborative work, the orchestral suite based on Spanish folk-tunes which they called *Mont Juic*, an attractive souvenir which has become well known. The two composers were together at what their later programme-note called 'a display of National Dances in Mont Juic Park' and Britten wrote down some of the tunes used.[24] For many years they were both secretive about who wrote which portions of the suite and the score at the Britten-Pears Library is entirely in Britten's hand. However, in spite of Berkeley's note in the published score to the effect that they were both involved in each movement, he told me that the first and second movements were mostly his and the last two mostly Britten's. On 11 January 1938, Berkeley wrote to Britten after hearing the BBC broadcast of *Mont Juic*: 'I must say I thought your two pieces more effective than mine . . .' And on 19 April 1938: 'I am very pleased with *Mont Juic* – the last movement is terrific orchestration and betrays the master hand?' In the final piece Britten exploits the orchestra in characteristic fashion but the rising triadic theme in Berkeley's first movement, and even some of its scoring, looks ahead to Britten's *Variations on a Theme of Purcell*. Norman del Mar thought it was 'absolutely impossible' to tell who wrote which portions but some people felt the Lament in C minor, the second movement, fitted the mood of Britten's pacifist music of the same period: its subtitle – Barcelona, July 1936 – refers to the start of the Spanish Civil War. But there was also a personal tragedy involved. Peter Burra, a writer and close friend of Peter Pears, was killed in a plane crash on 27 April 1937 and *Mont Juic* is dedicated to his memory. Burra was at Barcelona with Berkeley and Britten – all three of them met there for the first time – and was with them at the display of National Dances at Mont Juic, which impressed them all so much. He reviewed the Festival:

> Only two English composers were included in the Festival, but they represented us well: Lennox Berkeley and Benjamin Britten. Evidently neither of them is particularly interested in being English and they are equally far from looking for their inspiration in theory. In fact their work belonged to the small body which seemed to have its roots in genuine individual character . . . Lennox Berkeley's Overture (which received a brilliant performance from the Madrid Symphony Orchestra under the composer's direction) . . . is delightfully written with some dazzling orchestration and breaks out at moments into sheer lyrical beauty.[25]

[24] L. Berkeley, 'Views from Mont Juic', *Tempo* 106, September 1973, pp. 6–7. See also D. Mitchell and P. Reed, eds, *Letters from a Life*, Volume 1, pp. 537–40 and 586–7.

[25] P. Burra, 'The Barcelona Festival', *Monthly Musical Record* 66, June 1936, pp. 107–8.

Burra anticipated *Jonah* as an 'event to await with interest' and Berkeley obtained a ticket for him at Broadcasting House since he specially wanted him to hear it.[26]

Berkeley's collaboration with Britten opened up new avenues as he always admitted:

> Another musician to whom I owe a considerable debt is Benjamin Britten. When I came back to England after my student days in Paris, though I felt reasonably well equipped to embark on a career as a composer, I was still far from having found how to use what I had acquired to real advantage. I realised quickly that here was someone of greater musical ability than I, and from whom I could learn. Due to many conflicting influences, I was rather tied up in knots: he was able to undo them for me and encourage me to be myself, to write, in fact, the kind of music I really wanted to write, regardless of what the fashionable idiom of the time might be. I have done so ever since.[27]

At the moment when Berkeley came strongly under Britten's influence, Britten himself was much affected by W. H. Auden, whom he had met in July 1935 when writing music for the GPO Film Unit. It looks as if Auden's technical facility in verse encouraged aspects of Britten's own musical virtuosity. *Our Hunting Fathers* shows a considerable advance on the vocabulary of *A Boy was Born* and the subject arose from his developing pacifist and left-wing convictions. Auden's easy use of colloquialism in poetry can be compared with Britten's exploitation of traditional materials such as triads and scale patterns. Auden and Britten, of course, continued to work together during Britten's years in America, 1939–42. Berkeley, in England, kept in touch with Britten by letter – at an uncertain time of war when letters were liable to get lost – and they followed each other's works closely. However, they both suffered attacks from conservative critics. Even the 28-year-old William Glock felt that, in *Our Hunting Fathers*, Britten 'matched obscure sense in Auden's text with obvious nonsense in the music'.[28] Another reviewer in the *Monthly Musical Record*, identified only by initials, delivered a classic embodiment of the clichés then being peddled about Britten:

> The general impression is one of a dry cocktail cleverness, unrelieved by any real beauty of line. Of its technical accomplishments there can be no doubt . . . But such smartness and dexterity in the handling of the tools of his trade is a power that leads rapidly to decadence unless the composer has great things to say.[29]

Fortunately the composer did have 'great things to say' but this attitude of suspicion affected both Berkeley and Britten at a time when they were both responding to Auden and even setting some of the same poems. The chronology is hard to work out, but some intriguing connections emerge.

On 8 January 1937 Britten met Auden at the Lyons Corner House at Oxford Street and Tottenham Court Road. Auden was on his way to observe the Spanish Civil War, but he wanted Britten to have two new poems, so he wrote

[26] See C. Headington, *Peter Pears: a Biography*, London, 1992, pp. 63–5.

[27] L. Berkeley, 'A Composer speaks', *Composer* 43, Spring 1972, pp. 17–19.

[28] W. Glock, 'The Norwich Festival', *Monthly Musical Record* 66, November 1936, p. 206.

[29] E. R., 'Music Review', *Monthly Musical Record* 66, December 1936, p. 206.

them into copies of Britten's works which he happened to be carrying. Thus 'Lay your sleeping head, my love', which Auden had just written, was scribbled into the score of *Our Hunting Fathers*: it was published shortly afterwards in the Spring number of *New Writing*. Britten's diary refers to 'two grand poems' and concludes 'I've lots to do with them.'[30] He does not seem to have set 'Lay your sleeping head' but Berkeley did and dedicated his setting 'To Benjamin'. It is a tender love-poem based on a passing fascination recognised as such. This is one of Auden's best-known, presumably gay, love-lyrics, memorably illustrated in a late lithograph by Henry Moore which ironically depicts a man and a girl with long hair. The other poem Auden wrote out for Britten was included in *The Ballad of Heroes*: 'It's farewell to the drawing room's civilised cry' – very much in the mood of approaching war.

The tripartite involvements of another poem may be more complex. 'Night covers up the rigid land' was dedicated by Auden to Britten and written into a miniature score of his Sinfonietta. According to Humphrey Carpenter: 'This poem suggests that Auden was in love with Britten, but that Britten had rejected him, perhaps for someone else.'[31] Britten set the poem on 27 October 1937 but never published the song. However, Berkeley set the poem too, in the same year, and this was published in 1939. Berkeley's setting is dedicated 'To B.B.', perhaps recalling his own loss when it became clear that Britten had met the love of his life in Peter Pears. Auden's chagrin in the poem is clear enough – 'You love your life and I love you, So I must lie alone'. That was written in March 1936, the same month as 'Underneath the abject willow' a poem both for and about Britten. If Britten had rejected Auden's advances, which appears likely, this would reflect his dedication to his work and, at this stage, his frozen sexuality.[32] This was before Britten had met Berkeley or Pears.

This complicated situation can also be examined in notes as well as words. Britten set 'Night covers up the rigid land' at Peasenhall, Suffolk, on 27 October 1937, the same month as writing Nos. 1, 3 and 5 of of the Auden song-cycle *On This Island*. 'Night covers up' was not included in the cycle and is now to be found on the inside of the original cover of the manuscript of *On This Island*. Berkeley admired these songs, especially the Nocturne, and wrote to Britten: 'Incidentally I have got bitten with Wystan's poems and am doing another one. I promise not to do any more! Not that it matters – they are not as good as yours.' (undated letter) Presumably Berkeley had forgotten his own Auden songs composed at Oxford more than ten years earlier.

Both composers establish a regular pulse in their settings, which feels like a funeral bell for lost love. Britten chooses 6/8, with the piano texture opening out from one note, the tonic G. The recurring melodic phrase, in a transposed Phrygian mode, is particularly memorable:

[30] D. Mitchell, *Britten and Auden in the Thirties*, London, 1981, p. 141.

[31] H. Carpenter, *W. H. Auden: a Biography*, London, 1981, p. 188. See also H. Carpenter, *Benjamin Britten: a Biography*, London, 1992, pp. 81–2, and 127.

[32] D. Mitchell and P. Reed, eds, *Letters from a Life*, Volume 1, p. 379–385.

Example 19. Britten: 'Night covers up the rigid land'

This phrase is varied in the second stanza to modulate into D flat major, but the most striking variation is in the third stanza, where the high note reaches up to G instead of the F or G flat before. The words at this bar refer to the 'dark caressive head'. Did Britten set this knowing that the text described him? He certainly understood the crisis implicit in the fourth stanza, marked *agitando*, and arriving in the fifth stanza. Here Auden wishes for Britten a passionate love affair – 'O hurry to the fêted spot of your deliberate fall'. Constantly didactic about sex, Auden expounds the same theme in another poem dedicated to Britten, 'Underneath the abject willow', and again in *Letters from Iceland*.[33] In the song, Britten reacts with musical passion and even anticipates the sharp fourth suspensions and the tritones of the *War Requiem*:

Example 20. Britten: 'Night covers up the rigid land'

[33] W. H. Auden, *Letters from Iceland*, London, 1937, p. 238.

Britten ends his setting of 'Night covers up the rigid land' on tolling Ds, an empty dominant when no tonic solution can be found. The style is close to that of the Nocturne in *On This Island* and the achievement not far short. By contrast, Berkeley catches the mood of the poem without reflecting its rise and fall. His regular pulse is in 5/4 in E flat major. He starts with the dominant and, like Britten, ends with the dominant note on its own: perhaps the same symbol of frustration. Berkeley must have known Britten's setting; he dedicated his setting to him, and it looks as if they would both have realised what gave rise to the poem. Berkeley's response to lost love is more philosophical, more passive, than Britten's. Berkeley has established a mood in the descending phrase of the opening bars which has already allowed for the burden of loss. Thus, when the realisation of loneliness comes at the end of the fourth stanza, Berkeley can follow it with an altered and transposed recapitulation of the music from the opening. The touch of C major before ending ambiguously on a chord which suggests the sensuous added sixth is memorable (see Example 21 on p. 40). Berkeley's return to the music of his opening a major third higher in pitch facilitates direct comparison with a tune later appearing in Britten's *Albert Herring*, Act 1, scene 2, in the same key. This catches Albert in a mood of regret which makes it look as if Britten knew Berkeley's song – or at least proves that their musical thought was not far apart (see Example 22 on p. 41). This connection through *Albert Herring* (1947), although indicative of the two-way traffic between the two composers, is a footnote later to a unique crossing of paths between Auden, Britten and Berkeley through the medium of a poem which meant much to all three of them. Stravinsky may have considered that music was 'powerless to *express* anything at all' in the conventional sense, but in connection with a text and a context it can speak volumes.[34]

Berkeley's setting of Auden's 'Lay your sleeping head' has remained in manuscript – he was still using French manuscript paper but there is no date. The setting is a prototype for Berkeley's regular patterns where the piano part is unarresting to begin with, but the harmony changes subtly to qualify the vocal line and its shifting moods. Although the piano writing is mostly in the middle register, this is overcome by the emphasis on the vocal line, which carries the story rather like a ballad. Berkeley may have rejected the song because he felt that the amount of text had been too much for him in the layout he had chosen. He cannot have thought the setting too personal in its dedication since 'Night covers up the rigid land' was printed with the same inscription.

It was in April 1938 that Britten moved into the Old Mill at Snape, which he had bought the previous August. He shared this with Berkeley who remained in charge after Britten and Pears had left for North America in March 1939. With work-rooms at opposite ends of the house, Britten worked on his Piano Concerto, Opus 13, which he dedicated to Berkeley, and Berkeley worked on his Introduction and Allegro for two pianos and orchestra, Opus 11, which he

[34] I. Stravinsky, *An Autobiography*, New York, 1936, p. 53.

Example 21. Berkeley: 'Night covers up the rigid land'

dedicated to Britten.[35] They were both represented again at the International Society for Contemporary Music Festival held in London in 1938, Britten with his Frank Bridge Variations, Opus 10, and Berkeley with *Domini est terra*, Opus 10, the setting of Psalm 24 for chorus and orchestra which he had written the year before and dedicated to Boulanger. So both men dedicated their ISCM works to their teachers at the same time, with the same opus number. Berkeley's work was the shorter – nine minutes compared with Britten's substantial 25-minute set of variations.

On 4 December 1937, Britten wrote to their mutual friend, the singing-teacher and choir-trainer Ursula Nettleship: 'P.S. By-the-way – Lennox Berkeley has just written a fearfully good PSALM for chorus & orchestra. It's the goods all right. You must see it.'[36] *Domini est terra* shows a mellowing of style – more

[35] D. Mitchell and J. Evans, *Benjamin Britten: Pictures from a Life 1913–1976*, London, 1978. However, see pp. 85–6 for photographs of the two composers working together.

[36] D. Mitchell and P. Reed, eds, *Letters from a Life*, Volume 1, p. 528.

Example 22. Britten: *Albert Herring*, Act 1, scene 2

tonal, more consonant and less cluttered – perhaps through the influence of Britten, who also liked to pare music down to its basic essentials. Seventeen bars of introduction provide a dramatic entry for the chorus – the tactic of Handel's *Zadok the Priest*, that Berkeley was to use again in his *A Festival Anthem*, Opus 21 and in the *Magnificat*, Opus 71. There is less textbook polyphony than in *Jonah* and more unobstructed appeal when lines are homophonic or unison. The first performance of *Domini est terra* was at the Queen's Hall, London, on 17 June 1938 and then it was given at the Three Choirs Festival. It would have sounded well in Worcester Cathedral, and Philip Radcliffe, writing in *The Criterion*, responded sympathetically to Berkeley's reserve, even if his cautious remarks about Stravinsky were typical of the period in England:

> *Domini est terra* was austere and restrained, with some of the directness and economy of texture of later Stravinsky: it was, however, free from the angularity and dryness which often disfigure the latter's more recent works, and left an impression of quiet and individual beauty.[37]

Berkeley's ballet *The Judgement of Paris* was produced at Sadler's Wells on 10 May 1938, with choreography by Frederick Ashton. On 28 December 1937, Berkeley wrote to Britten from Paris: 'I am writing some rather voluptuous ballet music which I think you might approve of – anyhow I am enjoying it.' The five numbers were composed between December 1937 and February 1938. The ballet has not had a full-scale revival and when I asked Ashton about it he regretted that an enormous amount of material got lost from pre-war days since there was no ballet notation then and little filming.[38] However, it seems effective

[37] P. F. Radcliffe, *The Criterion* 60, October 1938, p. 73.
[38] Sir Frederick Ashton, interview with author, 3 August 1983.

dance music, with none of the jazz connections of Berkeley's earlier untitled ballet score. Other works from this period are still largely unknown, apart from the Cello Concerto (1939), which was not performed until 1982. The neglect of these works is surprising, since the piece after the Cello Concerto is the Serenade for Strings, Opus 12, widely acknowledged as one of Berkeley's masterpieces. As might be expected, the Cello Concerto is not far short of this standard. I discussed it, along with other early works, with the composer when I was establishing his list of works for the *New Grove Dictionary of Music and Musicians* in 1975. He preferred not to include it then. Later on, publicity was made of the fact that he appeared to have forgotten about it altogether. Berkeley's letter to Britten of 5 January 1940 shows that the Cello Concerto was written for Maurice Eisenberg, but he had returned to America after being based in Paris for most of the thirties, and the war must have disrupted plans:

> Eisenberg is in America now and says he will work at my Cello Concerto. I think in some ways it is the best thing I have done, but it's still so far from what I hope some day to do that I can't get very keen about it really. Whether I shall ever be able to do what I feel I might, remains to be seen, and I feel rather frail and incompetent about it, but it may gradually develop.

The belated premiere of Berkeley's first concerto was given by Moray Welsh and the Hallé Orchestra under James Loughran at the Cheltenham Festival on 17 July 1983. The first of the two movements is an expansive *Allegro moderato* in an adapted sonata-form design which luxuriates in four main themes, which are all well defined and memorable. The precisely planned entry of the soloist on a sustained high A anticipated by the horns is a superb gesture, and throughout the scoring is ideally controlled to allow the cello to come through. The confident strength of the ideas is quite at variance with Berkeley's usual disclaimers and this movement looks ahead to Symphony No. 1. The only disappointment is that in revising the score for the premiere Berkeley cut out the repeat of the second subject at the recapitulation – it was surely too late to alter a work he had forgotten he had written anyway and future performers should consider restoring this. The second movement is an introduction and allegro. The *Lento* opens with rising perfect fourths in the solo cello which, although not the main theme here, would recur in the Horn Trio, Opus 44. It leads to an *Allegro moderato* which becomes a kind of waltz. The two-movement scheme is related to the Introduction and Allegro for two pianos and orchestra composed just before – another pair of works – and is as carefully planned as that of the later Two-Piano Concerto, Opus 30. The neglect of this concerto by cellists is surprising considering its enthusiastic reception, which caused Bayan Northcott, after its premiere, to consider that it might have bridged the gap between Elgar's and Walton's.[39] The Cello Concerto is a true virtuoso piece right on the edge of the next period, when almost every work reached Berkeley's highest standard.

[39] B. Northcott, *Sunday Telegraph*, 24 July, 1983.

3. Maturity

The late 1930s brought three major British contributions to the literature for string orchestra. Britten's *Variations on a Theme of Frank Bridge* (1937); Berkeley's Serenade (1938–39); and Tippett's Concerto for Double String Orchestra (1938–39, but not performed until 1940). In 1975 I wrote in the sleeve-notes for the recording of the Serenade, conducted by Berkeley:

> Both in its title, and in its scintillating brilliance of sound, the Serenade recalls Mozart. But like some of the neo-classical pieces of Stravinsky the model is difficult to pinpoint, and Berkeley's first movement, *Vivace*, is just as close to Bach's Third Brandenburg Concerto in its exhilarating moto perpetuo. Like the Divertimento, although written four years earlier, the Serenade wastes no notes – a lesson learnt from Nadia Boulanger.[1]

But it could also be claimed that the example of Britten, rather than the influence of Boulanger, may have brought about the new open sound and natural flow of the works of Berkeley's maturity, which began with the Serenade (see Example 23 on p. 44). More specifically, Berkeley has learnt how to use major and minor triads and scales with the freedom of Britten from the Frank Bridge Variations onwards. The Serenade is a group of character pieces, comparable to Britten's separate variations, which use daringly contrasted styles and yet just cohere. Berkeley completed the first movement at Snape in 1938 and its accented chords shifting from D major to minor and back belong to the Mozart-Schubert tradition. The string texture is ideally spaced with the background activity in the middle range and the melody high up, answered periodically by the cellos and bases. The regular pulse has moved away from Stravinskian dislocations and Berkeley has attached himself to a wider orbit, laying claim to a position where he can inherit whatever he chooses in the Western tradition. Now it is not the derivations that are the main thing, but the new personality and its ingredients of which there are many.

The melody of the second movement is a kind of melancholy serenade with traditional guitar plucking effects (see Example 24 on p. 45).

[1] Divertimento in B flat, Op. 18; Canzonetta from the Sinfonia Concertante for Oboe and Chamber Orchestra, Op. 84; Serenade for Strings, Op. 12; Partita for Chamber Orchestra, Op. 66. London Philharmonic Orchestra/Sir Lennox Berkeley. Lyrita SRCS 74 (1975), CD reissue SRCD 226 (1992).

Example 23. Serenade, Opus 12

Vivace (♩=176)
Violins I
Violins II
Violas
Violoncellos
Contra Basses

The oscillating semitones in the fifth bar, developed later, are a hallmark of Berkeley's melody – the element which carried Berkeley away from his extended training in France towards what Mellers saw as an English independence. The third movement, *Allegro moderato*, is a kind of scherzo based on fragments over a regular 6/8. At figure 33 there is a wonderfully heard texture mixing *col legno* with *pizzicato*, leading to a melodic scrap based on a falling major sixth. This relates to the third of the Five Short Pieces, in the same key, and illustrates a tendency of Berkeley's to add further material as a movement progresses. In this case several distinct ideas are successfully held together by the unexpected way they emerge over a continuous rhythmic background.

Before turning to the unusual last movement it may be worth seeing how a kindred spirit introduced Berkeley to his principal publisher. He told me that it was probably in 1933 that he went to dinner with Lord Berners, in London, where Nadia Boulanger was also a guest and after that meeting Berners introduced Berkeley to his own publisher, J. & W. Chester. There are a number of connections between the two of them. Both came from an aristocratic background and Berners also grew up as a composer abroad – in

Example 24. Serenade

Rome during World War I – and was able to reach a public in England only later through his ballets in a simpler musical idiom. Berners was shattered by the Second World War, feeling that everything European he believed in was under threat, and Berkeley, completing his Serenade in November 1939, must have felt much the same. In October he got permission from the authorities to return to his flat in Paris even after war had broken out and it must have been depressing. 'Paris is much the same as London – pretty empty compared with normal times', he wrote to Ralph Hawkes, and José had been called up.[2] They never met again. This mood impinges inescapably on the last movement of the Serenade, where the situation is emphasised by a slow-motion quotation in the last few bars of the opening theme of the first movement. That was written at Snape, but by the time Berkeley had completed the work the war had started and Britten had gone to America with Peter Pears.

The lyrical quality of the last movement's opening bars brings a new intensity, which prefigures the composer of the Teresa of Avila songs eight years later. The

[2] L. Berkeley, letter to Ralph Hawkes from 1 Cité Chaptal, Paris IX, 22 October 1939.

mood seems to be religious. Berkeley had become a Roman Catholic in 1928 but, apart from *Jonah* and *Domini est terra*, it was only from the later war years that religious texts emerged in his output. The details of the initially four-part texture bear closer examination:

Example 25. Serenade

Surprisingly, the key, and even the mood, is that of the angel's farewell from Elgar's *The Dream of Gerontius*. The disguised perfect cadence to bar 3 is overt in bar 8 and the middle section has a pizzicato ostinato now far removed from Stravinsky. The climax – perfectly placed and built on a rising bass line over two-and-a-half octaves – rings with the unique clarity of high strings. The reminiscence at the end is poignant, inseparable surely from the circumstances of personal and national loss. However, looking back in 1975 to the premiere of Vaughan Williams' Fourth Symphony forty years earlier, Berkeley thought differently:

> Some thought the work was influenced by the troubled atmosphere of those pre-war days. This may be so – though I don't believe that exterior events necessarily produce an immediate reaction in music: some of Mozart's most serene work, for instance, was written at times of extreme stress.[3]

[3] *Radio Times*, 16–20 August 1975 – part of Berkeley's series of notes about every Prom concert that season.

On 4 February 1940 Berkeley wrote to Britten after the first performance of the Serenade which had been given at the London Contemporary Music Centre five days before:

> My thing went well, and was quite appreciated – it came off well, and on the whole I feel fairly satisfied, and to be quite honest I must say I think it was the best thing after yours [*Les Illuminations*, Opus 18].

Berkeley was then uncharacteristically outspoken about two other British composers in the same programme, finding Howells' Concerto for String Orchestra a 'conscientious sort of music, but its content completely secondhand and boring' and Berners' Adagio and Hornpipe from *The Triumph of Neptune* 'feeble and badly scored'. Berkeley must have had a response from Britten to the score of the Serenade since he wrote back, on 9 November 1940:

> I agree with what you say about the Serenade – it is rather uneven in quality, but I think too that the last movement is the best . . .

Berkeley was vulnerable to criticism, as Lady Berkeley has confirmed, and always took adverse reviews seriously. So it looks as if Britten, in America, may have had reservations that he did not hesitate to express – unfortunately since the Serenade is not 'uneven in quality' and was to become one of Berkeley's most frequently performed and admired instrumental works. However, just before leaving the USA, on 20 January 1942, Britten made amends. He wrote to Albert Goldberg, who had conducted the American premiere of his Piano Concerto with the Illinois Symphony Orchestra and Britten as soloist, and sent a score of the Serenade:

> Enclosed . . . is the score of Berkeley's which I have been meaning to show you. I do wish you could see your way to doing it. It is quite a slight piece, but very charming & ought to sound well on the strings . . . Let me know what you decide, because I'd like to tell him when I get back – he's had a tough time in the air-raids in London.[4]

The Serenade was in the same concert as the premiere of Britten's *Les Illuminations* with Sophie Wyss and the Boyd Neel Orchestra. In his earlier letter of 4 February 1940 Berkeley continued:

> The *Illuminations* are marvellous – even better than I had expected. It's grand music from beginning to end, and I don't know how to wait to get hold of a score . . . I think it's an absolute knockout, and the best thing you've done (of what I've heard) . . . You've had a wonderful press.

Berkeley had helped Britten by copying some of the score of *Les Illuminations*, and he and Sophie Wyss had made suggestions about French

[4] D. Mitchell and P. Reed, eds, *Letters from a Life: Selected Letters and Diaries of Benjamin Britten, Volume 1 1923–39*, p. 1014.

accentuation.[5] But in this first complete performance there were some songs that were new to him:

> I had a strange feeling (when listening for the first time to the ones I didn't know) of familiarity, as you might if you went to a place you had never been in before and found that you knew your way about.

This adds detail to an already involved relationship which, on Berkeley's side, showed elements of an inferiority complex. On 30 September 1937 Berkeley wrote to Britten:

> I'm afraid I go on liking your music better than my own. It just is better, and though it rather annoys me to admit it, I'm at the same time delighted because the music itself pleases and satisfies me so much.

This relationship is so unusual psychologically that it is worth recording the impressions of Berkeley's friends, colleagues and family at this stage. I asked the critic Desmond Shawe-Taylor, who had reviewed Berkeley since the 1940s and watched him develop, what he thought about the relationship between Berkeley and Britten:

> I think that really Benjamin Britten, although such a strong musical personality, had in fact absorbed something from that particular spare delicacy of Lennox's style and approach to music. But they were naturally related in tastes and – although Lennox had a stronger French influence through Nadia Boulanger and so on, which Britten didn't – nevertheless I think there was a close sympathy between their outlook on music. I think they probably enriched each other.
>
> **PD** Does Lennox suffer from the comparison?
>
> **DST** I think that, modest as he was to a fault, one would feel that he must have been aware of his less brilliant musical personality. And he so openly admired Ben's music and made no bones about it . . . In a curious way Lennox remained his own man and wasn't immensely influenced by whoever he had lately encountered even if it was somebody like Britten.[6]

Norman del Mar, who regularly conducted Berkeley, went even further in dissociating the music of the two composers, and felt that Berkeley did not live under the shadow of Britten:

> **NdM** However much he may have hero-worshipped Ben . . . I can't see the connection at all. I think of Lennox as coming from that Boulanger area and developing in his own way from there despite Ben and it doesn't seem to me that there is an influence or pattern which connects with Ben in his writing.
>
> **PD** They wrote for some of the same performers.
>
> **NdM** Oh yes. At the time when Lennox wrote the *Stabat Mater* for the English

[5] 'Lennox Berkeley talks about Benjamin Britten', BBC Radio 3, 2 November 1977, archive tape T53121.

[6] Interview with author, 28 November 1990.

Opera Group, which I think is one of his most successful pieces . . . there is perhaps . . . a connection between the two in that sort of sense. But even then there is no moment in the *Stabat Mater* where I would say 'that sounds just like Ben' . . . It sounds just like Lennox.[7]

Julian Bream, who worked closely with Berkeley in most of the guitar works, made some particularly astute comments:

I remember Ben saying about the Guitar Sonatina: 'You know, Julian, that is *almost* a very good piece.' I thought this was terrific praise from him because I never heard him praise any composer, except I think Shostakovich latterly. In Ben's book it must have been rather a good piece!

I think that Ben was a little bit irritated by Lennox's music – at times – but I also think he admired him. I think he felt that compositionally, in terms of form, there were some weaknesses in the construction. But there is also Lennox's slight waywardness that is part of the charm of his music . . . it's not music that has been construed.

One has to admit that Lennox was, harmonically speaking, a more sumptuous composer. His style was less austere. His music could sometimes have a sort of mellifluous quality which was rarely a quality in Ben's music. Ben may have thought that, in a sense, he was just going over the top . . . Lennox was his own man . . . finally I don't find a great deal of Britten's influence in his music.[8]

However, Basil Douglas, Manager of the English Opera Group, specifically remembered Berkeley saying that he liked Britten's music better than his own, which seemed very characteristic, and that when he was asked to write an opera for the English Opera Group, he wanted to do it as well as possible, which meant coming close to *The Rape of Lucretia* or *Albert Herring*.[9]

Michael Berkeley, who was born in 1948, saw the relationship between his father and his godfather from within the family later on, but the whole extraordinary mechanism was still very much in operation:

MB Britten was an absolute fundamental part of my childhood and my upbringing. He ran through my musical life like one of the two rails of a railway because my father was so involved with him both personally and musically, although by the time I was growing up they saw less of each other but they kept in touch. My father kept musically absolutely on top of everything that Ben did. He couldn't wait for a score to come through the post such was his admiration. And he was also enormously fond of Ben. It was a very close relationship at one time and he went on having that fondness for Ben. I think he felt he'd learnt a lot from Ben and there were always things in the scores he could learn from even later in life. I remember him pointing things out to me and just being in awe of the simplicity, the economy of means, the way that with just a few notes Britten could summon something up and it would be absolutely right.

[7] Interview with author, 21 December 1990.
[8] Interview with author, 28 January 1991.
[9] Interview with author, 28 November 1990.

> **PD** Your father said he liked Ben's music better than his own – a rare kind of humility?
>
> **MB** He was extraordinarily realistic. I don't think he actually felt inferior, because I think he felt that there were things he could say in his own way that were totally his. I never got the feeling of inferiority. I did get the feeling of – quite simply – open admiration.[10]

Malcolm Williamson saw Berkeley's attitude as an example of his humility and of his generosity to others. After the first performance of Williamson's *Hammarskjold Portrait* for soprano and strings (1974): 'Berkeley went home and wrote a letter praising me to the skies saying he wished he could write a piece of music as good as mine . . . My piece is not better than Lennox's. It was simply that it was typical of Lennox to draw attention away from himself. This was part of his asceticism.'[11] These testimonies put Berkeley's attitude into perspective. He should be assessed in terms of his music and not what he said about it.

On 21 April 1940 Berkeley wrote to Britten after having spent some five weeks in Paris, which the German army would enter less than two months later. Full of the success of *Les Illuminations* at the 30 January concert in London, Berkeley confronted Boulanger with his increasing enthusiasm for Britten – and found conflicts:

> Boosey and Hawkes lent me a proof of your *Illuminations*. I think the one called *Parade* is far the best. I couldn't get Nadia to be very keen – she doesn't seem to take your music easily. We had a terrific argument about it. She much admired the string writing, but thinks that you haven't found your real musical language yet – she doesn't feel that the harmony is sufficiently personal. I can see what she means, but it doesn't worry me so much – in fact I definitely disagree . . .

One does see what Boulanger meant since there is little distinctive about the harmony in early Britten. Earlier, on 19 June 1936, Britten's diary entry had admired Berkeley's music and noted an element missing in his own: 'To its advantage, it is under Stravinsky's influence, of course, but the harmony is extremely personal.'[12] However, the composer himself, in New York, cannot have been amused by such comments relayed from Boulanger. All the same it looks as if it was thanks to Britten that Berkeley had gained the courage to stand up to Boulanger and to realise himself. The equivalent mother-figure from whom Britten needed to escape seems to have been Mrs Britten herself, who died in 1937.

By the early 1940s Berkeley was having his own successes and many more were to come. The Sonatina, Opus 13, was written for the recorder player Carl Dolmetsch, and has become better known in performances for flute and piano, notably by James Galway, whose recording came more than forty years after it

[10] Interview with the author, 29 November 1990.
[11] Interview with the author, 22 February 1991.
[12] H. Carpenter, *Benjamin Britten: a Biography*, London, 1992, p. 84.

was written in 1939.[13] On 21 November 1939 Berkeley was able to write to Britten:

> Hardly any concerts nowadays. . . . I actually had one the other day though: Carl Dolmetsch played my Recorder Sonatina and it was quite a success. The last movement was encored and I actually got a good press about it.

This Sonatina was the first piece for single instrument and keyboard – it looks as if the first performance was with harpsichord – since the Violin and Piano Sonata No. 2 designated as Opus 1. The title of sonatina, as for the Violin and Piano Sonatina, Opus 17, seems appropriate, but there is more to it than that since all the inessentials have gone. The C major of the slow movement is absolutely serene and the major chord reigns.

Example 26. Sonatina for recorder and piano, Opus 13

This melody – the *Adagio* of the Recorder Sonatina – has much in common with the corresponding movement in the String Trio, Opus 19 (1943). The Lydian mode sharpened fourths, common in Bartók as well as Debussy and Ravel, coloured several of Berkeley's melodies from this period onwards and can be found in Britten's too, such as the third of the *Seven Sonnets of Michelangelo*, Opus 22 (1940). Britten's major key radiance, in slow tempi, is at its most characteristic in Nos. VII and IX of *Les Illuminations* and the sixth of *The Holy Sonnets of John Donne* (1945), 'Since she whom I loved', which should be compared with Berkeley's *Silver*, in the same key, from the Five Songs (de la Mare), Opus 26.[14] The four-bar phrase of the *Adagio* ends with a perfect cadence. The dominant chord on the second half of bar 4 contains the tonic, which is coming, as well as its own dominant components. It could be a quote from Purcell, which is where Britten may have found it too. A recently published Auden setting by Britten – 'What's in your mind', a poem Berkeley also set much later – uses this cadence exactly in the same key. It also appears in the sixth of the Donne Sonnets in the central section. Berkeley may have been aware of Britten's use of this cadential device, but they had both discovered the secret of rehabilitating traditional materials at a time when the more advanced composers were moving in the opposite direction. As a result, Berkeley began to lose the support of the modern music lobby without yet gaining wider public acceptance. Britten alone seemed to have it both ways by conquering an

[13] *James Galway plays Lennox Berkeley*, LPO under Berkeley, RCA Red Seal RS 9011 (1982).
[14] See Chapter 5 p. 93.

international audience through opera and, as we shall see, Berkeley tried to follow him in that direction later on.

Meanwhile, the very obstacles to public appreciation of Berkeley's larger works – what might be regarded as his rather withdrawn and private temperament – became an asset in his growing body of chamber works. In a broadcast talk on Gabriel Fauré, Nadia Boulanger's own teacher, Berkeley unintentionally made some observations which can be applied to his own work:

> The more closely one examines his music, the more one is brought to realise that the extreme sobriety of his manner hides a talent of a highly individual kind. There is an element of understatement in his music which has limited his public appeal. And it demands a correspondingly greater effort on the part of the listener than does music of a more extrovert character.[15]

In 1990 Basil Douglas looked back to the pleasures of singing songs to Berkeley's accompaniment at the piano. Their repertoire, for purely domestic occasions, included some of Berkeley's songs but a great deal of Fauré.[16]

What has been called Berkeley's restraint is a natural quality for chamber music, but his range should not be thought limited. Neither should Fauré's for that matter, as a staged production of *Pénélope* soon demonstrates. The String Quartet No. 2, Opus 15, shows the same simplification process at work when compared with No. 1 from five years earlier. On 17 July 1940 Berkeley wrote enthusiastically to Britten: 'I've written a new String Quartet, which I finished last month, and I think is miles better than anything I've done yet.' The variety of textures, the logical flow and the thematic invention can be compared to Ravel's example. The level is as high as the Serenade and the Recorder Sonatina but in a more exacting medium. Erik Levi, writing in 1983, justifiably found 'a ferocity in its outer movements that can only be related to its date of composition'.[17]

Around 1967 Berkeley introduced the work to the BBC Radio 3 audience:

> My Second String Quartet was written twenty-seven years ago. This is quite a long time in anybody's life and it was, I think, not surprising that when I was asked to give a brief introduction to its performance in this series I found that, apart from the opening phrase, I couldn't remember a note of it. I was therefore able to read through it almost as one would be able to read a work by someone else, wondering what I would think of this composer who would, I felt sure, bear little resemblance to me. I was astonished to find that he was closer to me than I thought and that, though there were big differences, the basic musical language had changed little. I don't know whether I should regard this as a good thing or not. It certainly made me take stock of how much or how little I

[15] BBC Radio 3 talk by Berkeley on Fauré in the early 1960s. Extract included in P. Dickinson, 'Lennox Berkeley', *Music and Musicians* 13, August 1965, pp. 20–23 and 54. Reprinted as 'Senior British Composers 2: Lennox Berkeley', *Composer* 36, Summer 1970, pp. 3–9 and 11.

[16] Interview with author, 28 November 1990.

[17] E. Levi, 'Sir Lennox Berkeley at 80 – Chamber Music', *W. H. News* no. 1, 1968.

> had advanced and of the extent to which I have used the enlargement of the musical vocabulary or of the technical methods that have caused such an immense difference between the music of today and that of even thirty years ago. The conclusion I reached, though important to me, can hardly be of much interest to anyone who may listen to this work today but it may be worth mentioning the influences that lay behind it at the time. I was much influenced in my younger days by French music of which I had a great love and to a large extent still have. It was the clarity, order and emotional climate, as it were, something more subtle, more lightly touched on than what I found in other music of the period that appealed to me. A certain type of harmony, too, deriving from the French composers of the late nineteenth and early twentieth centuries – Fauré, Debussy and Ravel – that one finds later in the music of Poulenc in particular. It was this that I felt that I could use in my own way. This is the idiom in which the music I was writing at that time was based and, though I hope I have now acquired a more individual musical language, I have never felt inclined to deny my immediate musical ancestry.
>
> The Quartet is in three movements. The first in traditional sonata form, with two main subjects, development and modified recapitulation, so easy to follow that any more detailed analysis is unnecessary. The slow movement, the part which I now prefer, is in free form finding its own shape rather than fitting itself into a conventional and perhaps over-worked pattern. The last movement consists of an introduction, a main middle section, and a coda which returns to the opening. I asked myself, after looking at this score again, how different, apart from any change in the actual idiom, would a string quartet be if I wrote one today. I think I would feel the need to give it a more fluid form, letting the ideas grow and develop more and avoid so much repetition. Also I would apply many things I have learnt and am still learning about music after nearly thirty years experience of composing and hearing my music played.[18]

There are many features of Berkeley's whole temperament in this introduction which have made it worth complete quotation. It shows again how consistently he disengaged himself from his earlier works and how precisely he was aware of his own uses of French traditions. His descriptive phrases such as 'clarity, order and emotional climate' and 'something more subtle, more lightly touched on' catch the characteristics of his music to perfection. The use of repetition in the Quartet is minimal and his criticism of it seems unjustified, but this approach is undoubtedly that of neo-classical Stravinsky, a strong influence at a formative stage, and these are all indicators of Berkeley's thinking in the late 1960s moving towards his Third Quartet.

Back in the early 1940s Berkeley's increasing command of continuity was put to the test in a more exposed public form – that of a symphony. In 1972 the composer explained his conception of the title:

> I think any composer can throw his work into . . . modified symphonic form. I think the word 'symphony' is no doubt out of fashion now, but I think it's only

[18] L. Berkeley, introduction to BBC Radio 3 broadcast of String Quartet No. 2, undated private tape not listed in BBC archives.

> the word because you'd make your own form and idiom in the symphony now anyway, wouldn't you? I think it's just a question of whether you choose to use the word or not.[19]

This could be argued, but Berkeley's Symphony No. 1, completed in 1941 and conducted by him with the London Philharmonic Orchestra at the Proms on 8 July 1943, does justify its title in terms of lyrical rather than dramatic development. This does not mean that the work lacks drama or the ability to sustain its length of over half an hour. Berkeley had made a start on it as early as August 1936, as a letter to Britten from Jersey indicated: this was Berkeley's first experience of air travel.[20]

The first movement opens sombrely (Example 27 on p. 55). The tonal centre of the whole work is C, but the opening unison contains menace in its minor thirds. The fourth and fifth bars employ bitonal harmony of a kind which Berkeley was attracted to at this period but which lapsed with his more contrapuntal later style. Bar 11 brings a further theme in the oboes, which is developed in a close fugato from bar 18. Two features of bar 17 are worth mentioning – the first of a series of second inversion chords, which occur with almost Straussian panache during this movement, and the succeeding dominant thirteenth chord. Both of these chords are taken out of any traditional context, not employed as dramatic revelations but more like fingerprints, or points of reference. (Berkeley's next opus goes further. In the Sonatina for Violin and Piano the second subject of the first movement seems to emerge entirely from the major second inversion chord which underpins it.) It is worth quoting this next melody, bar 49, since the movement's biggest climax, bar 188, derives from it (see Example 28 on p. 56).

The way in which the melody arises is revealing. First of all it looks like a counterpoint to the first subject in the bass (bar 45), but on closer examination it is simply the tail end of the second phrase of the first subject. This anticipation ends with a dotted rhythm which will become important through the second subject. At bar 49 Berkeley makes a tune out of the tail end and extends it characteristically by repeating and decorating it.

The development section begins at bar 105. Throughout it Berkeley makes both melodies and counterpoints out of the first-subject material. The start of the recapitulation at bar 211 is unobtrusive, with an ascending oboe phrase to disguise it. This section is both condensed and varied, easy to miss in a framework of continuous unfolding. The timpani has almost the last word with the dotted rhythm over luminous C major.

The second movement of the Symphony, the *Allegretto*, is a gentle waltz with three main themes in the context of a constant beat supported by groups of instruments in turn. The first theme is played by the oboe, over repetitions of a single chord (see Example 29 on p. 56). The second theme is just as memorable.

[19] P. Dickinson, ed., *Twenty British Composers*, London, 1975, p. 27.
[20] Berkeley, letter to Britten, 25 August 1936.

Example 27. Symphony No. 1, Opus 16

Its rising sixth, a favourite interval, is varied in the contrapuntal development it receives. At times Berkeley risks submerging his tune through the use of imitation, but the texture and scoring are such a delicate blend of pastel shades that it is all clearly audible. The third theme, over a pedal C, has its rhythm section in the timpani, decorations in the harp and first violins, and the melody itself in violas doubled with bassoon (Example 30, p. 57). This

Example 28. Symphony No. 1

Example 29. Symphony No. 1

theme seems utterly characteristic of Berkeley in relaxed mood. But of the three it turns out to be the dynamic one capable of sustaining a climax in the compressed recapitulation of this idyll and it is fastidiously scored.

The third movement, *Lento*, takes over from the mood at the end of the Serenade (see Example 31 on p. 58 and continued on p. 59). It is hard, in spite of Berkeley's remarks, not to see the war years reflected in its sparse desolation.

Example 30. Symphony No. 1

The movement opens with an ostinato containing a dotted rhythm which will feature in lighter guise in the finale. After an opening for strings alone the baleful voice of the cor anglais, as in the equivalent movement of the Second Symphony, conditions the atmosphere. At bar 25 the regular pulse in the horns

Example 31. Symphony No. 1

supports a gradual string crescendo, strongly sustained, building from two to four parts. The blue-note false-relation contributes tellingly to bar 28 but not systematically since reappearances of this material vary.

The three rising notes which open the *Lento* are those of the first subject of the first movement, but this time major, and the dotted rhythm continues in the finale, but in a different mood. In bar 8 of the first movement (Example 27) there is a curious anticipation of the rondo theme of the finale. Its first two bars, complete with timpani, might have come from a Haydn symphony. High spirits

Example 31. (cont.)

prevail. Apart from the recurring rondo gesture, there are three or four different attempts at a second theme in a similar rhythm:

Example 32. Symphony No. 1

These elements are loosely associated rather in the manner in which Charles Ives took popular tunes from memory with no intention of preserving their detail accurately. Later, at bar 113, a lyrical theme emerges from a clarinet descent: varied, this soon provides the strongest outburst of the movement at bar 127. Similar emotional heat recurs in the strings alone passage from 161, where bar 13 is inflated in a distinctly Mahlerian manner – especially the sharpened fourth, a high A, over the first inversion of E flat major at bar 172. The coda telescopes the opening rhythm to 6/8 for a snap ending.

In 1965, I pointed to the maturity of the First Symphony which I felt could easily become a popular work with the large public which at that time was only just coming to terms with twentieth-century music.[21] When I suggested to Norman del Mar that the Symphony was not really a light piece he disagreed: 'The slow movement is very serious. So much so that the sudden dramatic middle section takes one aback. But the rest of it is all what I would describe as lightweight, though I don't use that word in a derogatory sense.'[22]

Berkeley's technique is a personal combination of the instinctive and the calculated whereas Britten never used so many or such diverse ideas. This approach is closer to the method of Delius and, as Beecham knew, such music needs careful nurturing in performance. There are similar interpretative problems in other large-scale sonata-form movements by Berkeley, such as the Piano Sonata to be examined later. Discursiveness may have charms, but lingering is at the price of unity. The first recording of this Symphony with the London Philharmonic Orchestra under Norman del Mar is effective but occasionally lacks impetus. A recent landmark in the progress of Berkeley on CD is the Berkeley Edition under the direction of Richard Hickox. Its first volume contains the First Symphony and the Serenade in interpretations

[21] P. Dickinson, 'Lennox Berkeley', *Music and Musicians* 13, August 1965, pp. 20–23 and 54.
[22] Interview with author, 21 December 1990.

which are utterly convincing and scrupulous in every detail.[23] It used to be assumed that Berkeley's works on a smaller scale were the most characteristic but this performance of the First Symphony disproves that assumption. Berkeley met Del Mar when he was Sir Thomas Beecham's assistant and the three of them went together to the recording session with the Royal Philharmonic Orchestra which played Berkeley's music for the film, *The First Gentleman*, released in May 1948. In a letter to his publisher Berkeley reported:

> I'm glad to say that the recording went well and that everyone seems delighted with the music. Beecham behaved like a lamb and apart from one or two places where my timing had not been quite accurate and one or two technical mishaps (the film caught fire once – appropriately enough just after the music to one of the love scenes!) we had no trouble. I think you'll like it.[24]

At almost two hours this period drama is the longest of Berkeley's five film scores. Other composers such as Vaughan Williams, Bliss, Walton and Rawsthorne, apart from the film-music specialists, wrote for feature films and some of this music has been revived. From this point of view Berkeley should be worth investigation.[25]

In 1990, Norman del Mar, who had given many performances of it from 1951 onwards, regarded the Divertimento as 'totally successful' and could see no reason why Berkeley's attractive earlier works were not permanently in the repertoire. He regarded Berkeley as part of the *Boulangerie* and thought he had 'that light element which very little English music has in quite the same way'.[26] Nicholas Maw, too, found a 'strong French strain' in Berkeley's music, not specifically allied to Poulenc but more to Albert Roussel – and certainly not salon music.[27] In 1954 Alan Frank, in a telling phrase, admired Berkeley for finding 'a light way of expressing serious thought . . . illuminated by a Latin clarity'.[28]

It looks as though Berkeley could hardly have had the chance to learn from the performance of the First Symphony at the Proms before completing the concise Divertimento, premiered by the BBC in October, which – as so often in his output – makes the two works a pair. The first movement is a Prelude in a compressed sonata form. It announces its catchy main theme straight away in four-bar phrases shared between violins and a relay team of woodwinds. The

[23] Berkeley Edition, Volume 1, Symphony No. 1, Serenade, BBC National Orchestra of Wales, Richard Hickox, Chandos CHAN 9981 (2002). (Includes *Coronach* and Horn Concerto by Michael Berkeley.)

[24] L. Berkeley, letter to Douglas Gibson, J. & W. Chester, 19 January 1948.

[25] Berkeley is not even mentioned in J. G. Swynnoe, *The Best Years of British Film Music, 1936–1958*, Woodbridge, 2002.

[26] Ibid. Del Mar told me that Berkeley scores he conducted often had inconsistencies which had to be settled by the conductor in advance.

[27] Interview with author, 18 October 1990.

[28] A. Frank, 'Composer with Style and Grace', *Radio Times*, 25 June 1954.

bassoon figure, dotted, serves as a minuscule second subject; the dotted rhythm takes over as accompaniment; and returns in the trumpets at figure 7 to start the development. The return is in B flat, the tonic, with the first theme treated momentarily in canon and the second theme represented by only half a bar – merely its rhythm – correctly in the tonic. All is then over in a flash of woodwind.

The second movement, the Nocturne, is an A–B–A structure, centred on E flat. The middle section starts with a gently pulsating string accompaniment over which a clarinet solo and then the upper strings build a powerful climax with a sinuous melody. A characteristic pulsating rhythm returns in the horns, in the final A section, and to end with in the timpani. The third movement is a Scherzo which blows away all the gloom of the Nocturne. It is rich in themes and hesitations of the kind used provocatively by Haydn and Beethoven in sonata-form contexts. Surprisingly the movement is of symphonic proportions within the lighter scale of this Divertimento. There is no counterpart in the First Symphony. The finale, on the other hand, after its introduction, is very much after the mould of the symphony's last movement. In the work as a whole, nothing is out of scale. I remember Robin Orr, himself a Boulanger pupil, lecturing on this work to Cambridge undergraduates in the mid-1950s. He emphasised the skill of the scoring where every detail is fastidiously treated with the same endearing light touch as the overall conception. This is vintage Berkeley, where the finesse is Mozartian, with that composer's equanimity and style. To achieve this kind of success in other areas, Berkeley needed to introduce the instrument through which he came to music – the piano.

4. The piano

Some of Berkeley's earliest musical memories relate to the piano, as he recalled:

> My father was passionately fond of music and had been invalided out of the navy before I was born. He hadn't been able to learn music as a boy, or hear very much, so he acquired a pianola with all kinds of rolls of classical music – Beethoven sonatas and arrangements of concertos – which I heard at a very early age on this machine. That was my introduction to music.[1]

In addition to Hastings Berkeley's collection of piano rolls, Aunt Nellie Harris was a composer of songs and young Lennox used to accompany her. Her song, *Valse Lente*, and piano tango called *La Nena* have a nostalgic Edwardian charm which would not have been lost on her nephew. These experiences, combined with the singing of his godmother Sybil Jackson, were obviously significant. When he played himself he began by improvising but he soon had lessons which lasted throughout his school days. Berkeley seems to have had very little experience of playing in public and could never play the more demanding of his own works. Writing to Britten on 5 January 1940, he said:

> Since I finished the Serenade I've been working on some Piano Studies. They're real virtuoso music – I can't play a bar of them. I've also written a Mazurka, which I think you'd like. [The first of the three.]

All the same, Berkeley played one of the pianos in his Introduction and Allegro, Opus 11, for two pianos and orchestra at the Proms in the same year. The other piano was played by William Glock, later Controller of Music at the BBC (1959–73), and Berkeley commented in another letter to Britten on 9 November: 'I didn't play too badly considering my very poor technical resource as a pianist.'[2] This limitation, as we shall see, did not prevent him from having a special relationship with the instrument which has been particularly fruitful. As John

[1] P. Dickinson, ed., 'Interview with Sir Lennox Berkeley', in *Twenty British Composers*, London, 1975, p. 23. However, Hastings Berkeley rejoined the navy in 1914 and retired as a Captain in 1918.

[2] See L. Foreman, *From Parry to Britten: British Music in Letters 1900–1945*, London, 1987, p. 236 for Ernest Chapman's letter to Erwin Stein – both on the staff at Boosey and Hawkes – written after hearing the Prom performance and advising against publishing this work.

Manduell pointed out in 1990: 'No British composer has written more distinctively for the piano.'[3]

The major solo work, the Sonata, Opus 20, which seems to have had a long gestation period (1941–45), contains Berkeley's most substantial piano music, although the Four Concert Studies, Opus 14, are also on a high level, especially the *Andante* with its implied blue-note colourings. Colin Horsley's first recording of this set is outstanding.[4] The sources of Berkeley's style can be investigated in these works. Chopin stands out in the central section of the Berceuse from Opus 2, a debt which is overtly acknowledged in the Three Mazurkas, Opus 32, No. 1. The set was completed at the invitation of UNESCO for a concert in Paris on 3 October 1949 to celebrate the Chopin centenary: the first mazurka goes back to 1939[5] but only the third one was used on that occasion and it opened the programme of tributes by eleven composers. Once again, models are tantalisingly near although hard to specify but the partnership between Berkeley and Chopin is convincing and still operates in the late Mazurka, Opus 101.

The Six Preludes, Opus 23, were completed in 1944 and were originally commissioned by the BBC as interludes between radio programmes.[6] They have been popular even with pianists of moderate ability and would be more so if No. 1 and No. 3 were not harder to play than the rest. All the same, they form a concise anthology of the composer's techniques. No. 1 has the glittering passage-work he likes, with the delicacy of Ravel but employing Berkeley's own device of repeated and extended phrases. The use of decorative patterns involving both major and minor thirds fails to dislodge the A flat tonic, re-emphasised in the sixth Prelude which provides a gentle lyrical end to match the

[3] J. Manduell, Tribute at Memorial Requiem Mass, Westminster Cathedral, 20 March 1990.

[4] Berkeley: Piano Sonata, Preludes, Scherzo, Impromptu, Concert Studies, Lyrita Mono RCS9 (1959).

[5] Sir Thomas Beecham's library contained a manuscript copy of the first Mazurka, dated December 1939, which is now in Sheffield University Music Library.

[6] V. Drewry: 'Lennox Berkeley, some recent compositions', *Chesterian* 26, October 1951, pp. 1–4. The Six Preludes were dedicated to Val Drewry, who wrote: 'They were commissioned by the BBC to be used as interludes in underrunning programmes . . . but like many good ideas, it came to nothing, so the Preludes were published for all to use.' In this early article Drewry also notes Berkeley's attitude to his works written before 1940, which 'he regards with little affection; in fact he has discarded some of them altogether in a recent compilation of his works to which he has attached opus numbers: the items omitted are those he no longer wishes to be played or remembered'. Colin Horsely remembers making his first gramophone records on 78s for HMV and, when he had finished recording Prokofiev, Rachmaninov and Szymanovsky, he was asked at the studio whether he had anything else he would like to play. He proposed the Six Preludes, which were released in 1949 and outsold the others. Horsley did not give the first performance but recalled that the pianist at the Wigmore Hall premiere became ill after playing the first two and the composer had to finish off. (Interview with author, 30 November 1990.) Horsley had been in the habit of following his performances of the Preludes with a Stravinsky Etude. To avoid the need for this, he commissioned the Scherzo, Op. 32, No. 2, for his 1950 tour of Australia and New Zealand.

soft opening and closing of No. 1. No. 2 is in the key of the Sonata, A major, and its technique is worth further scrutiny:

Example 33. Six Preludes, Opus 23, No. 2

The F sharp in the left-hand pattern creates ambiguity between A major and F sharp minor. This is further confused by C natural and later F natural, which find their way into the melody by bar 5, and by bar 8 the F has become the dominant for a central section starting in B flat major. The second bar of this, bar 10, introduces a shape and a rhythm which is so persistent that it is superimposed onto the return of the opening theme later, with adjustments to make it fit harmonically. Bars 6 and 7 are relevant to passages in the Sonata. The doubling of a melody at the octave with a filled-in third or sixth between may have a surprising origin. According to Edward Lockspeiser in 1947:

> One cannot imagine that a young man with a strong bent for music reading modern languages at Oxford at that time – Berkeley had at first no intention of pursuing a musical career – could have come away without a devout admiration for Brahms. Brahms was the idol of that period as Mendelssohn was the idol of the Victorian period. It was the time, too, when the more curious minds were stimulated by the modern French and Russian composers, but the appeal of Brahms was supreme, and although much of Berkeley's music is almost anti-Brahmsian, there are several recent works of his revealing the ties of what one imagines to have been a strong allegiance.[7]

Lockspeiser goes on to instance both the Viola and Piano Sonata, Opus 22, and the Piano Sonata as examples, and he finds a 'somewhat gloomy and pessimistic side' to Berkeley's character with 'patches of dark brooding' at odds with his reputation for Francophile wit and elegance. This is an interesting suggestion but there is little evidence that Berkeley studied Brahms' scores in order to learn about musical structure and organisation. His symphonies and sonatas would be different if he had. Modern music, seen from Paris, must have been too preoccupied with Stravinsky and the ballet whereas thematic logic was at its most intense through Schoenberg and his followers. Boulanger's values were different. At times Berkeley seems to go back to another composer fashionable during his Oxford years and active in Paris before that – César Franck.

Britten was obsessed with Brahms and Beethoven as a teenager and then seems to have reacted against them;[8] Auden made fun of Brahms by writing a rude couplet about the Requiem on Britten's score of *Our Hunting Fathers* along with his poem 'Lay your sleeping head'; such reactions would have cut Berkeley off from what he might have learned technically from Brahms. What did remain was a melodic intensity and a mood – the spiritual qualities of the *Vier Ernste Gesänge*, Opus 121, or the Eleven Chorale Preludes, Opus 122, which Berkeley may have played during his organ study with W. H. Harris and certainly admired later.

The third Prelude is a delicate toccata (Example 34a, p. 67). As in the first one, the basic figuration alternates major and minor thirds. The key is F major and there are many fingerprints such as the dominant thirteenth ending bar 4; another one articulating the harmony in bar 6; the perfect cadence to bar 9, which introduces two bars of syncopation which never recur; the imitation at bar 5; and the tonal centres marked out through bass notes – D from bar 13 and A at 33 – all reached via a dominant. Bar 33 is a typical Berkeley inspiration (Example 34b, p. 68). After an awkward bar of uncertain tonal direction, bar 32 clears the way by modulating to a four-bar phrase centred on A major with a rising scale going off in slightly different directions each time and eventually

[7] E. Lockspeiser, 'The Music of Lennox Berkeley', *Listener*, 10 July 1947, p. 76.
[8] M. Schafer, *British Composers in Interview*, London, 1963, p. 119.

Example 34a. Six Preludes, No. 3

reaching C major – an irresistible indulgence of a Mozartian kind. The chromatic scales of the earlier part of the piece have lifted away and the C major turns out to be the dominant. One can imagine several ways of working out a short piece based on Berkeley's opening figurations. Britten, in solo piano works such as *Holiday Diary*, Opus 5, sticks rather aridly to the basic patterns and Tippett, too, uses more sequences in his earlier and later piano writing. Berkeley proceeds by a process of instinctive association. Sometimes, as in the next Prelude, this can involve other composers too.

In 1928 Poulenc wrote a *Hymne* as the second of his *Trois Pièces* for piano. Very much of a magpie composer, he may have borrowed the opening gesture

Example 34b. Six Preludes, No. 3

from Stravinsky's *Hymne* which opens the Serenade in A (1925) for piano. Here, and rather improbably, Stravinsky is almost quoting the second phrase of the opening melody of Chopin's Ballade No. 2 – Poulenc would have liked this situation and so would Berkeley. But it is Stravinsky's gesture and attack which Poulenc mirrors, as Berkeley perhaps does in the opening of his Sonata. Poulenc continued this approach by borrowing from himself – the *Hymne* appears in his *Gloria* and in the first Nocturne for piano – which is one of the ways in which a composer's free association can operate. What at first seems to be an incidental passage in the middle section of Poulenc's *Hymne*, although it soon gets blown up into a climax, has consequences. A fleeting moment in Poulenc prompts Berkeley's entire piece (Example 35, p. 69 and Example 36, p. 70). Berkeley's use of almost identical chords makes it certain that he played the Poulenc and may have intended the quotation as a tribute. Not only has he used the four chords untransposed but he has picked up the left-hand-over effect and used it for a counter-melody when the eight-bar phrase is repeated, a feature of Brahms' Rhapsody in G minor, from Opus 79, too.

With his veneration for neo-classical Stravinsky, Berkeley knew how to make use of a model, consciously or not. He refines Poulenc's texture by concentrating

Example 35. Poulenc: *Trois Pièces*, No. 2

on the chords, with the dotted rhythm above giving rise to his own melody. The major seventh chord in bar 1 is progressively softened – note the functioning dominant thirteenth implied in bar 3 – to the minor and major chords of bars 7 and 8. The dotted rhythm is extended as a neat link in bars 4 and 6 in the bass and bars 7, 15 and 16 in the melody. At the end of the Prelude, three of the four chords from the opening, transposed up a fourth, form the coda. The harmony alone has to be sufficient to recall the opening mood without the melody. It works, concluding a piece in which the main motivic element is the semitone found in the melody – bars 2, 4, 5 and so on – which acts as a foil to the whole tone in bar 1, with these two bars melodically reversed at the repeat in bars 31 and 32.

Berkeley admired Poulenc but with reservations:

> He was not a great composer, but some of his songs have a unique charm – 'La grenouillère' [Apollinaire, 1938], for example; the nostalgia of the poem is more than reproduced – it's enormously heightened. The harmony is conventional if analysed chord by chord, but not one phrase could be by any other composer, and the last-minute return to the tonic shows the kind of skill that only the ear can command.[9]

The fifth Prelude brings contrast with a rhythmic vitality new to the set. There is a connection with older French music since the diatonic opening tune starts with the notes of the Toreador's song from Bizet's *Carmen.* But the metre is mostly 7/8, with a middle section in 6/8 but reverting to 7/8 after seventeen bars. There is much sequence and short-term repetition with a carefully graded *diminuendo* and written out *ritenuto* – Brahms again – to end with.

In his sleeve-notes for Colin Horsley's recording, Berkeley calls the last Prelude an epilogue.[10] It does have this function but it also harks back to the

[9] L. Berkeley diary, 19 August 1966.

[10] Lyrita RCS 9 (1959).

Example 36. Six Preludes, No. 4

blues out of the Parisian ballet (Example 10, p. 22). In fact the sixth Prelude is a cross between a siciliano and a blues. The underlying rhythm is constant; the plain A flat major is calculated to match the first piece in a key scheme planned for the whole set; and dominant thirteenths and appoggiaturas abound. It must be the most indulgent music Berkeley had composed since his student days and it embodies the core of his increasingly sensual lyricism. The slow movement of the Piano Concerto, Opus 29, written two years later, in the same key, has a similar effect, although without recourse to the blue-note technique found in the Prelude. Considering the Six Preludes as a set, Colin Horsley told me that quite well-known pianists had found them much more tricky than they had expected – and with such clear textures any mistakes would be obvious.[11]

[11] Interview with author, 30 November 1990.

Example 37. Six Preludes, No. 6

Like all composers, Berkeley has built his style from a variety of sources, and his individuality is accounted for by the mixture itself and the strength of each ingredient. The blue-notes in the sixth Prelude are not quite typical – although we shall encounter prominent ones in the Piano Concerto and in *Nelson* – but the regular pulse, the repeated fragments, and the use of decorated dominant harmony are. The second-inversion major chords in bars 15 and 26 are another fingerprint and have the same broadening effect as those in the First Symphony. Blue-note inflections can be felt in bars 9 and 11. Having shifted the harmony up by a semitone at bar 20 – more like show

Example 37 (cont.)

business than Schubert – Berkeley again modulates abruptly at the end of bar 24 to D major, returning after one bar, almost as if he had been caught in a rare error of taste. Another sublimated popular music cliché is the climax at bar 15. It falls on the flat sixth of the key, written as E rather than F flat, and the dominant seventh in F, which underpins the second half of the bar, luxuriates in the modal contradiction of the B natural above it. That B natural has functioned melodically already in bars 2 and 6 and as C flat in bars 9, 10 and 11. Harmonically it colours the last six bars as the tenor part carries the tune to an ending in the bass, with the blue G flat as part of a final reference to bar 1. The point of these investigations has been to show how Berkeley built a personal style by a process of exploration, trial and ultimate integration. Like the Five Short Pieces a decade earlier, the Six Preludes function as a kind of microcosm of Berkeley's style at the time. In a letter on 9 November 1940, Berkeley told Britten how much he admired Bartók's *Mikrokosmos* and the *Music for Strings, Percussion and Celesta.*

Nicholas Maw, a pupil of Berkeley's at the Royal Academy of Music who then went on to Boulanger, first heard the Six Preludes in a recital Paul Hamburger gave at his school in the early 1950s. Maw immediately admired 'music, saying something which was real and true . . . I think it was said in a way which was so clear, beautifully done, almost like Japanese caligraphy.'[12]

Berkeley's description of his working methods supports the claim that his approach is more instinctive than ratiocinative:

> Perhaps it's a slight exaggeration to say that ideas never come to me when I'm not actually working. But if I'm not working I usually forget them so they might as well not have come in the first place . . . Sometimes I improvise. Generally this doesn't help because I find I am wandering and not getting to the precise facts of what is at hand. But sometimes the contact with actual sound at the piano helps to get me started.[13]

Thus the act of composition can be a kind of improvisation in itself. Delius has described his method at the time of *Sea Drift*: 'The shape of it was taken out of my hands, so to speak, as I worked, and was bred easily and effortlessly of the nature and sequence of my particular musical ideas.'[14] That was also Delius' approach to sonatas and, like some other twentieth-century composers, he avoided literal repetition. His continuity was rhapsodic in a way which bears some relation to the outer movements of Berkeley's Piano Sonata and his other works on a similar scale. But the Sonata itself is a landmark amongst British works in this form.[15] Malcolm Williamson recognised this in no uncertain terms:

> You know there are lots of composers but very few total composers. Lennox was a total composer. And this goes through, certainly, the Second and Third Symphonies, the Piano Concerto, the Two-Piano Concerto and that gigantic – I'm talking about the conception – Piano Sonata. It's an absolutely faultless, stupefying masterpiece. There's not a bad note in it. What more can I say than that?[16]

[12] Interview with author, 18 October 1990.
[13] M. Schaffer, *British Composers in Interview*, London, 1963, p. 119.
[14] E. Fenby, *Delius as I knew him*, London, 1936, p. 36.
[15] See Lisa Hardy, *The British Piano Sonata, 1870–1945*, Woodbridge, 2001, pp. 168–70.
[16] Interview with author, 22 February 1991.

Berkeley wrote the Piano Sonata, Opus 20, for Clifford Curzon but, after the premiere, many performances were given by Colin Horsley, who recorded it in 1959 closely supervised by the composer.[17] In his sleeve-note Berkeley recognised the value of recording:

> One of the great advantages enjoyed by the composer of today is that he is able to have his works recorded under his own supervision by artists who know him personally and to whom he is able to give clear guidance as to how he wishes his music to be played. Such records can present a composer's work to the public with a degree of authenticity hitherto unknown. What immense value recordings of this kind would have for us today could they have been made of the works of the great masters of the past during their lifetime! This record is the fruit of a long collaboration between composer and pianist, in the course of which each has grown to know the other's mind and musical personality.[18]

Berkeley describes the first movement as in 'traditional sonata form' but this is hardly the case since the material is varied at almost every opportunity. He admits that 'the recapitulation is a much shortened form of the exposition, only a few bars being exactly as before, and the second subject, instead of being repeated, appears in a considerably modified form'. Martin Cooper noticed this in 1959: 'It is characteristic of Berkeley that he demands of his listener the kind of musical awareness that accepts a hint, an almost disguised reference to what has gone before, in place of unambiguous repetition.'[19] Compare the opening of the first movement with the recapitulation, where the vital two-bar motif comes as the second half of a four-bar phrase re-emphasising the tonic (Examples 38 and 39, p. 75) The rising sixth is associated with a variety of attractive textures, some of an improvisatory kind which are hard to link in performance. The recording by Colin Horsley – 'the fruit of a long collaboration between composer and pianist' – allows this movement's momentum to waver. Perhaps this is the negative side of the influence of Chopin, or at least the way Chopin is too often played. There are no such worries about the second movement, the *Presto*, which is a character piece built from whirligig *moto perpetuo* figures and brilliantly carried out. The *Adagio* could equally be described as melodic and atmospheric perfection. Set in E minor, with freely moving triads forming an inner harmony over the tonic pedal, this is the type of slow movement at which Berkeley always excelled (Example 40, p. 75):[20] The Introduction to the rondo finale harks back to the Brahmsian filled-in octaves of the first movement and the second Prelude. Again, Horsley's performance is somewhat discursive, perhaps reflecting the composer's wishes, but this seems inconsistent with what Horsley remembered in 1990:

[17] Britten's letter to Berkeley of 4 June 1948 indicates that Curzon was ill and unable to play the Sonata as planned at the Aldeburgh Festival.

[18] L. Berkeley, Lyrita RCS 9 (1959).

[19] M. Cooper, 'Lennox Berkeley and his new Symphony', *Listener*, 19 February 1959, p. 351.

[20] The repeat of this material in the final section is in C minor. The bars in Example 40 are simply transposed. The third bar, in the left hand, has a D flat missing in the score. The 1974 second edition has not corrected this but confirms that the last note in bar 1 on page 3 is D natural.

Example 38. Piano Sonata, Opus 20

Example 39. Piano Sonata

Example 40. Piano Sonata

> Lennox liked things to be played in a classical way because he was basing the Piano Concerto, for instance, on Mozart's influence . . . and French music as well. He couldn't bear anyone to pull things about really. I remember him saying that Ravel couldn't bear this either, when I played some Ravel to him once. So he really had a classical approach.[21]

In a way the problem is built into music composed by a process of free association, which is why I made the comparison with Delius, but Raphael Terroni's 1982 recording seems more successful in conveying the sweep of the outer movements.[22] Christopher Headington, Berkeley's first composition pupil at the Royal Academy of Music, who made the first recording of any Berkeley for CD in 1988, also maintains continuity and catches the character of the work.[23]

After the Piano Sonata came the Viola and Piano Sonata, written for Watson Forbes and completed in the same year, and various vocal works, including the *Four Poems of St Teresa of Avila* and the *Stabat Mater*, which will both be discussed later. The vocal works helped to confirm the increasingly melodic dimension of Berkeley's style and paved the way for two concertos involving the piano – one for solo piano and orchestra, Opus 29, and another for two pianos and orchestra, Opus 30. This pair of works came in 1947–48, directly after the vocal pieces mentioned, themselves a pair completed in 1947, and they extend the important role of the piano in Berkeley's output to full concerto proportions.

The First Symphony was followed by the less ambitious Divertimento: this time the solo piano concerto came first and then the more extended work for two pianos. Both demonstrate a new confidence and the timing may not be a coincidence. The gloomy war years were over, admittedly followed by austerity, but for Berkeley in 1946 came his exceptionally happy marriage to Elizabeth Freda Bernstein who, in the words of Tony Scotland, was the 'orphaned only child of an enterprising Lithuanian clothier from Merthyr Tydfil who had escaped to the West from the anti-Jewish pogroms of late nineteenth century Tsarist Russia, and made a fortune as a boot dealer and landlord in the prosperous mining towns of South Wales'.[24] During the war Berkeley was an

21 Interview with author, 30 November 1990.

22 Pearl SHE 576, 1982. Colin Mason, in the *Listener*, 27 February 1956, felt that the Sonata had been influenced by Stravinsky's Serenade. The opening of the first movement can be seen as a cantabile but still declamatory reflection of Stravinsky's *Hymne*: all the more reason for a taut performance. However, Susan Bradshaw, who also found Stravinsky in the work considered the Sonata 'unusually successful in welding together its basically episodic ideas into a unified whole' (D. Matthews, ed., *Keyboard Music*, Penguin, 1972, p. 367).

23 Kingdom KCLCD 2012. This enterprising recording from a Berkeley pupil who knew the music intimately includes *Paysage*, only recently published – see note 42. Originally entitled *Paysage de France*, it was written in 1944 and dedicated to Raymond Mortimer. The back page of the manuscript contains a twelve-note row (G–A–D–G sharp–F sharp–C–B flat–F–B–C sharp–E–D sharp) which must have been written much later.

24 Personal communication. See also the leaflet introducing the Lennox Berkeley Society, founded in 1999 by Kathleen Walker and Jim Nichol. (See www.lennoxberkeley.org.uk)

The Berkeleys were married on 14 December 1946 at the Church of the Holy Apostles, Claverton Street, Pimlico.

Air Raid Warden in the thick of the blitz, although he had applied for a ground job in the RAF Volunteer Reserve and was not called up. In 1941 he was working for the BBC, at first in the European Service (French Department); then as an orchestral programme builder with the Music Department at Bedford; and finally, until 1945, in the Home Service Music Section in Marylebone High Street where Freda Bernstein was working as a secretary. Basil Douglas, then on the music staff, recalled that Berkeley was brought in primarily to construct programmes for the BBC Symphony Orchestra and was very efficient: 'His knowledge was tremendous and he learnt how one had to choose the pieces which fitted with the orchestration . . . He and Adrian Boult got on extremely well. His tastes were very catholic . . . If he got a chance of putting in some French music which he thought was under-rated . . . he would take it.'[25] Even more, Douglas was a witness to Berkeley's meeting with the third of the most significant influences on his life – Freda, after Boulanger and Britten:

> Freda was my secretary for quite a long time and it was lovely, after Lennox was appointed, because it was remarkable how often he kept popping into my office in order to talk about either his programmes or my programmes. Freda would be sitting there smiling very sweetly and I had no idea that there was anything closer happening but I did notice they were together quite a lot. The first thing I knew was the notice in *The Times* saying they were engaged. Everybody was highly surprised and very delighted.[26]

Colin Horsley remembered Berkeley's time at the BBC because he was reputed to have kept manuscript paper under his desk and was obviously longing to get more time to compose.[27] Since it was there that he met his wife it is no wonder that the vocal music conveys a spiritual radiance and these secular concertos a carefree, youthful, quality. Twenty years later Berkeley himself recognised this landmark:

> This month we shall have been married for twenty years. I feel that I've been so immensely lucky, and I know that to have lived with someone so good, so sweet and so generous has made me into a different person.[28]

The Concerto in B flat for solo piano was written for Colin Horsley and commissioned by him and Val Drewry. In 1990 Horsley told me that he considered the work as a chamber concerto in the spirit of Mozart and recalled that Berkeley particularly admired Mozart's K503 with its unison passages and used those in his own slow movement. He also remembered that when he was giving the early performances of this concerto the quality of pianos was not as good as later on and he attributed the neglect of the concerto partly to the fact that it was not a work that could be played on one rehearsal on the day of the concert.

[25] Interview with author, 28 November 1990.
[26] Interview with author, 28 November 1990.
[27] Interview with author, 30 November 1990.
[28] L. Berkeley diary, December 1966.

Horsley gave the first performance at the Proms on 31 August 1948 with the London Symphony Orchestra under Basil Cameron but he particularly remembered playing it at the International Society for Contemporary Music Festival in Palermo under Constant Lambert with the Rome Symphony Orchestra on 26 April 1949. The concert was at the splendid opera house in Palermo with a distinguished and enthusiastic audience. There were successful rehearsals in Rome beforehand but at the concert the piano was poor and – most unfortunate of all – Lambert, in poor health in the last years of his life, was the worse for wear with drink. However, the Concerto was well received by a conventional Sicilian audience and Lambert apparently admired it. Horsley recognised Berkeley's gift for melody but felt his music usually had to be heard more than once, something the composer himself has noticed.[29] Altogether Horsley thought he had performed the Concerto twenty-eight times in this country and abroad, although unfortunately he never recorded it.[30] He gave performances of the concerto under conductors such as John Barbirolli, Basil Cameron, Eugene Goossens and Charles Groves, all of whom admired it. And under the composer's baton: 'It was a joy to play with Lennox. It was very comfortable and I felt free and not on tenterhooks as you can be with an indifferent conductor. He conducted beautifully.'[31]

This tribute from a performer is valuable evidence, but Michael Berkeley later on expressed some reservations about his father's conducting:

> He was not a wonderful conductor. He could do it technically – he was a good enough musician – and I think it was interesting for people to have these performances just to see how he thought they should go . . . But he was neither strict enough, in the Stravinskian sense, to have a tight little beat which would drive the orchestra on nor flamboyant enough to make large gestures.[32]

This seems quite understandable and Berkeley realised the problem himself when he wrote in 1974:

> It was an exciting experience rehearsing the RPO and conducting the performance of my Third Symphony at the Royal Festival Hall but only because of the very friendly attitude of the orchestra who made allowances for my inadequacy as a conductor. I made a lot of mistakes in the rehearsal but I think not in the performance, though even then I realised that I lack the power of making the compelling gestures that a good conductor must have . . . It's ironic that many professional conductors confine themselves to classical music that the orchestra knows by heart anyway whereas the wretched composer-conductor has to face difficulties of this kind continually . . .[33]

[29] Interview with author, 30 November 1990.

[30] Letter to author, 12 May 1975. Horsley played all Berkeley's solo piano music, and he also commissioned the Scherzo for piano, Op. 32, No. 2, the Horn Trio, Op. 40, and the Concerto for Piano and Double String Orchestra, Op. 46, giving their first performances. The first recording is by David Wilde with the New Philharmonia Orchestra under Nicholas Braithwaite, Lyrita SRCS 94 (1978).

[31] Interview with author, 30 November 1990.

[32] Interview with author, 29 November 1990.

[33] L. Berkeley diary, 1974, following 21 November concert.

Plate 1 Lennox Berkeley in the twenties

Plate 2 Lennox Berkeley in the thirties

Plate 3 Benjamin Britten and Lennox Berkeley, 1938. Photo: Howard Coster. Copyright: National Portrait Gallery. Courtesy of the Britten-Pears Library, Aldeburgh

Plate 4 Lennox Berkeley in the forties

Plate 5 Freda Berkeley. Copyright: Camilla Panufnik

Plate 6 Lennox Berkeley rehearsing the Violin Concerto with Yehudi Menuhin, Bath Abbey 1961

Plate 7 Lennox Berkeley (standing) with painter Derek Hill (right) and singer Billy Patterson on a rowing trip to Iona

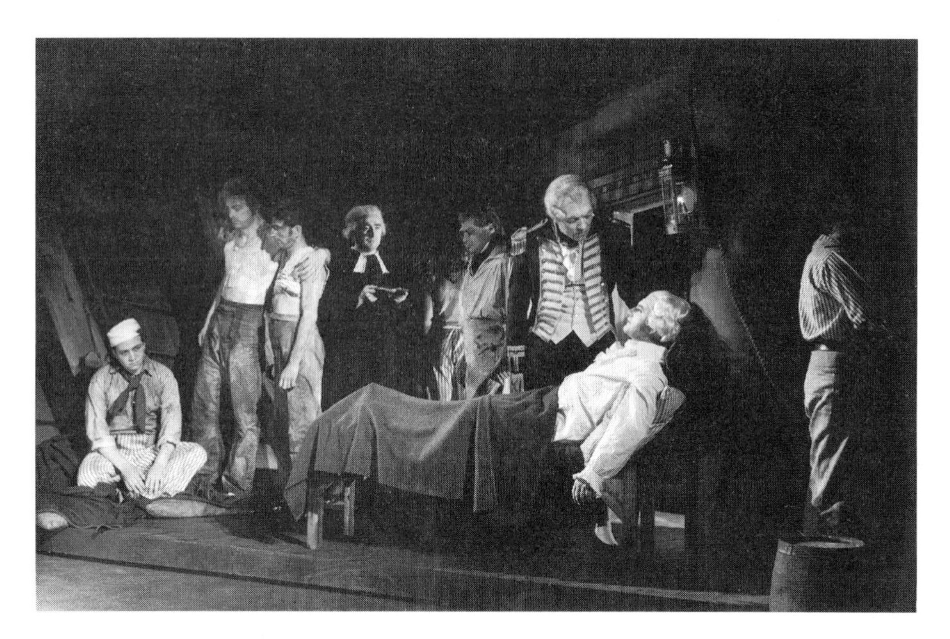

Plate 8 Deathbed scene from the 1954 Sadler's Wells production of *Nelson*

Plate 9 Scene from the English Opera Group's 1956 production of *Ruth*, with Una Hale, Anna Pollack and April Cantelo

Plate 10 Lennox and Freda Berkeley in Julian Bream's car

Plate 11 Lennox and Freda Berkeley

Plate 12 Dr Lennox Berkeley, Oxford 1970

Plate 13 Lennox Berkeley, Witold Lutoslawski and Peter Pears at the recording session for the *Ronsard Sonnets*, 1972

Plate 14 Lennox Berkeley with Nadia Boulanger, 1973

Plate 15 Lennox and Freda Berkeley with Desmond Shawe-Taylor, 1973

Plate 16 Peter Dickinson, Sir Lennox Berkeley, Alice Artzt and Lady Berkeley outside Keele University Chapel, 1975

Plate 17 Sir Lennox Berkeley

Plate 18 The Berkeley family: Julian and Michael (standing), Lennox, Nicholas and Freda, 1982

It does seem unfortunate that Berkeley, at the height of his career, lacked a dedicated conductor who could have done for him what Colin Davis did for Tippett at a crucial stage. All the same, Berkeley's own performances, like Copland's, are valuable as documentary evidence. Not all composer-conductors possess the authority of Mahler or Boulez.

The effortless invention throughout the Piano Concerto is at Berkeley's highest level. The sustained string chord at the opening of the first movement contains the major and minor third and is the background to the immediate appearance of the first subject:

Example 41. Piano Concerto, Opus 29

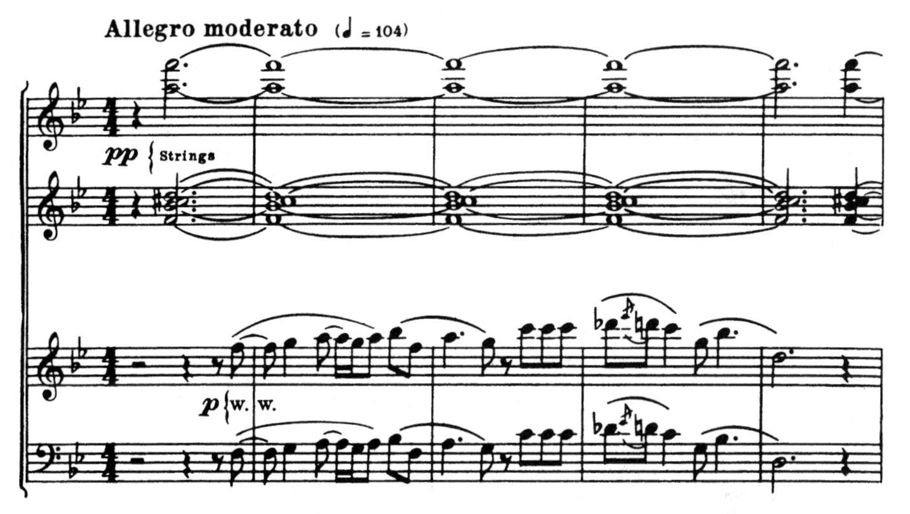

The syncopation adds rhythmic interest; the repeated-notes of the answering phrase, followed by a blue-note, are another motivic feature; and a dotted theme is added on the oboe as the orchestra builds towards the soloist's entrance. There is an ingenious moment when the piano strikes a loud, low C flat along with an orchestral staccato chord, so that the piano sounds through only afterwards. The same thing happens at the start of the real cadenza towards the end of the movement. The piano's first entry is like a short cadenza followed by the orchestral statement of the themes – varied of course. When the piano introduces the second subject (figure 10) there is a clear blues connection with B flat above the G major chord, in a neo-Gershwin manner (Example 42, p. 80). It is instructive to make a comparison between this and the second subject in the recapitulation (figure 26) (Example 43, p. 80). Now the first tune seems to have been overlaid, like a painter covering up his sketches and partially obliterating them as he goes along. The blue-note is lost this time and the reconceived cantabile theme is imitated in the orchestra. Berkeley is well aware of what he is doing, as his own sleeve-note shows:

Example 42. Piano Concerto

Example 43. Piano Concerto

> The recapitulation is far from being a repeat of the exposition as in so many classical concertos; though it uses the same material, it does so only in a modified form, nothing is now quite the same, the themes being alluded to rather than restated.[34]

The development section opens with a fugato which is followed by plenty of pianistic decoration in a rich variety of keyboard textures. Double octaves are not disdained, and the themes bear all the onus placed on them. The final perfect cadence uses an unexpected minor dominant chord. Berkeley's approach to sonata form is always unconventional and serves him well in chamber music too.

The slow movement is as perfectly realised as that in the Piano Sonata:

[34] L. Berkeley, sleeve-note to Lyrita SRCS 94 (1978).

Example 44. Piano Concerto

Muted strings intone a two-bar ostinato and for the first six bars this pattern alternates between two chords. Both contain secundal dissonance without imparting harshness. The main theme, with the soloist, is simply in middle-register octaves for the whole period of eighteen bars. At bar 6 the melody implies modulation, but the ostinato's denial is gently relentless. The harmony ranges more widely in a further four-bar phrase from bars 7 to 10 and so does the melody, with its climax as a rising major ninth. The harmony of bar 7 provides the later climax point of the movement. The ostinato returns at bar 11 prior to three bars of major chords – two of F and one of D – neatly contradicted by the melody until the third quaver beat of bar 14 and then a French sixth opens bar 15. Later there is a new theme for the soloist:

Example 45. Piano Concerto

The A flat and the G flat can again be felt as blue notes, but the modulation at the end of the four-bar phrase could have been by Mozart. However, by now the amalgam is pure Berkeley. The composer acknowledges his own technique when he refers, in his sleeve-note, merely to 'fragments of the original melody' bringing the movement to a close after the climax. The French sixth is again in evidence, low-register flutes purr gently, and the timpani ends with the falling minor third of the main theme. All this is Berkeley's instinctive invention at its most poetic. The Vienna-born British musicologist, Hans Redlich, admired this movement at the time and made a suggestion about its possible ancestry:

> The wistful brittleness of a Berlioz cantilena (Cf. Roméo et Juliette) is conjured up in the cantabile melody of the Piano Concerto's second movement with its curious quasi-vocal stresses, the dissonant backcloth of the murmuring strings and the obstinacy of their rhythmic pattern.[35]

Redlich also spotted Berkeley's habit of discursiveness by referring to his 'obvious virtuosity leading him occasionally to formal pliability' which 'eschews to a certain extent thematic relevance'.

Berkeley avoids any kind of pompous finale by setting the tone with a perky theme which would not be out of place in Prokofiev or Shostakovich:

[35] H. F. Redlich, 'Lennox Berkeley', *Music Survey*, June 1951, pp. 245–9.

Example 46. Piano Concerto

The blue-note connections of the first two movements are continued in this melody in bar 2 and the movement goes on to develop good-natured cross-talk between soloist and orchestra. Major second-inversion chords at strategic places in the orchestral tutti propel the piano into its descents and the second subject, in D major, is pure Berkeley:

Example 47. Piano Concerto

It is a personal gesture in every way. The string spacing is unusual, the added sixth rare in Berkeley, but the melodic gesture is his and the eight-bar phrase is ended with a dominant ninth and thirteenth. As the composer points out in his sleeve-note, the piano does not use this theme but contributes to a variant of it later on. Perhaps there is a suggestion of the block scoring of Stravinsky's *Symphonies of Wind Instruments* but in a less austere context – an impression which is confirmed by the piano's perky passage-work and the way in which the movement peters out.

In 1975, when the Piano Concerto was recorded, Berkeley wrote that the soloist David Wilde was 'really first class' and went on: 'I still quite like the piece, though there are things I would do differently and, I hope, better now.'[36] This is a mistaken impression – Berkeley could not have improved on the Piano Concerto.

The Two-Piano Concerto was commissioned by the Henry Wood Concert Society for Phyllis Sellick and Cyril Smith, who gave the first performance on 13 December 1948 with the London Symphony Orchestra under Malcolm Sargent, and it has a completely different layout. As on other occasions, Berkeley has shown the ability to write two works for similar resources without duplicating them in any way, much as Ravel wrote two piano concertos at the same period. This time there are only two movements and the first, lasting eight minutes, is in an unusual form. A slow declamatory opening for the soloists alone leads to an orchestral *Lento* which the soloists join later. The central section is an *Allegro* followed by an exquisite coda opening over a chord of C major. The whole movement functions as a prelude to the Theme and Variations, lasting over twenty minutes.

Redlich treats these two keyboard concertos on equal terms and is intrigued to find that Berkeley's theme for the variations is close to that of Wagner's early Symphony in C.[37] That was a new idea about the sources of Berkeley's style and it means only that something simple is bound to have connections with other works. My own suggestion is an English source, such as *Bobby Shaftoe*.[38] The resemblance applies only to the first four bars, which are repeated four times during the 34-bar theme. The model for the second movement may have been Britten's Frank Bridge Variations, but there are significant differences. Berkeley's variations are virtually through-composed in a carefully planned layout since he understood that simplicity and memorability were needed for the theme. The stylistic range is as wide as Britten's and the lighter moments also provide comedy, but the Britten connection should not be exaggerated since Berkeley obtained a copy of Aaron Copland's Piano Variations in 1938.[39] There was also the example of Stravinsky. But the Two-Piano Concerto brought a new expansiveness for Berkeley, who never puts a foot wrong in allocating acoustical space between the two soloists and the orchestra. Like Mozart, Berkeley can move in and out of intensity: the fourth variation is a serious fugue mounting to a sonorous climax but it gives way to a frolic in 6/8 before the menacing sixth variation with flutter-tongued flutes as a background to agonising phrases on the strings. There is parody as the seventh variation – a waltz – looks back to Chopin, Strauss or Ravel. The ninth variation, for orchestra alone, may feel like a relation of Ravel's *Pavane pour une infante défunte*, but this type of melody poised over a simple accompaniment is essentially Berkeley. It harks back to the central section

[36] L. Berkeley diary, August 1975.
[37] H. F. Redlich, 'Lennox Berkeley', *Music Survey*, June 1951, pp. 245–9.
[38] P. Dickinson, sleeve-notes, Lyrita SRCS 80 (1975).
[39] S. R. Craggs, *Lennox Berkeley: a Source Book*, Aldershot, 2000, p. 19.

of the *Festival Anthem* (Example 50) and prefigures some of the later liturgical music and all these tunes, including Ravel's *Pavane*, are in G major.

Desmond Shawe-Taylor accounted for the role of the piano in Berkeley's output with particular reference to the Two-Piano Concerto:

> He was quite a decent pianist without any pretensions whatsoever and yet he wrote frightfully well for the piano . . . That spilled over into the concertos to the extent that the Two-Piano Concerto, I think, is one of his best works . . . It has a second movement in variation form. That attracted him very much, his feeling for pattern, and often drew out the best in him.[40]

The success of the Piano Concerto encouraged Colin Horsley to commission another work, the Concerto for Piano and Double String Orchestra, Opus 46 (1958). This piece is virtually unknown and Horsley attributes its poor reception at the time to the fact that he had succumbed to a particularly virulent strain of Asian flu. This affected the premiere and no announcement about his indisposition was made to the Festival Hall audience at the concert on 11 February 1959.

Michael Berkeley stressed the importance of particular performers, pre-eminently Colin Horsley, in encouraging his father to write for the piano: 'I don't think there have been very many composers of great piano music in this country. I think actually that his contribution to the piano repertoire, despite the fact that Ben was a better pianist, is more important than Ben's.'[41] The piano was always a stimulus to Berkeley whose output contains the Sonatina for piano duet, Opus 39, and the Sonatina for two pianos, Opus 52, No. 2 – both at a high level – as well as shorter solo pieces such as *Paysage* which was written 'in honour of a redeemed France' and dedicated to Raymond Mortimer. Berkeley played this himself at the Fyvie Hall in London on 20 February 1945, when he also accompanied the Swiss soprano Sophie Wyss in two of his finest songs, *Tant que mes yeux* and *Ode du premier jour de mai.* He must have been relieved to celebrate the liberation of France.[42]

Berkeley employed the piano extensively in chamber music and songs but, by comparison, said he found the organ less sympathetic in spite of its essential role in his choral and liturgical music. When Nicholas Kynaston gave the premiere of the Fantasia at the Royal Festival Hall, Berkeley wrote that he was 'pleased with the piece, but I feel I shall never really like the organ – the sound is so often lacking in clarity – so blurred and indefinite. Only in quiet passages is it pleasing to my ear.'[43] This is an extraordinary reaction given the thoroughly satisfying and idiomatic way in which Berkeley employed the organ in his church music. The earliest surviving organ piece is an Impromptu written for

[40] Interview with author, 28 November 1990.

[41] Interview with author, 29 January 1990.

[42] *Paysage* was not published until 1991. The main theme is particularly memorable and the piano textures of the central sections are resourcefully laid out. The left-hand chord in bar 68 is wrong as F and B and is corrected in the manuscript to C and F below.

[43] L. Berkeley diary, 1 December 1976.

the Rev. Colin Gill 'on the occasion of his translation from Holborn to Brighton' in October 1941. It seems extraordinary that this piece was fiercely condemned in internal memoranda at the BBC.[44] It is a kind of celebratory postlude and its opening section announces the main theme chordally. The central section sets a version of the theme, like a cantus firmus, below moto perpetuo figurations which continue in order to articulate the chords of the theme as it moves to a climax. Those organ lessons with W. H. Harris at Oxford were not forgotten. The Three Pieces, Opus 72, No. 1, started life separately. The first was written for the Edith Sitwell Memorial Concert at the 1966 Aldeburgh Festival and the other two were commissioned to make a set of three for the Cheltenham Festival two years later, both performances given by Simon Preston. The Three Pieces made an impressive contribution before and after the Memorial Requiem Mass for Berkeley at Westminster Cathedral on 20 March 1990.[45]

There are other elements contributing to the composer's mature style, so it is necessary to leave the keyboard and go back in order to examine the role of vocal music.

[44] Information from Tony Scotland.

[45] For the recording of both the Three Pieces and the Fantasia see Jennifer Bate on Hyperion LP A 66061 (1983).

5. Voices

In a BBC Radio 3 interview in 1974, Berkeley confirmed his interest in melody and his wish to communicate:

> One has only to think what a composer has to do to a poem: he has to destroy or at best modify its natural rhythm. He cannot possibly adhere to its actual metre. He then has to translate it into another medium. His only excuse for doing such a thing is that he feels he can recreate its atmosphere and feeling in the language of music. And here he can, if he's a good enough composer, heighten its emotional impact. He may even be able to bring out and stress certain rhymes and assonances that will enhance the actual words, but it remains a risky undertaking on which one hesitates to embark. There are things, though, that have drawn me to song-writing. One of them is the opportunity that the medium gives for melodic music. Another, the fact that music combined with words communicates to the listener more quickly than does music in a more abstract form. I'm old-fashioned enough to want to communicate.[1]

In Chapter 2 it was possible to compare Berkeley and Britten setting the same poems by W. H. Auden. This is always a fascinating exercise since, whatever the idiom of the composer, something of the poet filters through which then gives quite diverse musical settings something in common.[2] Berkeley's stature as a composer of songs is consistently high at all periods. *D'un Vanneur de blé*, composed at Oxford in 1925, can be compared with *How Love came in*, which was written ten years later. Both have memorable tunes perfectly matched to the mood of a poem. The same is true of the other single songs which have been grouped together as Opus 14.[3] *Bells of Cordoba*, an English translation of a poem by Lorca, has a strong sense of atmosphere which is owed to the Spanish 3+3+2 rhythm and the repeated notes imitating bells. Berkeley employed the same kind of realism in *Lauds*, the first of the *Five Auden Songs*, Opus 53. As late as 1985 the composer, listening to a recording of a broadcast of *Bells of Cordoba*, felt it

[1] BBC Radio 3, 16 November 1974. Recital of Berkeley's songs by Meriel and Peter Dickinson including an interview with the composer.

[2] A number of my recitals and broadcasts with Meriel Dickinson were designed to illustrate this: notably settings of James Joyce, W. H. Auden, E. E. Cummings and Stevie Smith.

[3] Dating has been confused by putting all the songs, originally without opus numbers but certainly not rejected, into Opus 14b. Only two were not published: *Lay your sleeping Head* (Auden) and the O'Malley poem about a train called *Eleven-Fifty*, which Berkeley may have felt was rather close to Britten's earlier involvement with the documentary film *Night Mail*.

was 'one of the best things I ever did' and liked the 'feeling of bells'.[4] Its rhythm can be compared to the 3+2+3 of the slow movement of the Trio for flute, oboe and piano (1935) but the effect of the harmony is to suggest the hum notes and overtones produced by actual bells.

In many of these songs the melody floats over a repeated accompaniment pattern, also a feature of two exquisite songs to French texts. *Ode du premier jour de mai* is underpinned by a regular rhythm in 3/4 but this is varied with bars of 7/8, 5/4 and 4/4 so that the rhythm is as unpredictable as the direction of the modulations, although it starts with the freshness of the Villanelle in Berlioz's *Nuits d'été*. The same finesse, and real expressive power as well, can be found in *Tant que mes yeux*, dedicated to Sophie Wyss, for whom many British composers, including Britten, wrote songs. The melancholy mood of the poem by Louise Labé is caught with a melodic line hovering between major and minor, a continuous pulse, and some typically French *parlando* towards the end.[5] If *The Beacon Barn* appears less perfect than the French songs and the Auden settings, this is partly the fault of the weak text by Patrick O'Malley. But *The Beacon Barn*, like all these songs since *D'un Vanneur de blé*, avoids the obvious strophic layout. There are two places in its through-composed form where second-inversion major chords, as in the First Symphony, are used for punctuation – bars 9 and 14, one a loud climax, the other a soft coda. Britten did this too, in his Nocturne from *On this Island* at the same period.

It is one thing to write a completely satisfying song but quite another to make a balanced cycle, which Berkeley has seemed able to do almost as instinctively as he has written tunes. Composed in Paris in 1926, *Tombeaux* is a coherent group and in early 1940 Berkeley set A. E. Housman. The English Georgian composers of the twenties and thirties thrived on this poet, so it may seem out of character for Berkeley to join such a company. In fact the severe pessimism of Housman's lyrics of rejection and despair suited the composer's mood exactly, following the sad ending of the Serenade and before the brooding opening of the First Symphony in the climate of war and with Britten in America. In a letter to Ralph Hawkes, written in Paris on 22 October 1939, Berkeley refers to Britten's absence:

> I haven't heard from Ben for ages – I hope he's all right. I think he might really just as well come home – I don't think he would be interfered with by conscription – otherwise he may get stuck over there for years, and I'm afraid that he may lose the position he's already got in England if he remains in America throughout the war.

In a letter to Britten, written on 21 April 1940, Berkeley says: 'I'll send you a copy of my Housman songs – perhaps Peter might sing them.' And admits: 'I still feel pretty feeble compared to you, but I think I've improved a lot.'

[4] L. Berkeley, interview with author, 8 March 1985.

[5] The climax is built over sustained bass lines which imply a continuous tone that the piano cannot provide: the composer once suggested to me that the low C, page 3, line 2, bar 1, could be repeated.

The *Five Housman Songs* (1940), in their choice of text as well as the actual music, point to a searing emotional experience of a kind which rarely came to the surface in such an urbane and civilised man as Berkeley. There are two manuscripts in the composer's hand – first as Four Songs, then as Five Songs, with the last one added. The first is dated January 1940, but it was the second, complete set, with a dedication to Peter Fraser, that was in the possession of Peter Pears. There is no evidence that the songs were sung until after Pears sent me the manuscript in 1975: Ian and Jennifer Partridge performed them on BBC Radio 3 in 1978 and they were published in 1983.[6]

Every song relates to separation.

I And wide apart we lie, my love,
And seas between the twain.

II Such leagues apart the world's ends are,
We're like to meet no more;

III He would not stay for me . . .
I shook his hand and tore my heart in sunder.

IV One the long nights through must lie
Spent in star-defeated sighs . . .

V Because I like you better
Than suits a man to say,
It irked you, and I promised
To throw the thought away.
To put the world between us
We parted stiff and dry;
'Goodbye', said you, 'forget me'.
'I will, no fear', said I.

In 1990 Desmond Shawe-Taylor thought he had introduced Berkeley to Peter Fraser, who was in the RAF, and that their friendship started in happiness and ended in anxiety.[7] Berkeley and Fraser shared a flat from 1944 to 1946 and Basil Douglas recalled that Berkeley was deeply insecure at this period.[8] The manuscript of the orchestral Nocturne, Opus 25, is also dedicated 'To Peter', but not the published miniature score. This is a nightmarish piece with an angular major seventh motif and dramatic exchanges probably related to Berkeley's life at this period.

The technique of the fifth Housman song is pared down to a painful minimum, although the left hand often doubles at the octave to ensure the maximum harmonic comprehensibility:

[6] There are a few discrepancies between the two manuscripts: it looks as if D sharps and not C sharps were intended in the bass of bar 5, since the first manuscript rings these notes and the second one has C sharps. The published score is incorrect.

[7] Interview with author, 28 November 1990.

[8] Interview with author, 28 November 1990.

Example 48. Five Housman Songs, No. 5

The rhythmic figure in the piano is recurrent and it lets up for only a few bars in the central section. The texture opens from a single note, the tonic D flat. The melody exploits conflict as well as coincidence. At bar 4, for example, the E natural in the voice has no sooner been matched by an F flat in the piano than it rises to an F natural. This anticipates the F which is part of the harmony – a major seventh chord on G flat – in the next bar. This turns sentimentally to a dominant seventh on E flat but the effect is acutely gauged without conventional resolution, fitting the words: 'It irked you.' The chord at bar 9 starts as a French sixth but becomes a dominant, with minor ninth, in D minor. This resolves as expected at bar 10 only to provide painful clashes in the second half

Example 48 (cont.)

of the bar and later – a technique of dramatic intensification at least as old as Schubert's *Erlkönig* in the voice and piano medium. Another point of tension, bar 17, turns out to be a perfect cadence in B major and the rhythmic ostinato, still menacing, now moves to the bass. If this symbolises the inevitability of loss, it is remarkable that such intensity can emerge through such conventional devices with an excruciating power comparable to that found in the lieder of Hugo Wolf. It is hard to believe that songs like these could come from a composer who had not experienced feelings as acute as those depicted in the poetry at the time of composition. How unfortunate that Pears simply hung on to the manuscript instead of performing what is possibly the finest Housman cycle of all.

There are two further songs with piano from 1943: *The Ecstatic* (C. Day Lewis) and *Lullaby* (W. B. Yeats). Both deal with aspects of love, the former arousing and the latter sleeping. The piano part of *The Ecstatic* is *moto perpetuo* – comparable to the scherzo of the Piano Sonata and the central section of the Impromptu for organ (1941) – and the *Lullaby* is closely linked to the first theme of the opening movement of the Viola and Piano Sonata both in key and the predominance of the minor third.

It is worth following the thread provided by a text in Berkeley's works through the 1940s. The discontents engendered by love and the agonies of separation were evident in the Housman songs, linking them to settings by Ireland and other Georgian composers. By 1944, Berkeley has turned towards his religious faith as a source for texts in a more profound and personal manner than in *Jonah* or *Domini est terra*. The poet is the early seventeenth-century mystic Richard Crashaw and in *Lord, when the Sense of Thy sweet Grace* the language of carnal love is transmuted to a spiritual level:

> Lord, when the sense of Thy sweet grace
> Sends up my soul to seek Thy face,
> Thy blessed eyes breed such desire,
> I dye in love's delicious fire.

The manuscript of what seems to be Berkeley's first work for choir and organ bears a dedication to Trevor Harvey but the published score, like the agonised Housman songs, is inscribed to Peter Fraser. Curiously Crashaw, like Berkeley, was a convert to Roman Catholicism and he too went to Paris. In the seventeenth century it was a dangerous time for Catholics in England which, in the twenties and thirties, was an uninspiring habitat for young composers. As in several other choral works, there is a carefully graded build-up in the organ part leading to the entry of the voices. As a whole, *Lord when the Sense of Thy sweet Grace* is in the tradition of the choral anthem with organ, less ambitious than the *Festival Anthem* to follow, but equally notable for its quiet ending when the text implies rejoicing. Precedent for that can be found in the soft alleluias of Stravinsky's *Symphony of Psalms* and its quiet coda over a regular ostinato of the kind which Berkeley always found attractive. But this provides common ground nearer home in the work of Britten.

In 1943, Britten wrote *Rejoice in the Lamb*, Opus 30, to a commission from the Rev. Walter Hussey for St Matthew's Church, Northampton. This unconventional church work also features soft alleluias and muted jubilation, which makes Berkeley's idea about the artist not necessarily responding to his surroundings seem even less convincing. It was Britten who suggested to Hussey that Berkeley be asked to write the 1945 commission for the church's festival and later that year their two works were broadcast together.

Comparison between Britten and Berkeley is again illuminating. Britten had chosen poems by the eccentric eighteenth-century poet Christopher Smart, which produced rather unexpected secular results in terms of the Anglican church music tradition. Berkeley carried further his interest in the metaphysical poets by adding George Herbert and Henry Vaughan to his earlier setting of Crashaw, and opening his *Festival Anthem* with the sequence *Jerusalem et sion filiae*. This is the anthology approach, also found in Britten's cycles, but Berkeley was aware of a precedent in Vaughan Williams, as he wrote to Hussey, when he had already started with the Herbert verses from 'The Flower':

> The main reason why I chose 'The Flower' is that I thought immediately of a setting of the fourth verse (which I have actually written). I was not so particularly set on doing the whole poem. I now wonder . . . whether I could incorporate that verse in a setting of something more suitable to your purpose. Vaughan Williams has several times taken the text of his religious works from various things – the Bible, seventeenth and eighteenth-century poetry, and even Walt Whitman, all mixed up together! I wonder whether I couldn't take something more liturgical and include my little verse from 'The Flower' in it, or do you think that impossible? I always find that the choice of a text for this sort of thing is more difficult than writing the work![9]

[9] W. Hussey, *Patron of Art*, London, 1985, p. 95.

Berkeley successfully enclosed the Herbert setting as the core of the work and it is a typical Berkeley melody, sufficiently self-contained for him to make a version for cello and piano, published in 1955, and for him to allow Jennifer Bate – at my suggestion – to make an organ arrangement in 1981. Britten's tenor aria in *Rejoice in the Lamb* is also about flowers, which Christopher Smart calls 'the poetry of Christ', and Herbert wants to be in paradise 'where no flower can wither' (Example 49, p. 94 and Example 50 p. 95). Berkeley is writing a melody, whereas Britten is contributing a character piece to a suite, one of his favourite forms: Berkeley's accompaniment is merely the articulation of chords, either clearly diatonic or slightly clouded by inessential notes. Compare the treatment here with Berkeley's setting of 'Silver', the last of the Five Songs, Opus 26, to poems of Walter de la Mare – a poem which Britten set in his teenage de la Mare cycle, published much later as *Tit for Tat.* Notice the similarity between Britten's accompaniment in Example 49 and Berkeley's in 'Silver'. If the Britten was Berkeley's model, then he has improved upon it.[10] In the tenor aria in *Rejoice in the Lamb* Britten is working with motifs where each phrase of the vocal line extends its range and the accompaniment is doubled in thirds as a consistent texture throughout. Britten's melodic shapes unfold without any eventual repetition whereas Berkeley uses an A–B–A design. For his recapitulation he unusually has ten bars of exact repetition then tellingly brings in the choir, more fully harmonised with a luscious dominant thirteenth in the bar after figure 18, where the organ carried the line before.[11] The Berkeley conveys a devotional atmosphere, even a specifically Roman Catholic one. This is the Gounod or Franck tradition in Berkeley's French past and it successfully skirts sentimentality. Britten uses the minimum of means to achieve a lyrical atmosphere and, as usual, those means he has chosen are rigorously worked.

[10] This may not be the right comparison. Perhaps the impact of the sixth song, *She whom I loved,* in Britten's *Holy Sonnets of John Donne* (1945), has affected Berkeley's *Silver,* the last of the de la Mare set composed in 1946. They are both in the same key of E flat major and Britten almost consistently sustains the two-against-three between voice and piano using this rhythmic conflict, along with harmonic ones, to symbolise the anguish of the lover's loss of his beloved. Berkeley's *Silver* is a dream about the moon, in an entirely calm thin light, and he dares to end his cycle with it; Britten's more monumental subject requires sterner resources. If Berkeley is responding to this Britten song, he is able to turn a similar technique to different ends.

[11] There are differences of detail between the anthem and the arrangement of this tune as the *Andantino* for cello and piano. The same is true of Jennifer Bate's arrangement for organ, which was discussed with Berkeley in detail and recorded on Hyperion A66061 (1982). On 13 June 1986 the composer heard a version for trumpet and piano played by Francis Dickinson and myself. This was intended to demonstrate that, like Ravel's *Habanera,* Berkeley's *Andantino* was the kind of piece which could be arranged for many different single instruments with piano. My earliest connection with Berkeley was through his publisher when I wrote to point out some misprints in the score of the *Festival Anthem.* The managing director, R. D. Gibson, replied to say that in every case my suggestion was correct and that the composer 'particularly asked us to express his appreciation of your kindness in drawing attention to these points, but regretted that you had been put to the trouble'. (Letter, 3 January 1956) A characteristic response. For a recording of this work and other sacred pieces see *Lennox Berkeley: Choral Music,* the Choir of Clare College, Cambridge, directed by Timothy Brown on Meridian CDE 84216 (1991).

Example 49. Britten: *Rejoice in the Lamb*, Opus 30

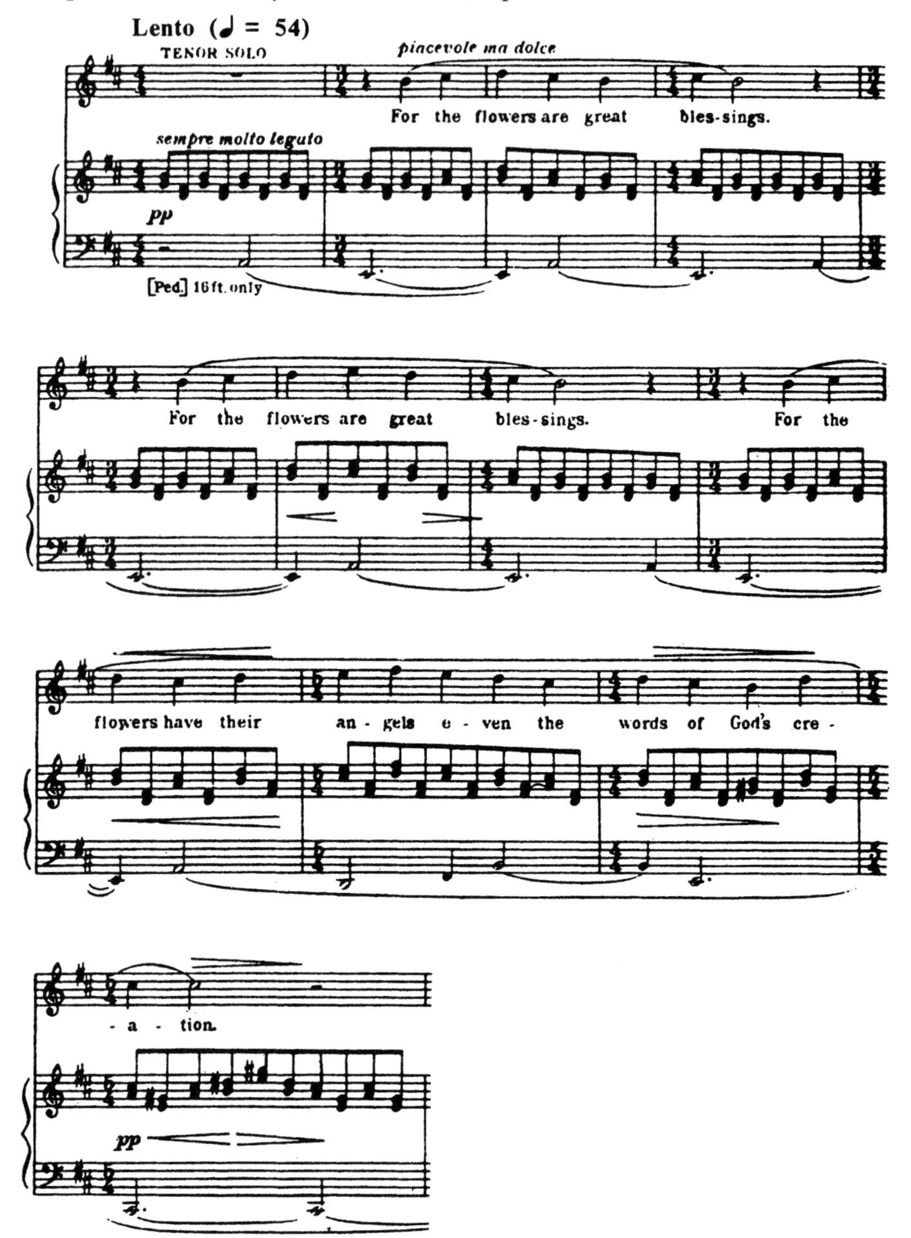

Example 50. Berkeley: A Festival Anthem, Opus 21

Comparisons do not end with these two reflective arias. Britten's minimalism at the start of *Rejoice in the Lamb* causes everything to emerge from a pedal-point middle C. Compare this with the forty-six bars of C major which form the opening crescendo of his Te Deum in C (1935). How different from Berkeley's expansive opening *Lento.* When both settings become rhythmic, Britten employs varied metres derived not from Bartók or Stravinsky but probably Holst's Dance of Spirits of Earth in *The Perfect Fool* (Figure 51, p. 96). Berkeley's rhythmic organ texture has the same perfect fourth bass as Britten's and the same type of diatonic dissonance. (Figure 52, p. 97). The vocal entries in Berkeley following the organ introduction are mostly in two parts but sometimes more. Britten's diagnosis of the choir's capabilities implies that his rhythms will be got right with the least trouble since the singing is mostly in

Example 51. Britten: *Rejoice in the Lamb*

unison. As a final comparison, Berkeley's closing section opens with an organ flourish and the choir enters with a triadic theme enriched by G sharps in D major. This is another example of both composers using the transposed Lydian mode but this time the Britten comparison is not backwards to *Rejoice in the Lamb* but forwards to *Billy Budd* – the lively chorus in Act I, scene 2 (Example 53, p. 98, Example 54, p. 99). As with 'Night covers up the rigid land' and Albert's aria in *Albert Herring*, Berkeley may have provided a pre-echo to something in Britten. This is further evidence, which will be confirmed later, that a composer is not *sui generis* and that a partnership such as that between Britten and Berkeley has been productive both ways.

Berkeley's secular vocal works are by no means confined to the voice and piano medium. One of the most striking is the second set of *Four Ronsard Sonnets*, Opus 62, for tenor and orchestra. The composer's admiration for the sixteenth-century French poet, Pierre de Ronsard, goes back to his Oxford days, when a *Sonnet de Ronsard* – now lost – was performed at the University Musical Club on 4 December 1924. Much later, Berkeley's first set of *Four Ronsard Sonnets*, Opus 40, was commissioned by Peter Pears for him to sing with Hugues Cuenod. They gave the first performance in 1953 but Berkeley revised the work and Pears and Ian Partridge gave this version at the Aldeburgh Festival in 1977. Ten years after the first set of *Ronsard Sonnets*, the BBC commissioned the better-known second set, which Berkeley dedicated to the memory of Poulenc, who had died in January 1963. Pears gave the first performance at the Proms with Berkeley conducting the BBC Symphony Orchestra, but this set was revised too. It looks as if Pears found the scoring overloaded so he commissioned a version for chamber orchestra. This is the version which was recorded

Example 52. Berkeley: *A Festival Anthem*

Example 53. Berkeley: *A Festival Anthem*

Example 54. Britten: *Billy Budd*, Act I, scene 2

by him, again under Berkeley, in 1972.[12] It was an interesting release, showing Pears' dedication to Berkeley and to new works by Lutoslawski and David Bedford. All three composers met at the sessions, as the photographs with the LP show. Bedford had been a pupil and at this time Berkeley regarded Lutoslawski as 'the most deeply musical composer of the more advanced type'.[13] This is quite understandable in any case, but especially in view of Pears' masterly rendering of *Paroles tissées*, which was written for him and exemplifies Lutoslawski's unique method of notation.

Berkeley's sleeve-note describes the poems he chose:

> They are love poems considered among the most perfect of their kind in the French language. Each of the four represents a different aspect of the lovers' feelings – the first, 'Ce premier jour de mai', joy and confidence; the second, 'Je sens un douceur', sweetness and tenderness; the third, 'Ma fièvre croist toujours', anger at the cruel treatment of the poet by his mistress; and the fourth, 'Yeux, qui versez en l'âme', serenity.

The first two songs show a preference for quintuple metre, not always quite steady under Berkeley's direction, and the accompaniment figure of the second song turns out to be the same as the main motif of the first one. There is plenty of orchestral colour, even in the reduced version, and the set as a whole is well conceived as a vehicle for Pears – without ever sounding like Britten.

The role of Pears in Berkeley's vocal music is an important one and shows that his advocacy was by no means confined to Britten although, as we have seen, he missed the opportunity of performing the Housman Songs. The manuscripts of two other Berkeley songs, both dated 1943, were in the

[12] Lutoslawksi – *Paroles tissées*; Berkeley – *Four Ronsard Sonnets*; Bedford – *Tentacles of the Dark Nebula.* Peter Pears, the London Sinfonietta, conducted by the composers. Decca Headline LP HEAD 3 (1973).

[13] L. Berkeley diary, 20 January 1972.

possession of Pears and Britten – *Lullaby* (W. B. Yeats) and *The Ecstatic* (C. Day Lewis) – and it looks as if they were forgotten too. This neglect is surprising since Pears sang in the English Opera Group commissions which included Berkeley's *Stabat Mater* and the now unknown *Variations on a Hymn by Orlando Gibbons*, Opus 35, at the 1952 Aldeburgh Festival, apart from his connection with both sets of *Ronsard Sonnets*. Again with the English Opera Group, Pears sang in the Wigmore Hall concert reading of *Nelson* in 1953 and played Boaz in the production of *Ruth* three years later. It was Pears who commissioned *Songs of the Half-Light* for the 1965 Aldeburgh Festival and premiered the *Five Herrick Poems*, Opus 89, for tenor and harp, at the 1974 Festival. These were revised in 1976 and apparently there were problems with the harp part.[14] Further, in 1955 Pears and Britten made a recording of Berkeley's 1935 Herrick setting, 'How Love came in'.

Berkeley's association with Pears was significant and productive, but there were other singers who had a role in his vocal music, notably Sophie Wyss, who gave the first broadcast performance of *Tombeaux* with Anthony Bernard's London Chamber Orchestra as early as 1929 and premiered *Tant que mes yeux* and *Ode du premier jour de mai*. Finally the legacy of Berkeley's songs prompted Stephen Banfield to claim:

> One might even argue that Berkeley's acceptance and furtherance of a fundamentally traditional song-maker's craft places him and not Britten most directly in the post-war line of succession of English song.[15]

[14] Christopher Headington, *Peter Pears: a Biography*, London, 1992, p. 266.
[15] Stephen Banfield, *Sensibility and English Song*, Cambridge, 1985, p. 389.

6. Religious music

In one of his radio talks Berkeley indicated the religious sources of his inspiration:

> Music does not speak to the intellect alone. Its most important contact with the listener is of another order for it belongs first and foremost to the spiritual world and the best music is that which communicates the most strongly and the most urgently on that level.[1]

In 1990 this was confirmed by one of his pupils, Nicholas Maw, who felt that Berkeley had 'an affinity with a most unlikely character such as Bruckner' and that 'in a very humble way he was doing what he could do and doing it as well as he could do it in the eyes of God'.[2] Malcolm Williamson went further in claiming that every work Berkeley ever wrote was religious and that, whatever the subject, Berkeley was – like Palestrina – a religious composer 'who could conceive of life in no terms other than religious terms'.[3] John Tavener, another pupil, felt this too:

> It is impossible to manufacture true 'devotional' music and it seems to me that Lennox Berkeley's greatest music is his religious music . . . The most important things about a person are usually the least easily described: Lennox's expression, for instance, when, unknown to him, I have seen him after Mass in Westminster Cathedral.[4]

Michael Berkeley came to know one of his father's best known vocal works as a student at the Royal Academy of Music when he conducted the *Four Poems of St Teresa of Avila.* He was deeply moved by 'Let mine eyes see Thee' as 'just a perfect little piece of music. It perhaps brought from him some of the strongest emotions – the sacred went straight to his heart and the music came straight back out again.'[5]

Music to religious texts both in the concert hall and increasingly in church

[1] Included in R. Nichols, BBC Radio 3 interval talk: Sir Lennox Berkeley Memorial Concert, Aldeburgh Festival, 21 June 1990.

[2] Interview with author, 18 October 1990.

[3] Interview with author, 22 February 1991.

[4] J. Tavener, 'Lennox Berkeley at 70', *Listener* 10 May 1973, p. 625.

[5] Interview with author, 27 November 1990. Michael Berkeley referred to various recordings of the *Teresa of Avila Poems* and stressed that 'Let mine eyes see Thee' is sometimes taken too slowly and too romantically, which his father disliked.

seems to be the core of Berkeley. Two vocal works which he wrote in 1947 have for long been considered as among his finest and most characteristic: the *Four Poems of St Teresa of Avila*, Opus 27, and the *Stabat Mater*, Opus 28. The Teresa of Avila songs were written first but the premiere – by Kathleen Ferrier – was not until after that of the *Stabat Mater*. Both are the sacred works of a believer and it is not difficult to see why Berkeley found St Teresa of Avila (1515–82) an attractive subject. The Spanish saint and author was a member of the Carmelite sisterhood and an energetic reformer of the order who travelled around to found new convents. She was famous for mystical visions and apparently courted martyrdom by preaching to the Moors.

When Berkeley turned to religious sources of inspiration he began to find a new seriousness of purpose, as Andrew Porter observed in his sleeve-note for Pamela Bowden's 1960 recording of the *Four Poems*:

> Almost every facet of his musical personality is here seen at its finest: his melodic invention; the sheer prettiness of his writing; its elegance and unaffected distinction; his unerring sense of form in shorter works – and beyond these, a more earnest, sober vein expressed with a quiet passion and intensity.[6]

The response of Desmond Shawe-Taylor, shortly after the first broadcast of the *Four Poems*, is instructive in several ways:

> There is no happier or more attractive talent than his in contemporary English music and his long neglect by the recording companies and the British Council is something of a scandal: I hear that records have at last been made of the Divertimento and I hope that this is only a beginning. Sensitive, unforced and always 'musical' in the sense that we call an artist 'painterly', Lennox Berkeley knows just what he wants to say and says it without emphasis, fuss or irrelevant paraphernalia . . . His orchestral writing shows a freedom and resourcefulness, a sunny invention and lack of strain, which place such works as the Symphony, the Divertimento and the Serenade in a category now sadly underestimated; their aim is neither to improve nor to argue, but simply to give pleasure to the cultivated ear, and it is characteristic of our age to suspect such an aim of triviality.[7]

This shows that Berkeley was recognised by perceptive critics from the 1940s onwards, but the recordings called for by Shawe-Taylor took twelve years to materialise – and it was at least another twelve years before adequate orchestral recordings began to appear.

Shawe-Taylor compared the *Four Poems of St Teresa of Avila* with Britten's *Holy Sonnets of John Donne*, Opus 35 (1945). This is relevant to the religious intensity and B minor tonality of the first songs of both cycles, but in other aspects the two composers diverge. Britten, as always, is rigidly concentrated, with a single texture set in the piano part and adhered to throughout each song. His setting of *Batter my heart*, the second song of the cycle, is over in a

[6] HMV 20 series, HQM 1069 mono/HMV DLP 1209.
[7] D. Shawe-Taylor, 'Music', *New Statesman*, April 1948.

flash, *presto agitato*, but Berkeley turned it into a thirteen-minute cantata with this title, his Opus 60, No. 1 (1962), commissioned by the Riverside Church Choir of New York and Director Richard Weagley. It looks as if the mystical intensity of the Teresa of Avila songs and Berkeley's response with a comparable conviction suggested new directions in his work. The ingredients are not easy to define, but the details are worth examination in what is effectively a four-movement scheme suggesting a concentrated sonata or symphony.

Example 55. *Four Poems of St Teresa of Avila*, Opus 27, No. 1

The opening motto is rooted to the unison B, the tonal centre of the first song, but not in conventional scales. Berkeley spells his leading-note as B flat. The first two-bar unit is repeated, with slight rhythmic differences, then rising whole-tone scales in contrary motion lead into the voice – not on the tonic B but in a more intense vocal register on F sharp, one of a number of focal points on a bare fifth. The four-note figure conveys the mood powerfully, as the composer must have recognised when he referred to it at the opening of his

Example 55 (cont.)

third opera, *Ruth*, using it as a way in to a suitable language for the biblical story. The motif may have its roots in Britten – it appears in the *Lacrymosa* which opens the *Sinfonia da Requiem*, Opus 20 (1940):

Example 56. Britten: *Sinfonia da Requiem*, Lacrymosa

These derivations, almost certainly at a subconscious level, are not flaws in Berkeley. Such things abound in classical and romantic music, and this one may be no more significant than the connection between the pounding repeated Ds at the opening both of Lutoslawski's Cello Concerto (1970) and Britten's *Sinfonia da Requiem.*

Example 57. Berkeley: *Four Poems of St Teresa of Avila*, No. 1

The C naturals in the B minor context colour the sound and – nine bars after figure 1 – the clash between C sharp and C natural is a characteristic modal contradiction. Tension is maintained as the climax, *largamente*, approaches over a pedal D and arrives with the high F natural in the voice.[8] This high note was an afterthought, not sung by Ferrier at the first performance, but a great improvement as the voice falls a minor ninth and the music modulates to the dominant at figure 2.[9] Notice that in this cadence the chord functioning as dominant contains B flat rather than the expected B natural. After this strong opening paragraph the setting falls into further episodes appropriate to the text. Five bars before figure 3 the scale with B flat and C natural is the basis of a melisma for the voice which is used in the instrumental interlude which follows:

Example 58. *Four Poems of St Teresa of Avila*, No. 1

Figure 4 sustains a type of recitative. The descending figure which opens the vocal phrase 'And I will build' is carried down all the strings as the texture extends towards the tonic B in the bass at figure 5 with the principal motif. Three bars and five bars after figure 5, the first chord contains both B flat and B natural over the C natural in the bass – a bitter-sweet Berkeley dissonance well matched to the erotic-spiritual imagery of the text. Added sixths appear in the harmony – a chord to which Messiaen gave religious associations, and one which will end the fourth song – as this song proceeds to a kind of spiritual consummation at figure 6. (Example 59, p. 107) This occurs on a dominant seventh in the key of F with the significant C in the bass. Three bars of unaccompanied vocal line are then sustained by this implied harmony with a suggestion of the thirteenth falling on the next two downbeats, but the later E flat making a blue note – one which, as D sharp, will become the tièrce de Picardie ending. The motto – the first four bars of the song – is evoked softly as an echo of the almost minatory power of the love of God at this electric intensity.

The second song is a musette in G major in a clearly spaced open texture redolent of Mahler (Example 60, p. 108). The B flat/B natural polarity noticed in the first song and operating there as tonic and leading-note now reappears with the same pitches as major or minor third. Everything about the scoring is atmospheric and luminous. It is dawn and there are shepherds in the fields who

[8] F natural is clearly intended, and is sung in the HMV 1960 recording by Pamela Bowden, but early editions of the published score have no accidental.

[9] A private recording of the first performance of the *Teresa of Avila Poems*, with Kathleen Ferrier, was discovered in the Berkeley household and issued on BBC Artium LP REGL 368 mono (ZCF 368 cassette) in 1979. The sound quality is appalling but it gives a good idea of the Ferrier mystique applied to these songs. There were later recordings by Pamela Bowden, Bernadette Greevy and Sarah Walker but there are none at the time of writing.

Example 59. *Four Poems of St Teresa of Avila*, No. 1

seem to hear the voices of angels. The first seventeen bars sustain open fifths so the voice is free to decorate with either major or minor third, retaining the mood of a folksong. An interrupted cadence, four bars after figure 3, sets the key of the central portion as F major. Nine bars after that the melody rises to a B flat in this different context. Five bars before figure 5 there is an

Example 60. *Four Poems of St Teresa of Avila*, No. 2

instrumental excursion to D flat, suggesting the tonality of the next song. When the aerated texture of the opening returns in G major, there is a new triplet rhythm carried by the violas in harmonics. Four bars before figure 8, this is shared by other strings to provide a plagal cadence, effected as a solo violin deftly runs up two and a half octaves in a brief coda:

Example 61. *Four Poems of St Teresa of Avila*, No. 2

The third song is in D flat major, but again with some significant variations of this scale to provide a blue-note flattened third:

Example 62. *Four Poems of St Teresa of Avila*, No. 3

As in the first two songs, a two-bar unit is repeated as an introduction for the voice. If the first song was a sacred consummation, this one is a religious *liebestod.* The tritone relationship with the previous G major and the use of the lowest contralto register combine to create a new depth. The opening progression in the strings – carefully kept below the voice until bar 11 – occurs five times unchanged. The opening chord is not actually D flat major but a first inversion of B flat minor which, in context, lends a feeling of added-note sensuality. It is not until figure 1 that the tonic arrives with a perfect cadence:

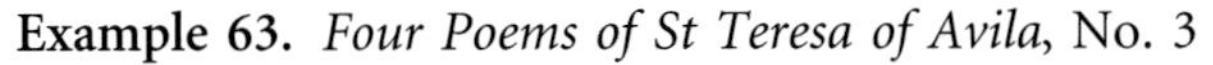

Example 63. *Four Poems of St Teresa of Avila*, No. 3

At figure 1 the first violins have the song's melody, but the minor third in it is harmonised this time as a conventional dominant thirteenth. The flat sixth, as A natural, comes into play for the first time two bars later as a new harmony for the motto repeated in the first violins. This progression, which will end the whole song in the voice and in the instrumental postlude, is prominent in much of Liszt and on a grand scale in Tchaikovsky's *Eugene Onegin*. Emotionally, it works. The A natural relationship now generates a rising figure in the strings four bars before figure 2. At figure 2 the E flat major, poised on a first inversion conventionally approached via a dominant seventh, lingers over 'Sweet Jesus' but the motto comes back four bars later and its second half is repeated to point the real goal of this religious ecstacy as the voice swoops down to 'death' over a chord containing C natural and B flat over B natural in the bass:

Example 64. *Four Poems of St Teresa of Avila*, No. 3

That chord, which has a precedent in Ravel, neatly resolves into an A major context, with some sharpened fourths and inflected thirds, which leads to the opening phrase of the song again. The semitone of the main motif conditions the expectancy of the coda in the two-note bass ostinato.

Berkeley's choice of text is in the tradition of Catholic mysticism. Richard Crashaw, whom he set in *Look up sweet Babe* as well as *Lord, when the Sense of Thy sweet Grace*, wrote a Hymn to St Teresa. The erotic connotations accurately reflected in Berkeley's music were recognised long before by Italian painters such as Bernini in his *Ecstasy of St Teresa* (1645).

The final song opens in the B minor of the first one, but over a cheerful baroque moto perpetuo bass with fanfare figures above (Example 65, p. 113). There are melodic connections between the first and last songs through the E sharps in the first phrases of both of them and there are harmonic connections too, where Berkeley's dominant thirteenth – two bars before figure 3 – sustains a paragraph of great buoyancy based on the fanfare rhythm. This comes to an end at figure 5, where a syncopated figure in E flat major ushers in a section which comes remarkably close to being a swung version of the third song (Example 66, p. 114). At figure 7, B flats and B naturals are momentarily in conflict and a recapitulation is launched at figure 8. Since ecstasy is again the goal, the key veers towards the relative major and one bar before figure 11 reveals the last blue-note false-relation before reaching a radiant fortissimo D major followed by a soft coda which comes to rest on a mystical added sixth.

More detailed observation further substantiates the impression of closely unified motivic working arising from an instinctive but accurate response to the world of these poems in the translation by Arthur Symons. It is not difficult to see why St Teresa appealed to this leading spirit of the decadent movement. As for Berkeley himself, he has enjoyed reading religious authors of all periods. In an article in *The Times* in 1962, he specified St Augustine, Von Hügel, C. S. Lewis and Teillard de Chardin, but added characteristically:

> But I have not always been lucky; mystical experience does not necessarily go hand in hand with talent and some books on the subject have seemed to me amongst the most tedious ever written. The liveliest writer in this category is surely St Teresa of Avila; even in translation the vigour of her writing, her imagination, humour and directness are captivating. Her personality would emerge even if she were writing wholly, as she is sometimes, about purely mundane matters.[10]

[10] L. Berkeley, 'The Sound of Words', *The Times*, 28 June 1962. Another revealing article in

Example 65. *Four Poems of St Teresa of Avila*, No. 4

Berkeley often wrote works in pairs – the First Symphony and the Divertimento; the Piano Concerto and the Two-Piano Concerto; the Violin Concerto and Five Pieces for Violin and Orchestra; even *Nelson* and *A Dinner Engagement* at the same time. The *Four Poems of St Teresa of Avila* and the *Stabat Mater* were written close together and it is in the light of Berkeley's new openness to mystical religious emotions that the latter should now be approached.

which the composer records his enjoyment of Evelyn Waugh, Nancy Mitford and Anthony Powell: his favourite contemporary French author was Julien Green.

Example 66. *Four Poems of St Teresa of Avila*, No. 4

Berkeley often wrote for some of the same performers as Britten. Kathleen Ferrier had sung the title role in Britten's *The Rape of Lucretia* in 1946 and she gave the first concert performance of the Teresa of Avila songs in the penultimate year of her life. Berkeley's connection with Britten continued when he asked Berkeley to write a work for a tour of the English Opera

Group, which planned to give concert performances as well as theatrical productions. The result was Berkeley's *Stabat Mater*, written for six solo voices, eleven instruments and percussion, and dedicated to Britten. Berkeley conducted the first performance at the Kleiner Saal of the Tonhalle in Zurich on 19 August 1947 and Britten conducted the first British performance for the BBC the following month and the first concert performance at the Aldeburgh Festival in 1953. Before that, when Berkeley sent him a copy of the score, Britten wrote: 'I am so glad that Chesters have done you proud, with such a lovely cover. The piece really deserves it too. I hope it will have lots & lots of performances & bring you the fame that it merits.'[11]

Zurich had already heard some of Berkeley's music when Sophie Wyss and Antony Hopkins performed some of his French songs the previous April.[12] In 1950, Robin Hull waxed lyrical about Berkeley's twin religious works and found they had features in common:

> The coalescence of music and text is carried out with consummate skill. Moreover, the artistic unity between the two is so integrated with the instrumental elements that the whole concept forms an indivisible entity. The unforgettable beauty found in these pages is, in truth, partly a matter of sheer inspiration, but it derives no less from that quality of inevitability which is among the rarest and most supreme in music. The significance of the issue is not only that the texts are handled with a mastery amounting to perfection, but that the perfection itself is of a kind which Berkeley alone could have achieved.[13]

Colin Mason, in 1956, found the *Stabat Mater*

> one of the most beautiful of all his works . . . and worthy of its creator in every way . . . not least in the writing for this difficult instrumental ensemble, of which Berkeley alone, among the other composers who have written for it, has shown the same mastery as Britten.[14]

Martin Cooper, in 1959, felt that the Teresa of Avila songs and the *Stabat Mater* 'showed an awareness of the human predicament and a spontaneous dramatic quality which were quite new in his music, and the *Stabat Mater* combined these with bold yet lucid writing for a sextet of soloists'.[15]

In spite of such accolades the *Stabat Mater* remains a neglected work which occupies the kind of position in British music since 1945 that Satie's *Socrate*

[11] B. Britten, letter to Berkeley, 11 January 1950.

[12] Details from the actual concert programme, courtesy of the Tonhalle Orchester, Zurich.

[13] R. Hull, 'The Style of Lennox Berkeley', *Chesterian* 24, April 1950, pp. 84–7.

[14] C. Mason, 'The Progress of Lennox Berkeley', *Listener*, 27 September 1956, p. 485. Mason refers to the 'tremendous imaginative release wrought in Berkeley by Britten's influence' but finds Berkeley a 'strong and individual personality'.

[15] M. Cooper, 'Lennox Berkeley and his New Symphony', *Listener*, 19 February 1959, p. 351. This article introduces the Second Symphony, Op. 51 (1956–57), which Berkeley revised considerably in 1976 for the recording, Lyrita SRCS 94 (1978), with the composer's sleeve-notes. In a letter to me, written on 29 February 1976, Berkeley said: 'My immediate task is the revision of my Second Symphony which is going quite well. I've never been satisfied with it and have hated the idea of leaving it as it was.'

held in French music after the First World War.[16] The comparison perhaps goes further – compare the open fifths over a regular beat at figure 2 in Berkeley's opening movement with the music which accompanies the death of Socrates at the end of Satie's work. The 6/8 movements of the *Stabat Mater* can be compared with Satie's similar rhythm in his second song. The severe two-part counterpoint often harks back to Berkeley's setting of Cocteau's poem about the tomb of Socrates in his early cycle, *Tombeaux* (1926) (Example 4, p. 11). Matters should not be taken too far. However, Satie and Berkeley, in their respective works to serious texts, share deliberate understatement and a kind of emotional restriction. Within a narrow range a great deal can be said – an ancient tradition in French music. Both Satie and Berkeley relate to Fauré, and all three have drawn something from plainchant, which, in Berkeley's case, colours his liturgical music.

But this kind of musical dépouillement can be misunderstood. In a changing climate in the mid 1960s Jeremy Noble found that Berkeley 'at times achieves the ritual anguish the poem calls for, but in attempting to provide contrast falls into a too-sweet sub-Poulenc vein that doesn't quite match'.[17] Noble had earlier commended Palestrina's solution for its homophonic unity, but neglected totally different approaches such as Verdi's vivid treatment with full orchestra. As for Poulenc, both he and Howells set the *Stabat Mater* after Berkeley and may well have been aware of his example.

Berkeley breaks up the sequence *Stabat Mater dolorosa* into ten sections of two three-line stanzas each. This makes the work about three times as long as Verdi's, but it is not as extended as Rossini's example. All the same, the elements which Noble found 'too sweet' seem to come from Berkeley's sometimes Italianate treatment of a Latin text and his awareness of the Catholic tradition of mass settings. The more melodic passages reflect Berkeley's growing sense of cantilena, which was leading towards opera.

Right at the start Berkeley sets the pace with a regular pulse in the harp as a subdued background for chords and falling phrases. Imogen Holst, in 1954, identified with the work and was specially interested in it because the Rural Music Schools Association had commissioned the composer to make an arrangement with a reduced accompaniment for string quartet, string orchestra and piano:

> The greatness of the *Stabat Mater* depends not only on the skill of its craftsmanship but also on the deeply-felt conviction that underlies the whole conception of the work. At the beginning, the silence is broken by the relentless repetition of the slow stroke of a pizzicato E. The bare fourths and fifths of the introduction bring with them a recollection of the thirteenth century; but while moving to and from

[16] Not all reviewers were as enthusiastic as these. It is a sharp reminder of the British musical climate at the time that Ralph Hill, after acknowledging the importance of the occasion, could write in the *Daily Mail* on 27 September 1947: 'This is not an easy work to assimilate at first hearing. Although it contains a lot of very beautiful and expressive music, some of the writing, particularly for the voices, seems unnecessarily crude and angular.'

[17] J. Noble, 'Music in London', *Musical Times* 106, April 1965, p. 279.

their chromatic passing notes add an intensity to the harmonies; it is the twentieth century's own contribution to that early austere framework.[18]

What might be called a penitential response to the *Stabat Mater* – a modern composer deliberately restricting his means – is also found in Szymanowski's setting of 1928, which reduces his normally opulent harmonic idiom to bare fifths, isolated melodic lines and a restrained atmosphere. Szymanowski's work was nevertheless given at the International Society for Contemporary Music Festival in Brussels in 1930 and at the Three Choirs Festival two years later. Imogen Holst was right to identify something new in Berkeley's bare fourths and fifths which carry through into later works of all types and especially the liturgical music.

The opening of the *Stabat Mater* establishes E, and then E major, as the centre to which the work will return. This is the key of the outside sections of No. III and of most of No. VIII and the work's coda returns to it impressively as the voices fade away. The sections of the *Stabat Mater* are mostly connected in terms of traditional related keys and this helps to provide continuity between contrasted textures which range from austere counterpoint to fully scored passages making the most of the full ensemble. After the opening centred on E, a heavier pulse arrives at figure 2, making a diminuendo on the dominant leading to the loud entry of the voices in D minor:

Example 67. *Stabat Mater*, Opus 28, I, figure 3

Each of the first two-bar phrases ends on an open fifth and the vocal layout is largely based on four parts with one doubling, but not consistently in the same part. There is a spacious momentum about the music as it builds to the climax on the words 'Pertransivit gladius'. The horn dramatises the sword by rising into high register followed by chromatic descents. This semitone obsession goes

[18] I. Holst, 'Lennox Berkeley's *Stabat Mater*', *Making Music* 24, Spring 1954, pp. 8–9. Further arrangements exist. Christopher Headington made an orchestral version (BBC Music Library, misc. sc. 3102) and Michael Berkeley expanded the string quintet into string orchestra, a version which was first performed at the Queen Elizabeth Hall on 12 May 1978 in a Park Lane Group concert for Berkeley's seventy-fifth birthday.

through to the end of the section when the viola's F sharp drops to F natural for D minor after five bars of uncertainty.

The second section is a duet for two sopranos in 6/8, who overlap each other's range and are sometimes scored in unison. It is in B minor with modal touches but nevertheless some clear cadences in an overall ternary form. E major is established at the start of No. III with a close-position high triad in the strings. So clear is the key that at the end – a condensed recapitulation where the composer gives the singer's melody to the horn – the tonic is avoided in favour of a partial added-sixth chord with the dominant in the bass. It was the ending of this section, the baritone solo to the words 'quis est homo?', that Berkeley discussed with Britten – and then declared his independence: 'Ben Britten suggested that I should change the ending in order not to make the soloist finish on such a low note, so I did, but afterwards decided that I preferred my own ending and changed it back again.'[19]

Berkeley ingeniously avoids full stops at the end of all sections: No. II ends with an open fifth, the B a dominant to the E major following; the B in the bass of No. III at the end is a dominant to the next E opening No. IV; that in turn ends with a unison F sharp – a leading-note to No. V in the key of G; No. V ends with a unison B as leading-note to the C major of No. VI; No. VII is close in the relative minor, but ending on a kind of half-close – an E minor triad plus added sixth and major ninth; this evaporates to the pure E major again of No. VIII, sufficiently traditional in conception to accommodate an interrupted cadence into figure 32; No. IX is transitional in tonality and contains the work's most dramatic passages; No. X opens with seven bars of preamble, based on the new sound of the bass clarinet, but figure 10 establishes D major, which remains as a centre until figure 44, when the voices alone lead back to the Es of the opening again.

There are pictorial references in No. IV. Homophony breaks into polyphony at 'Vidit Jesus in tormentis' and the sound of scourges is anticipated in the high bassoon at figure 14. Six bars after figure 15, a death ostinato begins and carries through after the voices have intoned 'Dum emisit spiritum'. No. V, the 'Eia Mater', is Berkeley's most Rossinian moment in the entire work – oddly enough the same major-minor ambivalence noted in the Teresa of Avila songs operates through the B flat/B natural in the first vocal phrase. It comes again and also forms the final cadence (Example 68, p. 119). There is a second-inversion chord under the fourth bar of the melody and another one used traditionally beneath a mini cadenza five bars before the end of the section.

The C major chord opening No. VI has no fifth – like the one at the end of the *Symphony of Psalms*, a work which profoundly affected Berkeley. It is typical that he should be influenced by the religious Stravinsky, whereas different works might be cited for the inevitable Stravinsky influence on Copland, Tippett, Walton, Britten and others. The opening motto of a falling major seventh in the flute becomes almost unrecognisable as a low bass solo, soon freely extended.

[19] L. Berkeley, letter to Douglas Gibson, J. & W. Chester, 16 May 1949.

Example 68. *Stabat Mater*, V, bar 3

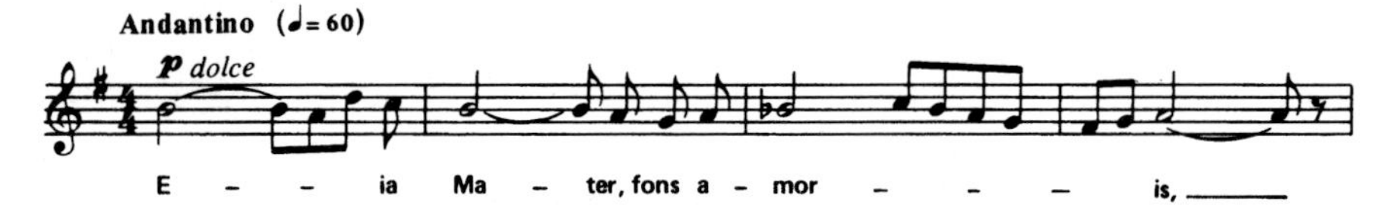

No. VII, as a contralto solo, harks back to the Teresa of Avila songs and its continuous 6/8 emphasising strings shows kinship with the third movement of the Serenade:

Example 69. *Stabat Mater*, VII

Turning to *a cappella* for the opening of No. VIII, 'Virgo virginum praeclara', is reminiscent of Verdi's similar treatment in his *Stabat Mater* at the words 'Eia Mater'. Only the middle eight bars are accompanied, and then the final four. The melody at figure 35 quotes part of the first section – from three bars before figure 4. The dramatic content of No. IX has already been mentioned – more coloratura than anything in the Teresa of Avila songs, more Verdian in response to the terrors of judgement. The high horn semitones are very characteristic of Berkeley's melodic elaboration:

Example 70. *Stabat Mater*, IX, 5 bars after figure 37

The use of consecutive first-inversion chords under the climax at figure 39 is unusual for Berkeley, although conventionally effective in launching the soloist's high B flat. The tension decays over a bass ostinato.

No. X opens with a kind of recitative for the bass clarinet, but at figure 40 D major is established along with the ostinato pattern which movingly dominates the final lamentation:

Example 71. *Stabat Mater*, X, figure 40

Flute and horn open in a counterpoint containing modal contradictions, such as the minor third below and the major third above, and the Purcellian cadence figure noted before is used. At figure 41 the full ensemble enters and the voices follow one by one, emphasising the threnodic mood. After the climax just before figure 43, regular crotchet movement maintains up to the unaccompanied vocal entries at figure 44. The final bars for the voices are based on a mixture of G major and E minor – the continuous Gs suggest G, but the D sharps propose the E minor which is coming. The last chord in the voices is a bare fifth against which the opening music is superimposed:

Example 72. *Stabat Mater*, X, figure 44

Phrases rise, as if heavenwards, over a tonic pedal – compare this with the 'Louange à l'Immortalité de Jésus' which ends Messiaen's *Quatuor pour la fin du temps* in the same key. Finally the major is achieved, a high chord in string harmonics, and the harp far below moves from F sharp to E. (Example 73, p. 123.) Or, in the words of Imogen Holst: 'At the very end of the work, the falling semitone of the minor second is transformed to a major second with a gesture that banishes all desolation; while the strings' high-held harmonics on the chord of E major shine with an unwavering serenity'.[20]

[20] I. Holst, 'Lennox Berkeley's *Stabat Mater*', *Making Music* 24, Spring 1954, pp. 8–9.

Example 72 (cont.)

In 1966 Berkeley examined the problems of composing for the liturgy and it will be convenient here to follow this strand through before returning to the 1950s and his operas:

> How, it may be asked, does a composer approach the task of writing religious music? Does he adopt a different tone of voice, or use a special idiom? I would say that in the case of music that is religious in subject matter but intended for the concert platform there is no problem. I cannot imagine that any composer in these circumstances would want to modify his ordinary musical idiom. The great masters of the past certainly did not. But in writing music to be performed in

Example 73. *Stabat Mater*, X, 6 bars after figure 45

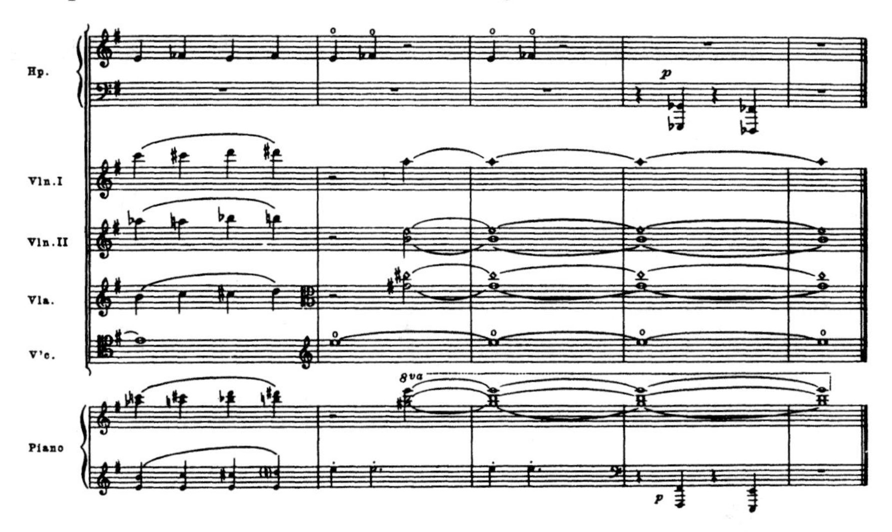

church as part of the service, some modification might be desirable. Speaking for myself, I have found that I wanted to make it somewhat more impersonal, so that it would merge into the liturgy, and not create a violent contrast or cause too much distraction . . . Being a Roman Catholic, I have naturally been drawn to the Latin liturgy and felt at home with it: it is part of my life, and I have wanted to bring to it what I have to offer, however unworthy.[21]

I asked Lady Berkeley if the religious works seemed to her to be the most important part of his output, which was also admired by Britten:

Possibly, yes. He chose to write anthems for the church . . . and settings of the liturgy. I think they were tremendously important to him . . . I came across a card from Ben saying he thought the *Missa brevis* was marvellous and he'd like to hear it done by the Westminster Cathedral Choir where it would have its best performance.[22]

A random glance at the list of music for church services provided each Saturday by *The Times* in 2002 shows that in the period since the first edition of this book in 1988 Berkeley's church music has conquered the cathedral lists.[23] The *Missa*

[21] L. Berkeley, 'Truth in Music', *The Times Literary Supplement*, 3 March 1966. This is an important article, as close to Berkeley's credo as anything he wrote. He extols Mozart, whose later music 'reaches an almost superhuman level of order and perfection, a pure unclouded heaven to which he alone had the key', and insists that 'all music is firstly apprehended by the senses, and the rigidly intellectual approach (all too common today) excludes an essential part of it'.

[22] Interview with author, 28 January 1991.

[23] Taken at random, the 'Sunday Worship' list in *The Times* on 23 February 2002 has three entries for the *Missa brevis* and two for the *Mass for Five Voices*.

brevis can often be found three or four times a week and the anthems are there too. Berkeley sometimes appears more frequently than Vaughan Williams and even Howells. This reflects the spiritual core of the composer himself and needs to be taken into account in defining his musical personality. Useful comparisons can be made with Poulenc, also a pious Roman Catholic, where Berkeley himself can be our guide. In 1966, after hearing Poulenc's *Quatre motets pour un temps de pénitence*, he wrote:

> I thought [the motets] among his best works . . . I thought of him with great affection. *The Times* critic says the work was let down by occasional touches of facile sentiment, but how grateful one is, in these days, for sentiment of any kind; it is at least a relief from the showy gimmickry of the avant-garde.[24]

Before that, in an obituary tribute, Berkeley appreciated Poulenc's integrity and the breadth of his interests:

> By the death of Francis Poulenc we lose a composer of a type that is rare today, for his talent was above all natural and spontaneous. He never sought to bring anything new to music other than the novelty of his own personality, and wrote unashamedly as he felt, paying little heed to musical fashion . . . Unlike some artists, he was genuinely interested in other people's work, and surprisingly appreciative of music very far removed from his. I remember him playing me the records of Boulez' *Le Marteau sans maître* when that work was much less well-known than it is today.[25]

Berkeley's three Opus 43 choral pieces from the mid-1950s show a move in the direction of liturgical music. The first, *Crux fidelis*, is a Latin motet for SATB unaccompanied, using one of the antiphons for Good Friday, which is dedicated to Imogen Holst. The other two, *Look up, sweet Babe* (Richard Crashaw) and *Sweet was the Song* (W. Ballet), are very much in the choir and organ tradition and both are carols. But they are impeccable examples of Berkeley's style with individual touches all along. *Look up* has a memorable melody, initially a treble solo, set over regular organ figures with occasional organ phrases weaving in and out. The climax is of mystical intensity, based on a verbal conceit built around the holy child's birth in the East, and the organ responds wth dissonant harmonies of a kind rare in cathedral music in the 1950s. Berkeley shows great resource in the interaction between choir and organ. Both these carols are perfect miniatures. The rocking 'lalulas' of *Sweet was the Song* may seem conventional, but they are treated in a personal manner.

Berkeley's *Salve Regina* is a simple setting for unison voices and organ written for the Society of St Gregory. This is specifically Catholic and, like his hymn-tunes, reduces Berkeley's idiom to the minimum. On the other hand *Thou hast made me* is a Donne setting written for the St Cecilia's Day Service of the Musicians' Benevolent Fund which brought together several Anglican cathedral

[24] L. Berkeley diary, 6 February 1966.

[25] L. Berkeley, 'Francis Poulenc: obituary', *Musical Times* 104, March 1963, p. 205.

choirs for what must have been an impressive occasion at the Church of St Sepulchre, Holborn Viaduct, on 22 November 1960. Donne's poem expresses the fear of death and looks to God as his only deliverance. Berkeley rises magnificently to its final magnetic image: 'Thy Grace may wing me to prevent his art, And thou like Adamant draw mine iron heart'. Triumphant unison voices strike a false relation with the organ on 'Adamant' and the exhilarating cadence is totally original.

On 12 March 1960, the Feast of St Gregory, Berkeley's most popular mass setting was first heard at Westminster Cathedral. The *Missa brevis* is dedicated to Michael and Julian and the boys of the choir and has a special significance since the composer's two eldest sons were both in the choir at that time. It followed close on the heels of Britten's *Missa brevis* for boys' voices and organ, which was also written for Westminster Cathedral, but there are no discernible connections except possibly the use of variable metres in the Gloria. Berkeley probably attended the premiere of Britten's mass at Westminster Cathedral on 22 July 1959 since he wrote to him: 'I was so delighted with the Mass – it is really beautiful and extremely characteristic.'[26] As for his own *Missa brevis*, Berkeley told Britten that he regarded it as 'essentially a liturgical piece . . . at too low a temperature, so to speak, for the concert hall. I agree that the Agnus Dei is the best movement.'[27]

By now Berkeley's vocal writing is becoming more polyphonic in the centuries-old traditional church music manner. The Kyrie opens with the voices in imitation over the organ's low D pedal point. This dissolves momentarily to pure G major at 'Christe eleison'. The Gloria sports varied metres of a kind that would have taxed some cathedral choirs at the time. Both Sanctus and Benedictus open polyphonically and both end on a luminous unresolved dominant seventh. The Agnus Dei confirms the sobriety of Berkeley's liturgical idiom, which is ideally suited to its purpose and gained Britten's admiration. The polyphony has unexpected elements where voices enter on pitches which are not obvious. Once this approach is mastered by choirs the writing sounds completely convincing, and again the melodic approach is memorable.

There are more works which carry forward this spirit into the composer's last years. Berkeley's *Mass for Five Voices*, Opus 64 (1964), was commissioned by Cardinal Heenan, Archbishop of Westminster, and there are *Three Latin Motets*, Opus 81, No. 1 (1972) dedicated to Alec Robertson, the critic and authority on Catholic church music, which had their first London performance at Westminster Cathedral. About the first of these, 'Eripe me, Domine', Berkeley wrote:

> I have always found the text very moving [in the Good Friday liturgy] and if I can put even half what it makes me feel into the music I shall be happy. This of course can only come about naturally – one can't do it by any act of the will – so I hope it has happened.[28]

[26] L. Berkeley, undated letter to Britten.
[27] L. Berkeley, letter to Britten, 17 January 1961.
[28] L. Berkeley diary, April 1971.

This makes it clear that Berkeley was not just setting a text but expressing his faith. Three works commissioned by the Anglican church followed. The most familiar of these is *The Lord is my Shepherd*, written for the 900th anniversary of the founding of Chichester Cathedral in 1975 and dedicated to the Dean, Walter Hussey, who had commissioned Berkeley's *Festival Anthem* for St Matthew's, Northampton, in 1945. Hussey also commissioned Walton to write a *Magnificat and Nunc Dimittis* for the occasion and discusses the arrangements for this in his book – but there is no mention of *The Lord is my Shepherd*.[29] However the Berkeley has become far more popular, and by 2002 there were six recordings.[30]

This short anthem opens with a placid organ figure over a pedal point as a backcloth to a quietly ecstatic treble solo which expresses the contentment of Psalm 23 to perfection. The key of G major seems to have had a special significance for Berkeley. Other examples in this mood include the central section of the *Festival Anthem*; the ninth variation of the Concerto for Two Pianos; and the 'Esurientes' section of the *Magnificat*. Apart from the unaccompanied Latin motet *Judica me*, Opus 96, No. 1 (1978), dedicated to Berkeley's loyal publisher and friend Sheila MacCrindle, there is a *Magnificat and Nunc Dimittis*, Opus 99 (1980), for John Birch at the Southern Cathedrals Festival. This shows Berkeley still exploring as he enters his last decade. The *Magnificat* opens with soft tone-clusters in the organ, but the voices are largely diatonic. Some of Berkeley's late music shows a decline, but there are still many original touches here in the exchanges between voices and organ. His last completed work was the simple carol *In Wintertime*, Opus 103, commissioned for the Festival of Nine Lessons and Carols at King's College, Cambridge, in 1983.

Berkeley's achievements in liturgical music for both the Anglican and Roman Catholic rites, now being more widely recognised, unexpectedly give this allegedly Francophile composer roots in the most extended musical tradition the British Isles has ever known. The sources of this rich heritage can be glimpsed in Berkeley's earlier concert works on sacred texts, even before the *Four Poems of St Teresa of Avila* and the *Stabat Mater*, but the extent of his later commitment could hardly have been predicted. It is now necessary to return to the 1950s to follow Berkeley's career in opera where the sacred element is present in *Ruth*.

[29] W. Hussey, *Patron of Art*, London, 1985.

[30] For many of the sacred works under discussion see *Lennox Berkeley: Choral Music*, the Choir of Clare College, Cambridge, directed by Timothy Brown, Meridian CDE 84216.

7. Grand opera

In a perceptive article introducing Berkeley's third opera, *Ruth*, in 1956, Colin Mason noted how composing for the theatre had altered Berkeley's position amongst British composers of his generation:

> Three years ago, when Lennox Berkeley was fifty, his reputation . . . might have been thought likely to remain for ever where it then stood. A contemporary of Bush, Rawsthorne, Rubbra, Tippett and Walton, he would always have been, if not the last, almost certainly one of the last two of them, to occur to most averagely knowledgeable persons asked to name the six most important or interesting composers of that generation. Now, suddenly, in the last three years, he has remarkably extended his musical range. He has become known to a wider public, his musical achievement and potentialities seem altogether greater, and his name now might well be among the first three on a good many lists.[1]

Twenty-seven years later, in a tribute to Berkeley for his eightieth birthday, I made the same point:

> How does the work of Lennox Berkeley fit into British music of the last fifty years? Obviously he is an elder statesman among British composers, still working as he enters his eighty-first year. Equally clearly he has become a member of the big four – Britten, Tippett, Walton and Berkeley – although to make a claim of this sort for such a modest and unassuming man may seem forced.[2]

Mason went on to discuss Stravinsky as the first catalyst in Berkeley's development – via Boulanger – and then to cite Britten as the next. He even saw the connection with Britten as working both ways, although without the evidence provided in this study. Mason also assessed Berkeley's temperament:

> He has always been a composer particularly responsive to, and to some extent dependent on, musical stimuli from other composers, and his music is often most compelling, and most personal, when most like somebody else's.[3]

The diagnosis of dependence, including the function of Boulanger as parental figure, seems accurate and has already been discussed. Berkeley did need to deify

[1] C. Mason, 'The Progress of Lennox Berkeley', *Listener*, 27 September 1956, p. 485.
[2] P. Dickinson, 'Berkeley at Eighty', *Radio Three Magazine*, June 1983, pp. 4–6.
[3] C. Mason, ibid.

his heroes, especially Boulanger and Britten, in ways that had personal as well as musical significance. But it is difficult to see how a composer can be most himself when sounding most like someone else. Even in Britten the inevitable influence of other composers shows through. It looks as if Mason was reacting to Berkeley and Britten through their common ground rather than their differences. Experiences they shared included writing film scores and incidental music for radio and theatre. In the period of their interaction – from 1936 until the 1950s – Britten's technique showed a controlled relevance which is not found in Berkeley, which is why I have suggested a comparison between his method and the instinctive free association of Delius.

But Mason was right in finding that Britten's influence brought a 'tremendous imaginative release in Berkeley' and generous in thinking that *Nelson* 'fully sustained the musical quality of the *Stabat Mater* with a still further extension of emotional range and power'. The example of Britten was universally known – *Peter Grimes* (1945), *The Rape of Lucretia* (1946), *Albert Herring* (1947), *Billy Budd* (1951) and *Gloriana* (1953). All these, not to mention his version of *The Beggar's Opera* (1948) and *The Little Sweep* (1949), took place before an opera by Berkeley had reached the stage at all. And in the year of the premieres of both *A Dinner Engagement* and *Nelson* – 1954 – came Britten's next masterpiece, *The Turn of the Screw*. This competition was truly stupendous from a composer who had established his stature and embodied his concerns through operas which have continued to hold the stage against all the odds, gaining ground through the later twentieth century and beyond. Britten, for his part, encouraged Berkeley by putting three of his operas on at Aldeburgh and Berkeley felt able to ask for his support when Sadler's Wells was considering *Nelson*. Basil Douglas, manager of the English Opera Group, confirmed this: 'I worked quite hard for *Nelson* because Sadler's Wells were dragging their feet in a rather disgraceful way, we all thought in the Opera Group, and with Ben's help I arranged a concert performance in the Wigmore Hall. That was full and *very* successful. Sadler's Wells were impressed . . . the next season, *Nelson* was put on.'[4] In 1975, Berkeley looked back to his first encounter with Britten as an operatic phenomenon:

> I think I can claim to be one of the first to hear *Peter Grimes* – or rather, part of it. Soon after he returned from America, Britten played me the first act on the piano. Though I was greatly impressed and moved by what I had heard, I was not surprised, for I knew that technically and emotionally he was capable of such an achievement. But I didn't suspect that the opera would become a world success so quickly . . .[5]

Of course Berkeley was not the only composer to follow the operatic lead of the composer of *Peter Grimes* and be forced into his shadow. Walton's *Troilus and Cressida* came in the same year as *Nelson* and in the following year came Tippett's *A Midsummer Marriage*. Both of these revealed the difficulties of the medium for composers with little experience of the theatre and required either revision or a long period of time to reach revival.

[4] Interview with author, 28 November 1990.

[5] L. Berkeley, *Radio Times*, 30 August/5 September, 1975, p. 39.

Britten had built up his operatic technique through writing film scores and music for plays and radio features during the 1930s. It is not generally realised that Berkeley followed his example here too, at a time when many of the most prominent British concert composers all wrote for films. Berkeley wrote five film scores between 1942 and 1957 and incidental music for eight radio or theatre productions from 1943 to 1960. This activity, along with his other commissions, kept him composing rapidly through the 1940s and 1950s and gave him experience with music in theatrical and visual contexts. What is surprising is that Berkeley started on *Nelson* in 1949, soon after the experience of the two works to sacred texts and the two concertos involving pianos, and that he wrote *A Dinner Engagement* during the same period – presumably for light relief – and several other works too. In fact he wrote a pair of operas, one grand and one comic, and carried off both with acclaim.

A Dinner Engagement, relatively easy to mount, has been regularly performed: *Nelson*, in spite of its warm acclaim and accessible subject, has never been revived. This is diffcult to explain, but what gradually emerged as the neglect of *Nelson* must have had an impact on the composer. Just as the early adverse reviews may have caused him to overreact and withdraw *Jonah*, this time he never returned to grand opera – until it was too late. In 1959 he doubted his ability to sustain a full-length ballet and instanced Britten's difficulties with the full-length *Prince of the Pagodas.*[6] *Ruth* is a biblical-pastoral series of tableaux, with some intimations of what church parables would later become in Britten. *Castaway* (1967) was designed as half a double bill with *A Dinner Engagement*, but lacks the same light touch in Berkeley's more severe late 1960s idiom. However, the premiere of *Nelson* was the highest point of Berkeley as public composer, tackling a major episode in British history. It is worth looking at its reception, which, like some of the articles from the fifties, was both sympathetic and understanding. This was quite different from the response to *Jonah* seventeen years before:

> Berkeley has written a singers' opera in the best sense, generous and uninhibited in its treatment of the voices and possessing melodic appeal. The musical characterisation of the main characters, including Lady Nelson, is remarkably successful.[7]

> The first impression was that [*Nelson*] has many qualities likely to ensure it permanence . . . This opera is by a long way the biggest thing Mr. Berkeley has yet done. He has for a good many years been striving for perfection of craftsmanship and elegance, but here something more ample, more impassioned, more profoundly felt was required of him, and his gifts proved capable of stretching into the new demands at once . . .[8]

> It is a theme full of the dramatic elements that make a good opera plot . . . The music is entrancing, and there are things both moving and startling in the score, generous expanses of subtle music and keen points of dramatic emphasis . . .[9]

[6] *The Times*, 2 April 1959.
[7] M. Cooper, *Daily Telegraph*, 23 September 1954.
[8] E. Blom, *Observer*, 26 September 1954.
[9] S. Goddard, *News Chronicle*, 24 September 1954.

> *Nelson* follows the heroic tradition of opera seria as handed on to recent times by Verdi . . . The invention is copious, fresh and symphonically delightful. Berkeley rightly thought it no shame to use broad melodies and well-tried devices. Whatever he wrote, it could never be other than aristocratic.[10]

Thus the rather conservative critics in the leading London newspapers welcomed Berkeley because his grand opera was approachable, although Eric Blom would have welcomed more 'glorious singable stuff'. The use of words like 'elegance' and 'aristocratic' began to make Berkeley type-cast in a rather limiting way, since an aristocratic approach to the theatre was at odds with the kitchen-sink drama beginning to appear – a very different kind of kitchen from that in *A Dinner Engagement.*

Wilfrid Mellers felt, on the strength of the concert performance with piano at the Wigmore Hall in advance of the Sadler's Wells production, that *Nelson* would be 'the culmination of Berkeley's career'.[11] Expectations of this kind were hard to fulfil and the *Musical Times* of November 1954 revealed some critical confusions. Donald Mitchell reviewed *The Turn of the Screw* and *Nelson* in the same London Music column.[12] The former he found 'remarkably successful from first note to last' and the latter 'strictly a failure' qualified by the 'fine things in it'. On the other hand Denis Stevens, in the same issue, reviewed the broadcasts and found that Britten's work 'displayed once more the brilliance of ideas dimmed by oppressive and circumscribed methodology'. But in *Nelson* 'Berkeley has given us vigorous, full-blooded music of a new kind, with ample melodic interest and a genuine feeling for the demands of the stage'.[13]

Fifty years later the operatic achievements of Britten are part of history, but *Nelson* can be reassessed only on the basis of a BBC studio recording made to mark the composer's eightieth birthday in 1983 and a concert performance given by the Chelsea Opera Group under Grant Llewellyn at the Queen Elizabeth Hall, London, on 7 April 1988. A generation of critics not born when *Nelson* was written responded with enthusiasm. Hilary Finch concluded that 'British opera houses, unlike Nelson himself, have not, it seems, done their duty. For this is a distinctive, sharply-profiled work, purposefully structured . . . compelling to hear'.[14] Michael John White recognised 'a brilliantly alive, sophisticated score'.[15]

[10] *The Times*, 24 September 1954.

[11] W. Mellers, 'The Music of Lennox Berkeley', *Listener*, 24 June 1954, p. 1113.

[12] D. Mitchell, 'London Music', *Musical Times* 95, November 1954, pp. 612–13.

[13] D. Stevens, 'Radio Notes', *Musical Times* 95, November 1954, p. 606.

[14] H. Finch, *The Times*, 9 April 1988.

[15] M. J. White, *Independent*, 9 April 1988. Edward Greenfield, in the *Guardian*, 9 April 1988, found 'the performance amply backed up my memories of thirty years ago, with its neat yet lively dramatisation of the love-triangle around Admiral Lord Nelson. There is nothing half-hearted or limp about the piece. Even the love-scenes tend to be urgent, passionately committed . . . strategically placed in Nelson's life.' Rodney Milnes, in the *Financial Times*, 9 April 1988, admired 'the characteristically long, even endless melodies, punctuated with succulent modulations' and 'a wealth of hearty nautical music'. He found Nelson 'full of good music and central to its period' and then blamed the libretto for 'too much narrative and too many characters'.

In January 1949, Berkeley prepared himself for *Nelson* in an unusual way. He met Rear-Admiral Charles Lambe (later to become Sir Charles Lambe, Admiral of the Fleet and First Sea Lord), a keen amateur pianist, who was about to sail to the Mediterranean in his flagship, *HMS Vengeance*. Lambe invited Berkeley to join him in order to pass through the waters where the Battle of Trafalgar had been fought in 1805. The Admiral even had two grand pianos installed in his day cabin where the two of them played Mozart and Schubert duets on most days of the voyage.[16]

Act I of the opera opens in Naples, where a large crowd has assembled outside the Palazzo Sessa waiting to welcome Nelson on his return from the Battle of the Nile. The hosts for the party inside the Palazzo are the British Ambassador, Sir William Hamilton, and his wife Emma.[17] The excitement built up results in an anti-climax since Nelson has slipped in almost unnoticed and is pointed out afterwards. He is not very imposing and the guests find him 'a strange little hero'. Emma Hamilton's mother, Mrs Cadogan, calls him 'a fierce sun in eclipse'. Nelson refuses to join the dancing couples and talks to Emma and her mother. He is persuaded to consult Madame Serafin, an old Neapolitan fortune-teller, because he is anxious about the future. She prophesies the fatal choice between love and duty, and sees that Emma and Nelson will never be parted.[18] So soon this is rather surprising, but after they have spent some time together their attachment develops and some of the guests are aware of it. The act ends as it began with the crowd calling for Nelson.

The first act, in a single scene, alternates recitatives, arioso and breezy choruses. The variety of material unfolding rapidly produces a hectic pace which alone must hold things together since there is little purely musical cohesion. The guests sing a kind of blues, an expectation motif, in the same key as the last of the Six Preludes, A flat major:

Example 74. *Nelson*, Act I, figure 21

[16] E. Thomas, letter to the *Independent*, 30 December 1989, p. 22, with corrections from Tony Scotland.

[17] Tony Scotland points out that this moment may have had a certain resonance for Berkeley since his grandfather Sir James Harris, British Consul at Nice, had a palazzo in Genoa. It was here in 1875 that Berkeley's father, a young naval officer aboard *HMS Rapid*, first met and fell in love with Berkeley's mother, Aline, then a girl of twelve.

[18] A. Pryce-Jones: *Nelson*, libretto, London 1954. The published libretto has the choice as that between 'love and death' and Madame Serafin's phrase about Nelson and Emma never being parted has been altered in revision. Cuts in the libretto are reflected in the revised performing material.

Apart from a reminiscence before Emma bids Nelson farewell in Act III, this memorable tune inexplicably never recurs. Nelson, whose unimpressive first entry is associated with a rising sixth in the orchestra, begins to make use of that interval in his own music:

Example 75. *Nelson*, Act 1, figure 22

Dance music is heard from the ballroom and, as in Berg's *Wozzeck* or in *Peter Grimes*, is used as a diatonic counterfoil to the main drama – consulting the fortune-teller and the developing fatal passion between Nelson and Emma.

By Act II the exposition of the situation is over and consequences begin to emerge. This allows Berkeley to elaborate the emotions of the characters in a way he has obviously found congenial. Right from the start the approach is more motivic, there is more counterpoint, which is fully exercised in ensembles of Mozartian complexity within broad harmonic control. Act II opens in London with Lady Nelson depressed about Nelson's affair with Emma, which is now public knowledge. The orchestral introduction anticipates the first notes of her gloomy aria in a five-part texture based on the same motif, which is related to the opening of the first of the *Four Poems of St Teresa of Avila*:

Example 76. *Nelson*, Act II, scene 1, opening

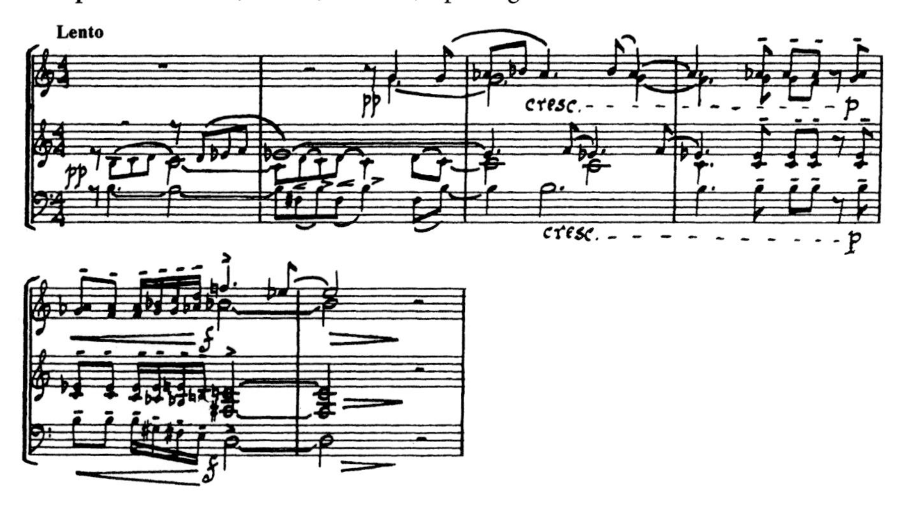

Example 77. *Nelson*, Act II, scene 1, figure 1

In her next aria, dominated by 5/8 time, Lady Nelson urges her husband to leave London with her, knowing it is too late. When Sir William Hamilton and Emma arrive, Nelson forces his wife to challenge Emma, who responds by declaring her love for Nelson, who takes it all rather passively. As could be expected, Fanny was no match for Emma, a scheming country girl who rose in society as a courtesan. Each character then recognises the inevitable in an ecstatic quartet, 'This then is the end of our love'.

Example 78. *Nelson*, Act II, 7 bars after figure 22

This is vintage Berkeley, poignantly affecting as Lady Hamilton sings of her love in the present and Lady Nelson of hers in the past, both with equal ardour. Emma's mother, Mrs Cadogan, comes in on all this with 'What is this madness?', only to find that she has started a brilliant *scherzando* sextet. A *sotto voce* quartet ends the scene with Emma and Nelson in rapturous accord but Mrs Cadogan and Hardy in staccato protests which fail to have any effect. Invention is sustained right through this scene where alluring music glosses over disrupted lives.

The second scene develops the character of Hardy, over a rhythm which turns out to be the call of duty – Nelson's, of course. A few weeks before the Battle of Trafalgar, he is asked if he will leave Emma and serve his country at sea. He agrees to obey orders in a rather conventional aria of resolution and follows that with a series of love-duets with Emma. At the words 'How can my spirit kindle a halting tongue?' Nelson opens the love-duets with a new theme which recalls the rhythm of the expectation motif from Act I (Example 74) as well as a hint of its blue note (Example 79, p. 135). The exchanges between Nelson and Emma are now uninhibitedly passionate and suggest a new source for Berkeley – Puccini. This enthusiasm goes back to 1940 when, on 5 January, Berkeley wrote to Britten: 'I love *Gianni Schicchi.* You're the only person I can really share enthusiasm with about that kind of music – most people are so

Example 79. *Nelson*, Act II, figure 61

infernally highbrow and inclined to turn up their noses.' When Nelson's orders to sail arrive from London the mood changes and so does the harmonic style.[19] Emma's 'Oh, that is too hard' is sung to rising minor ninths, the opening interval of the whole opera, and Nelson sings an aria of dedication. The libretto is based on the prayer which Nelson wrote in his cabin early on the day he was killed:

> May the Great God whom I adore
> Enable me to fulfil the expectation of my country.

We have already noticed the connection between this melody and one Berkeley wrote in 1929 (Example 7, p. 15). There are Stravinskian modal contradictions in the accompanying chords and a false-relation in the melody (Example 80, p. 136). That concludes what is probably the most consistently successful act of the opera and at the time even Donald Mitchell considered it 'first-rate lyric drama in Mr. Berkeley's best creative vein'.[20]

The last act has three scenes. In the first, at Portsmouth, the fleet is preparing to embark for the Mediterranean. There is a crowd outside the George Inn but it disperses as Emma and her mother, in disguise, meet Nelson and Hardy. Emma sings of her first meeting with Nelson as the orchestra recalls the expectation

[19] The revision provides two replacement bars based on rising chromatic bitonal chords at figure 72.

[20] D. Mitchell, 'London Music', *Musical Times* 95, November 1954, pp. 612–13.

Example 80. *Nelson*, Act II, figure 75

motif from Act I. The second scene is on the Victory where the surgeon is attending to a group of wounded sailors: it is preceded by an extended orchestral interlude portraying some aspects of the battle at sea. The mood of the wounded sailors, anxious to be back in action, is well caught but soon after it is established Nelson is brought in wounded. The music is pruned to the barest minimum to depict anguish and loss in the hour of victory (Example 81, p. 137). The scene ends with a succession of threnodies for the male voices, the last of which Winton Dean considered 'undoubtedly one of the peaks of Berkeley's achievement'.[21] There is another orchestral interlude before the final scene, in which Hardy tells Emma the news back at Merton. After much slow music Emma rallies in a final aria of determination which ends the opera in a mood of exultation (Example 82, p. 138). This aria is in Berkeley's most confident and ebullient manner, although Colin Horsley remembered that it was the producer who asked for it to be added.[22] The E natural is a Lydian mode fingerprint of the kind we have observed in both Berkeley and Britten since the late 1930s. Its effectiveness, allied with Berkeley's other characteristics intermittently evident in *Nelson*, causes one to wish the composer had more consciously and consistently built a Berkeley language for the purposes of his most extended work. There are parts of the third act which bring back Redlich's charge of irrelevance, or at least not making the most of opportunities which

[21] W. Dean, 'Lennox Berkeley and Nelson', *Listener*, 16 September 1954, p. 461.
[22] Interview with author, 30 November 1990.

Example 81. *Nelson*, Act III, 2 bars before figure 62

Berkeley himself had already created.[23] An outstanding melody, like the expectancy motif from Act I, languishes as an untapped resource, although Berkeley was too wayward to be Wagnerian about such matters. But there are oddities which reveal a lack of control. In the second scene of Act III the surgeon attends three wounded sailors. The texture is a kind of parlando over a regular 6/8, which mirrors the urgency of the situation during battle. At figure 55 a strong cantabile phrase is given to the surgeon – a tune capable of being the basis for an ensemble or long section – but it is only a coda set to the words 'One more turn to the binding' referring to the bandages. A similar diffuseness applies to the scenes after *Nelson*'s wounding and death, although these sequences make an impression of empty desolation which is entirely appropriate.

The final judgement about all this would have to be made in conjunction with an actual production. It looks as if the librettist, the writer and critic Alan Pryce-Jones, lacked experience in opera and the later cuts are an improvement.[24]

[23] H. F. Redlich, 'Lennox Berkeley', *Music Survey* 31, June 1951, pp. 245–9.

[24] Alan Pryce-Jones (1908–2000) was editor of the *Times Literary Supplement* from 1948 to 1959. He wrote a book on Beethoven and made an English translation of *Der Rosenkavalier*. Latterly he lived in America working for the Ford Foundation and as a journalist. (Obituary, *The Times*, 25 January 2000.)

Example 82. *Nelson*, Act III, 6 bars after figure 79

Michael Berkeley was a child of five and six when Nelson was being produced and looked back in 1990:

> I remembered very clearly that going on and him being very excited about it . . . because it was a new opera in London there was quite a lot of attention in the papers . . . I remember even then that there were problems with the libretto which caused him a certain consternation . . . I don't think there was ever a period again quite like that. My feeling is that he was riding the crest of a wave at that time.[25]

Lady Berkeley commented in 1991:

> I think it's sad that it didn't have a better production or a better libretto. There was some wonderful music in it and Lennox realised that and I think he was very disappointed that it didn't go on.[26]

[25] Interview with author, 29 November 1990.
[26] Interview with author, 28 January 1991.

I then mentioned to her a review of the first edition of this book by Stephen Banfield, who discussed what he called 'the celebrated personal diffidence' and found *insouciance* in Berkeley's idiom but nevertheless felt that

> . . . modesty betokens not *insouciance* but strength of character, even a traditional code of honour. This, surely, is where *Nelson* comes in, and where we must recognise that his creative horizons were far from diffident; modest men do not tackle such a hero on the operatic stage, maybe even identify with him (a possibility which no-one seems to have given any thought to).[27]

When I put the idea of Berkeley identifying with Nelson to Lady Berkeley she dismissed it, but added:

> He'd always admired Nelson as a character: he'd read Carola Oman's book, which is a wonderful picture of the period, and of course his father was a naval officer. He always would have liked to have gone into the navy himself, had he not been colour-blind – I think the navy would have suffered![28]

It is tempting to look for reasons for a composer's choice of subject and to draw some conclusions. *Nelson* is an epic tale with scenes at sea; the story of *Jonah* involves the sea; and, as it happens, Berkeley must have written some of *Nelson* at the cottage he owned on the Norfolk coast not far from Burnham Thorpe where the future admiral was born. More to the point may be the two operas involving the sea by Britten – *Peter Grimes* and *Billy Budd*. Berkeley was trying to follow Britten into the public domain and with two operas at once. Colin Mason, in 1956, suspected from studying the score of *Ruth* before the premiere that it would not 'affirm a positive vocation on Berkeley's part for the stage'. He even felt that *Ruth* would work better as a cantata and went on to discuss flawed libretti in all Berkeley's operas so far. Mason felt that Berkeley's second full-scale opera would decide the issue and awaited that 'with the keenest interest'.[29] It was not to be. The three operas Berkeley wrote in the 1950s can be regarded as the end of his attempts to follow Britten's lead. By evolving his own kind of neat comedy in *A Dinner Engagement* and continuing his own personal approach to the sacred in *Ruth*, Berkeley manged to circumvent direct competition. In any case he found himself out of sympathy with later Britten. In 1975 he went to *Death in Venice* at Covent Garden:

> To my great disappointment, I can't really get to like the music and find long stretches of it boring though skilfully contrived. It simply doesn't move me . . . there's a lack of melody which is all the more disconcerting in that Ben has shown in his earlier music that he can combine melodic material with a perfectly valid and individual style.[30]

[27] S. Banfield, 'The Cultivated Ear', *Musical Times* 132, January 1991, p. 709.

[28] Interview with author, 28 January 1991. However, according to Tony Scotland, when Berkeley was about eleven and considering entry to the Royal Naval College at Osborne, it was his maths which let him down.

[29] C. Mason, 'The Progress of Lennox Berkeley', *Listener*, 27 September 1956, p. 485.

[30] L. Berkeley diary, 27 June 1975.

In 1979 he saw *The Turn of the Screw* again at Cheltenham which confirmed his assessment: 'I've always thought this is Ben's masterpiece – it seems to me the most perfect of his operas'.[31] Berkeley had reservations about *Curlew River*, which he saw in the same year at Orford Church, but he recognised it as a landmark:

> I found it expressive and of a rather austere beauty. It marks the beginning of a new phase in Ben's music – very different from his former style. The hymn *Te lucis* sung by the monks as they go in procession almost steals the show.[32]

After the English Opera Group mounted *Ruth* in London in 1956, Berkeley wrote further works for the Aldeburgh Festival – *Songs of the Half-light*, Opus 65, and *Five Herrick Poems*, Opus 89, were for Peter Pears and *Castaway*, Opus 68, his final completed opera, was produced in 1967. In 1975 Berkeley attended a concert at the Aldeburgh Festival:

> Ben was in his box for the first part of the concert, looking very frail and much aged by his illness. I would have dearly loved to speak to him but have the feeling that I'm no longer much approved of, and in any case one feels particularly afraid of intruding while he is still so clearly very far from well. Later I went to speak to Ben in his box at a *Peter Grimes* performance, he was very charming and seemed to have acquired a new serenity, perhaps because of the suffering and frustration he has had to go through. I was much moved by meeting him after so long a time.[33]

On 8 August 1965, Berkeley wrote to thank me for writing a long article in *Music and Musicians*: 'It was good to bring in *Nelson*, which has been rather forgotten – the trouble is that I should now want to rewrite so much of it if it were to be revived. I do think it has good things in it, but I'm not satisfied with it as a whole.'[34] Berkeley did make minor revisions and cuts but in any case his reaction should always be seen in the context of his usual reticence. So often lukewarm reactions to new operas concede that good things are contained within them. In this case performances of the orchestral Suite from *Nelson* might make a start towards revival.

In the midst of all this operatic activity in the fifties Berkeley still found time to write chamber music. The Horn Trio, Opus 44, and the Concertino, Opus 49, will be discussed later in terms of the new ingredients emerging in Berkeley's style. But the Sextet for clarinet, horn and string quartet, Opus 47, is another successful example of Berkeley's effortless fluency at this period. It was a BBC

[31] L. Berkeley diary, 6 July 1979.
[32] L. Berkeley diary, 8 June 1979.
[33] L. Berkeley diary, 6 June 1975.
[34] P. Dickinson, 'Lennox Berkeley', *Music and Musicians* 13, August 1965, pp. 20–3 and 54. I did not see the Sadler's Wells production but, after studying the score, wrote that *Nelson* offered 'everything traditionally expected of grand opera. The subject is heroic, elaborate spectacle is invited by crowd scenes, and several facets of romance are explored in the triangle of Nelson, Lady Nelson and Lady Hamilton. Above all, the score is full of tunes, and offers some of the most direct and spontaneous music Berkeley has written.'

commission for the opening concert of the 1955 Cheltenham Festival when it was played by the Melos Ensemble. Berkeley's own sleeve-note is tersely factual:

> The first movement is in traditional sonata form, having two main themes of which the first predominates in various guises, indeed the movement ends with a transposed version of the notes with which it began. The slow movement consists of a fugal opening, played by the strings, in which each voice enters a fourth above the previous one; this is followed by a passage for the clarinet and horn alone, after which the strings resume with a modified version of the first part. The third movement is more concerned with rhythm; it is in a livelier and somewhat lighter mood than what has gone before. Though the melodic element is much in evidence throughout, rhythm becomes more important in this final section. Here, alternate bars of 5/8 and 3/4 continue until the latter take the upper hand and bring the movement to an end.[35]

Berkeley often described his instrumental movements as 'in traditional sonata form' but the themes are varied at subsequent appearances and as usual there is considerable subtlety about the way in which this is done – a process which Julian Bream referred to as the composer's waywardness.[36] The second movement of the Sextet, with its opening for string quartet alone and then a section for clarinet and horn alone, recalls the approach of the Concertino written shortly afterwards with its two duos as the two central movements. Nothing is quite predictable but all the details, such as the final chord of the slow movement, fall neatly into place after a few hearings. As Berkeley says, rhythm is the backbone of the concise finale where the listener has no time to miss melodic elements which come round only once. The Sextet is another polished example of Berkeley's individual kind of neo-classicism with a Mozartian elegance too. We shall return to the chamber music of this period in Chapter 9.

[35] L. Berkeley on Lennox Berkeley/Alan Bush, Music Group of London, Argo ZRG 749 (1974).

[36] Following Berkeley's designation of 'traditional sonata form' in the first movement, the second subject appears in the clarinet at figure 3; the development starts at figure 7; the recapitulation at figure 12; and a coda at figure 15. The horn, in augmentation, tellingly anticipates the clarinet's final reference to the theme. The string writing in the *Lento* is consistently contrapuntal. The fugal opening even has a chromatic counter-subject and it is this, extended, which moves towards the climax after figure 1. There is a rare moment of homophony in the strings against the horn solo from figure 5. At times the finale feels like a rondo but references to the opening theme are often inexact. The *cantabile* string theme at figure 3 is not a second subject and a new theme in the first violin two bars before figure 7 takes over in the most prominent of various episodes. Pitch-class or even thematic analysis is challenged by these techniques of free association.

8. Operas comic and biblical

In a letter to his publisher in 1954, Berkeley wrote: 'I think you will like the little opera – it is very light and meant only to divert, but that I think it will do'.[1] The librettist, Paul Dehn, explained that *A Dinner Engagement* 'was conceived through a series of actual dinner engagements at Lennox Berkeley's house and my own. On these occasions we always spoke glowingly of each other's food so that when the English Opera Group commissioned us to write a light one-act opera, it seemed proper that the action should be set in a kitchen.'[2]

The one-act opera, dedicated to Basil Douglas, was first performed on 17 June 1954 at the Jubilee Hall in the Aldeburgh Festival by the English Opera Group Chamber Orchestra under Vilem Tausky and three further performances followed at Sadler's Wells Theatre in London. The producer was William Chappell, who had designed and danced in *The Judgement of Paris* in 1938, and the plot was a topical subject in the post-war years of austerity and the welfare state, where the imposition of death duties made some aristocratic families embarrassingly hard up. In *A Dinner Engagement*, Lord and Lady Dunmow are desperately trying to keep up appearances, remembering their former grandeur when he was Envoy Extraordinary and Minister Plenipotentiary to the Grand Duchy of Monteblanco – a subject on which he becomes hilariously boring. The Dunmows are planning a dinner party for the Grand Duchess of Monteblanco and her gourmet son, Prince Philippe: unfortunately everything goes wrong, but in spite of it all he eventually agrees to marry the Dunmows' daughter, which causes everything to go right.

Straight away a series of conventional situations is set up in the context of the Dunmows' kitchen, where all the action takes place. These are observed with the finesse of Nancy Mitford's U and Non-U usage and appropriate gradations in between.[3] There is, in effect, a brief overture which introduces the Prince's 'Mon aimée' theme from much later in the opera and a fussing motif for Lord Dunmow as he starts to prepare the dinner. The errand boy comes with vegetables and demands to be paid in cash because his boss, Mr. Buckingham, insists on it. The Mr. Buckingham descending phrase provides a ridiculous motif which reappears.

[1] L. Berkeley, letter to Douglas Gibson, J. & W. Chester Ltd, 9 March 1954.

[2] P. Dehn, *Opera* 5, June 1954, pp. 335–8.

[3] N. F. Mitford et al., *Noblesse Oblige: an Enquiry into the identifiable Characteristics of the English Aristocracy*, London, 1956. Also in *Encounter* in 1955. These appeared after the production of *A Dinner Engagement.*

The daily, Mrs Kneebone, arrives apologising for entering by the front door rather than the back one in a catchy aria with just a touch of the music-hall appropriate to her Cockney background:

Example 83. *A Dinner Engagement*, Opus 45, scene 1, figure 11

The witty twists of unexpected modulations, shifting up or down a semitone, give this number great zest. So do its syncopations. Lord Dunmow reminisces in his aria 'In the summer of my time' which opens with, but does not exploit, a 3+3+2 rhythm within its 4/4. He explains to Mrs Kneebone the importance of the dinner they are preparing but she responds to this at the wrong social level by boasting of how she once served bridge teas for a certain Mrs Ellibank in Wimbledon. Although Lady Dunmow makes it clear that this sort of pretentious gentility was not exactly what she had in mind for the Grand Duchess, Mrs Kneebone is undeterred in an aria which, like the libretto, thrives on the minute social observation characteristic of John Betjeman. The melody is close to Berkeley's third Mazurka and it resurfaces again in the late Bagatelle, Opus 101, for two pianos. It catches exactly the flavour of the situation by implying ridicule of sponge fingers, café music and serviettes (*sic*) folded like fans.[4]

[4] This tune seems so familiar that it has to have been used before. One possibility is the opening theme of Shostakovich's First String Quartet, Opus 49 (1935). This repeated-note melody opens the third of the Mazurkas (1949) but it is anticipated by the Java in the film *The First Gentleman* slightly earlier. But Berkeley and Shostakovich may have a common source.

Example 84. *A Dinner Engagement*, scene 1, figure 22

The Dunmows' daughter, Susan, arrives and is not allowed to help but is asked why she is not in her bedroom in front of her looking glass. In a simple aria, often based on root position major and minor chords, she explains (Example 85, p. 145). The melody skirts the underlying harmony – C major with a minor dominant chord at first, and then a few false relations – with a charming simplicity of the kind to be found later in Malcolm Williamson's one-act opera to Oscar Wilde's story *The Happy Prince* (1965).

The Dunmows urge Susan to consider marrying the Prince; they explain 'It would help us so'; and cadence on a bare fourth with clear implications of bleak austerity if she does not. When pressed for details about the Prince, the Dunmows recall him affectionately some years ago – but only as a baby. An amusing set piece is the trio when Lady Dunmow reads the cook-book recipe in French and her husband translates, with Mrs Kneebone admiringly caught in between. Susan enters with her dress on all wrong and too much make-up. She is reproached forcefully – underlined by effective timpani glissandi – but all this time the food is getting burnt in the oven. At this moment the Grand Duchess and the Prince arrive – to a four-part fugue, which ends the scene.

At the opening of Scene 2 the orchestral motif perfectly describes the Duchess picking – even pecking – her way through the kitchen. She is intrigued and

Example 85. *A Dinner Engagement*, scene 1, figure 29

points out that she has never actually seen one before. The repeated notes and rising major third seem to expand the opening of the second movement of Stravinsky's Symphony in C into a regular pattern:

Example 86. *A Dinner Engagement*, scene 2, figure 56

Lord Dunmow goes through his routine of reminding everybody how important he used to be and then has to explain that unfortunately the dinner has been burnt. The guests want to see what they call the grounds, so the charade continues as they inspect the minute back garden. Somehow – improbably in such a small house – the Prince manages to get Susan to himself. Because he is French-speaking, the French atmosphere set by Berkeley can have free reign and is completely appropriate:

Example 87. *A Dinner Engagement*, scene 2, figure 79

This duet comes after a gastronomic argument about how much mustard-seed there should be in pickled walnuts and then there is a case of mistaken identity – Susan is the Dunmows' daughter and not their servant. The easy relationship between tune and accompaniment, in the tradition of Massenet, indicates reconciliation. The French atmosphere extends further when the Prince woos Susan by singing a Monteblancan shepherd's song in French (Example 88, p. 147). The harp chords form a minimal background but control the key, subtly suggesting modulation to the dominant followed by a twist to D minor from the tonic of A flat. Even something as simple as this sounds like Berkeley, full of his fingerprints. The scoring is for single woodwind, horn, harp, percussion and strings, with a piano part for the recitatives played by the conductor. It demonstrates the composer's flair for exploiting chamber music textures and colour.

The wooing of Susan by the Prince is interrupted by the Duchess insisting

Example 88. *A Dinner Engagement*, scene 2, figure 90

that they kiss and settle everything. The errand boy intrudes with calculated incongruity, which reminds the Duchess of the underlying financial realities. As for Susan, the Duchess says: 'Let her beauty be her dowry', and this is followed by the work's largest ensemble as a celebration. There is a final subdued duet between Susan and the Prince when he recalls that she probably told her parents earlier on that she would not marry him under any circumstances. This simplicity denotes the happy ending which was obviously coming – the rhythm is a Berkeley trademark going back to the second of the Five Short Pieces in the same key (Example 89, p. 148).

Above all, *A Dinner Engagement* works on stage with opportunities for clear characterisation where both libretto and music are in harness. Conventional situations taken from *opéra comique*, or *opera buffa*, are varied sufficiently to be interesting – diverting, to use Berkeley's own term. It is feasible to link the effortless success of *A Dinner Engagement* with the composer's own temperament and equable way of life, in contrast to the heroics and public gestures of Lord Nelson. The opera is peculiarly English, a successor to Gilbert and Sullivan, where Berkeley has been able to distance himself from some of the conventions through a kind of neo-classical perspective, which has liberated him from taking anything seriously. Like Sullivan, Berkeley has succeeded in a medium 'meant only to divert' and for which he virtually apologised.

Berkeley may have been conscious of Poulenc in writing *A Dinner Engagement*, although there are those, such as Donald Mitchell, who find *Albert Herring* in it. Either way, English and French sources are submerged in Berkeley's own finesse. After the English Opera Group put *A Dinner Engagement* on at the 1954 Aldeburgh Festival and elsewhere, Britten wrote to Berkeley: 'We are all *delighted* that DE is such a success. We did it 3 times in York & everyone loved it there too . . . There are most lovely things in the piece, my dear, which give one enormous pleasure & we are proud, both Festival and Group, that you wrote it for us.' Then Britten continued, as on

Example 89. *A Dinner Engagement*, scene 2, figure 107

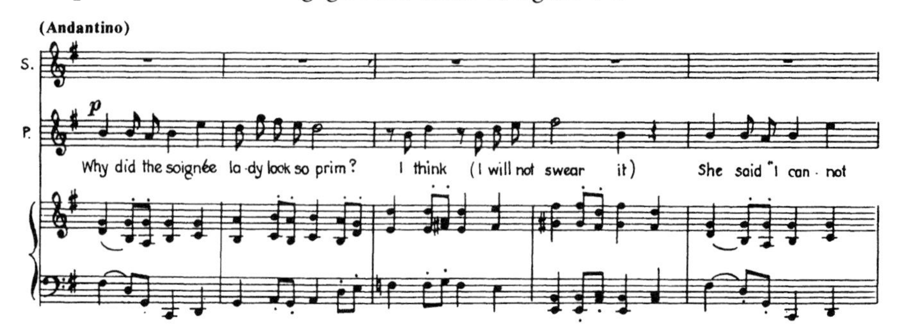

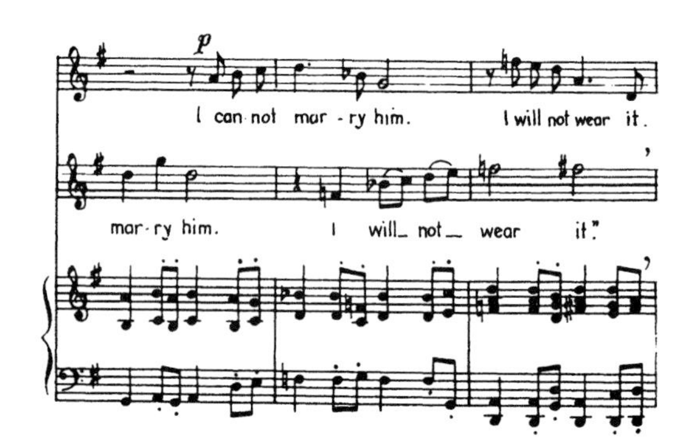

other occasions, in ways that suggest his own involvement in what Berkeley was writing: 'There are are one or two moments which either seem obscure or too long, & I'm not sure whether that is the 'tempo' or the writing. I want to hear it again with a score . . . can I make some suggestions before Sadlers Wells if it seems necessary?'[5]

Britten clearly valued Berkeley's contributions to his enterprises and was concerned about the poor performance given to an earlier Aldeburgh commission, Berkeley's *Variations on a Hymn by Orlando Gibbons*, Opus 35, at the Festival in 1952. He consoled him by saying that nevertheless 'a great deal came across – & a great deal of enjoyment was felt by many people I have talked to. Thankyou so much for writing such a lovely piece for us. Apart from the pleasure, it was a great honour for the little Aldeburgh Festival to have a new piece from your pen . . . it is so lovely for us to have all these musical expressions of your connection with & feelings for Suffolk!'[6]

Berkeley's third opera, *Ruth*, Opus 50, was again for the English Opera Group

[5] B. Britten, letter to Berkeley, 6 July 1954. Britten must also have made some suggestions about *Ruth* at an early stage since Berkeley wrote from Blois, Orleans, on 10 September 1955, to say that he needed the third lady in the cast for dramatic reasons and preferred the piano to the harpsichord since it would carry better in the theatre.

[6] B. Britten, letter to Berkeley, 27 June 1952.

who gave it under Charles Mackerras at the Scala Theatre, London, on 2 October 1956. It begins almost exactly where Berkeley left off with the first of the *Four Poems of St Teresa of Avila*:

Example 90. *Ruth*, Opus 50, scene 1

This is the principal motif of the opera, although it disappears in the later stages. It represents, as it did for St Teresa, the intensity of dedication to a cause. The use of the motif is sufficiently consistent – unusually so for Berkeley – that it could be claimed that the language of the Teresa of Avila songs has been developed to support the entire eighty-minute opera. Berkeley has also learnt from his earlier operas. As in *Nelson*, the chorus plays a lively role and as in *A Dinner Engagement* the scoring is ingenious. The small band of two flutes, horn, piano, percussion and strings never overwhelms the singers and the piano continuo is just as carefully integrated.

The libretto is taken from the book of Ruth in the Old Testament. The librettist, Eric Crozier, had already worked with Britten in *Albert Herring*, *The Little Sweep* and *Billy Budd*. The text in all Berkeley's operas has come in for criticism. Judging from the vocal score in 1956, Colin Mason felt that Berkeley had 'accepted librettos with serious flaws' where 'the opportunities for several of the best musical sections are unconvincingly contrived'.[7] He set these strictures alongside the fact that musically *Ruth* 'clearly belongs amongst his finest and most important works, emphatically confirming his vocation as a vocal and choral composer . . .' However, Donald Mitchell, who saw the English Opera Group's production, found *Ruth* 'a distinguished work' and felt that 'composer and librettist were surprisingly successful in making a stage piece out of somewhat improbable, though undeniably very beautiful, material'.[8] It is a pity that the impression of *Ruth* as a static sequence of tableaux has been allowed to predominate. The same problem causes little diminution in Wagner's reputation. A rare chance to test *Ruth* in production occurred

[7] C. Mason, 'The Progress of Lennox Berkeley', *Listener*, 27 September 1956, p. 485.
[8] D. Mitchell, 'London Concerts and Opera', *Musical Times* 97, November 1956, p. 597.

during the Cheltenham Festival in 1983, the year of Berkeley's eightieth birthday and his last year as President of the Festival. The setting was Tewkesbury Abbey, which, in spite of a rather reverberant acoustic, added a dimension which would have been lost in a secular theatre.

The opera has three scenes. In the first Naomi is returning to Bethlehem with her two daughters-in-law, Orpah and Ruth. Naomi has had consistently bad luck since she left Bethlehem originally with her husband and two sons to live in Moab, but all the men died. Now Naomi is returning to her homeland and tries to persuade her daughters-in-law to leave her there and return to their own people. Orpah goes back but Ruth dedicates herself to remaining with Naomi whatever happens.

The second scene reveals some local hostility to the Moabite girl when Naomi is recognised after her long absence. Fortunately they have arrived on the estate of Boaz, a distant relation, who protects them and provides all they need. In the final scene the harvest home is celebrated and Naomi, wishing to recoup her own and her family's fortunes, urges Ruth to offer herself in marriage to Boaz. After some uncertainties – there were more in the Old Testament story – this strategy is successful and the rest of the scene contains exuberant rejoicing.

The opening *Lento* of Scene 1 develops the principal motif in two-part counterpoint and punctuates the phrases with piano chords of A, F sharp, and E flat major – all without their fifths – before returning to the principal key of B minor for Naomi's entry:

Example 91. *Ruth*, scene 1, 3 bars after figure 2

The tone of the music for the two women establishes serious issues as Naomi tries to persuade her daughters-in-law to return and prays to God for help. Orpah's aria, 'Ah must I leave thee? Must we part?', although tender, suggests that she might not have been much help anyway. Ruth is made of sterner stuff and her own aria of dedication to Naomi's cause, 'Whither thou goest', is as powerful in its way as the third of the Teresa of Avila songs. The tempo marking is faster but the determination emerges. It may not be an accident that a stroke as effective as this shows derivation from earlier appearances of the principal motif (the five-note cell B–C sharp–D–A sharp–C):

Example 92. *Ruth*, scene 1, figure 21

This aria uses the principal motif, but reverses the order of the first three notes – D–C sharp–B–A sharp–C – transposed a perfect fourth down. The rhythmic motif on 'go' further propels the course of destiny and, since Ruth's gesture is altruistic and generous, the aria ends on a chord of C major but, like the introduction to the finale of Stravinsky's *Symphony of Psalms*, with a B flat. The association between C major and purity will recur.

After she has been recognised by her kinsfolk, Naomi sings 'Ah, call me not Naomi, let Mara be my name'. Mara means bitter, and her anguish accumulates over an aria which is the first of several set to a regular pulse. The short adagio interlude which follows refers to the principal motif and leads to a choral section making use of the rising figure in Ruth's dedication aria: mutterings based on this end the scene.

Scene 2, set in Boaz's harvest field, introduces the effective jollity of the workers leading to a choral theme, mostly unison, which is typical (Example 93, p. 152). The fresh D major in the voices is in contrast to the accompaniment where there are C naturals in the rising phrase which ends, characteristically, in a chord which can be derived from a dominant thirteenth. When resentment is expressed at the appearance of the Moabite woman, Ruth, in the fields, the workers assert 'This is the foreign woman' to the principal motif (Example 94, p. 153). Tension builds up to the entrance of Boaz, who quells their objections and apologises for them, and Ruth also explains 'I had no wish to anger them' in an extended aria which becomes a duet and finally a trio. The melody – another one over a regular beat – might be thought to reflect the *Lento* of Poulenc's Sonata for Clarinet and Piano, except that the Poulenc was written later (Example 95, p. 153). Recitatives and more arias of the reflective type slacken the pace at this stage. The piano continuo chords relate to open fifths and major and minor triads from other parts of the opera. At figure 36 a C major chord – not in the vocal score – marks the goodness

Example 93. *Ruth*, scene 2, figure 8

of Ruth as Boaz promises recompense from Israel's Almighty Lord. He continues to sing against the background of the chorus – the D major theme of Example 93 – which ends the scene. It opened in G major, but the last chorus is in D major, followed by a short coda. This leads away from the D major of the chorus and the G of Boaz's last phrase to settle on B major – another chord without fifth – plus G major – also without fifth – superimposed high above.

Scene 3 opens on G with reiterated bare-fifth chords and scurrying passages *allegro vivace*. This suggests action but the frenzy is the internal one of Ruth's

Example 94. *Ruth*, scene 2, 10 bars after figure 13

Example 95. *Ruth*, scene 2, figure 23

anxiety over her next step, when she offers herself to Boaz at Naomi's suggestion. Naomi encourages her in a concise aria which rises to a climax contemplating Ruth's entry into the house of Israel.

Now Ruth has to wait until all the harvest festivities are over before she can approach Boaz as intended. If Naomi's 'Fear not' aria is slightly sanctimonious, of the order of Gounod or Franck, then that too is part of Berkeley's French Catholic heritage. The choral jubilations, by comparison, seem particularly English. By the time we reach 'Wintertime is time to plough, Aie the wind does bite' there is no question about it. When the dance element comes in, at figure 32, there is a suggestion of the Tippett of *A Midsummer Marriage.* Few opportunities have arisen to compare Berkeley with Tippett since the emphasis here has been on Britten. But both Berkeley and Tippett have set *The Windhover* by Gerard Manley Hopkins – Tippett in 1942 and Berkeley in 1968. Comparison between the two settings shows more in common between the Berkeley of *Ruth* and the early Tippett. The choruses in *Ruth* use Tippett's type of varied metres, without his sense of unbarred sprung rhythm, and a kind of diatonic polyphony where a rough voice-leading effect may be more important than the actual notes. This is not always the case with the choruses in the third scene of *Ruth*, which are often homophonic, but the build-up to Boaz's solo invocation is cumulative and exciting. The solo is unaccompanied at this climactic point, as in *Belshazzar's Feast*, but here the tension decreases:

Example 96. *Ruth*, scene 3, figure 37

The chorus's response is a rapt pianissimo in the tradition of Berkeley's many soft alleluias. Each phrase moves up a step, like the opening chorus of Britten's *Paul Bunyan* (1941), which Berkeley could not have heard (Example 97, p. 155).

Now that the celebrations are over, Boaz retires and Ruth can approach him. The wait has been extended and her heart is pounding – a decorative baroque arioso has a heavy bass and an ornate flute melody. This is the climax of the opera, comparable to the actual rape in Britten's *The Rape of Lucretia*, and approached with the same sense of destiny. The situation in *Ruth* is of course without violence and quite different in emphasis. The contrast may imply something about the temperaments of the two composers. Lucretia is raped by Tarquinius, considers herself compromised and takes her own life. As Berkeley wrote: 'In Lucretia we have the very prototype of innocence and virtue finding, in suicide, the only escape from the consequences of lust and brutality.'[9] By contrast, Ruth offers herself to Boaz, who accepts her, creating a happy ending. This harmonises with Berkeley's eventual family life and spiritual serenity, with *Ruth* dedicated to his wife, as against Britten's need to deal operatically with individuals at odds with their society as pacifists or homosexuals or both. In 1990 Michael Berkeley commented on this contrast:

[9] L. Berkeley, 'Britten's Characters', *About the House*, vol. 1, no. 5, 1963, p. 14.

Example 97. *Ruth*, scene 3, figure 38

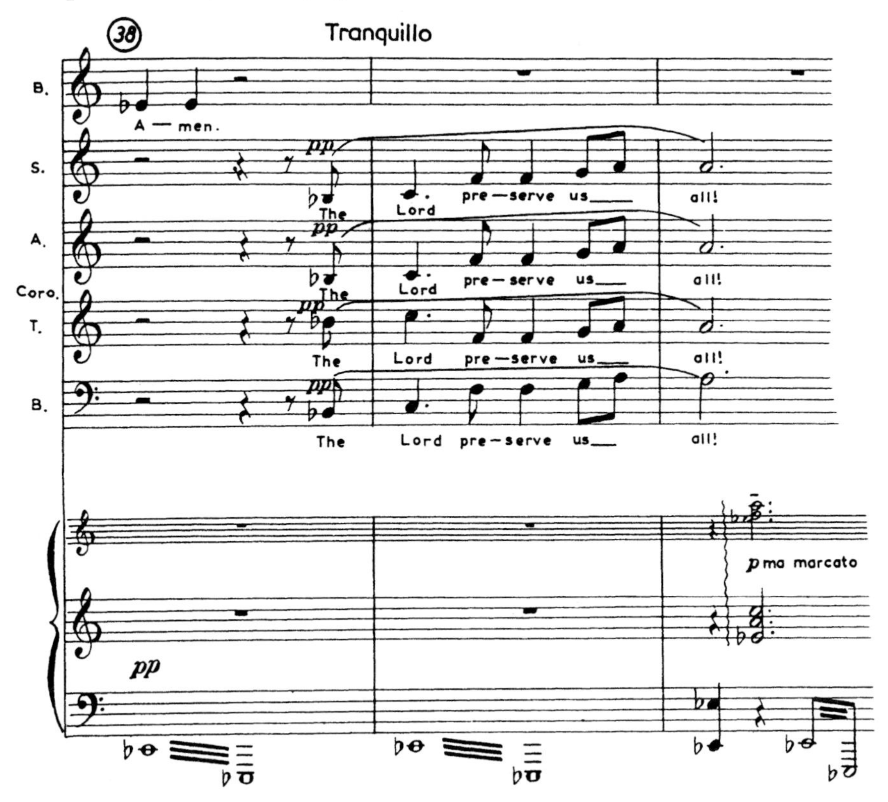

One of the powerful things about Britten is that the subject matter grows out of extraordinary personal turmoil – the corruption of innocence, Britten trying to deal with his own sexuality. I don't think my father was the sort of composer who ever confronted that in his music. It has an élan and a style but it doesn't signpost you into areas of enormous human turbulence.[10]

As Ruth approaches Boaz, Berkeley recalls the dedication aria from Scene 1. This is a masterly flashback, showing as it does how far Ruth is prepared to go in her devotion to Naomi. It works perfectly, as Ruth explains her hopes. What is more extraordinary is the response by Boaz at figure 43 in his own aria 'Thou comest in the stillness of the night' (Example 98, p. 156). This is a kind of passacaglia based on a twelve-note row, almost certainly only the second time Berkeley made use of the technique. The row is not treated consistently, as will be seen in the next chapter, but the new sound has a special role in changing the atmosphere at this stage in the opera. It tightens things up – so does the main motto slightly varied in the recitatives which follow. Three bars after figure 48,

[10] Interview with author, 29 January 1990.

Example 98. *Ruth*, scene 3, figure 43

the row is loosely recalled in sequence, followed by the introduction to a duet over a Purcellian ground bass in C minor. The duet is harmonically rich, founded on major and minor triads, and coincides with Boaz's increasing warmth over what would otherwise seem to be merely a kind of arranged marriage:

Example 99. *Ruth*, scene 3, 2 bars after figure 49

There is excitement and anxiety as Boaz prepares to tell his people. As the crowd asks whether Boaz will marry Ruth, the orchestral response is restrained, perhaps in order to highlight what is coming. This is another new sound in the opera – an absolutely triadic accompaniment to a tune which nobody but Berkeley could have conceived. It depicts goodness with the same ecstatic gratitude as the slow movements of Messiaen's *Quatuor pour la fin du temps*:

Example 100. *Ruth*, scene 3, figure 56

The soloists and chorus join in making an ensemble out of this as expressive as the end-of-love quartet in Act II of *Nelson*. There only remains the approval of the people and more rejoicing. Bare-fifth motifs reappear; Naomi and Ruth include the rapid rising figure from the dedication aria in scene 1; and otherwise the principal motif is conspicuous by its absence. Since it has been associated with anxiety this seems entirely suitable.

All of Berkeley's operas have been worth considering in some detail but there obviously have to be reasons for their neglect. Desmond Shawe-Taylor, a sympathetic critic, was not sure that opera drew the best out of Berkeley, but he found *Ruth* the most typical as a sacred drama in a pastoral context:

> None of his librettos really quite hits the mark in a firm way. Even *Nelson*, the most ambitious, was flawed although it went through various modifications . . . Perhaps the subject was a bit on the strong side for both the librettist and the composer . . . I like *Ruth* very much. I don't think of it as an opera but as a scenic cantata. Certainly it has more of Berkeley himself in it than the other operas, except stray passages.[11]

[11] Interview with author, 28 November 1990. In a letter to me on 11 January 1991, Eric

After the Aldeburgh premiere Berkeley wrote to his publisher:

> You will be glad to hear that the performance of *Ruth* went very well at Aldeburgh. I am now rather inclined to leave the work as it is, as I feel that the only really unsatisfactory things are matters of production and do not very much concern the music itself. I am anxious that the work should be brought out as I think it is in many ways the best thing I have done and I feel it should be available for concert performance . . .[12]

John Manduell, who ran the Cheltenham Festival when Berkeley was President and included many of his works, identified different problems:

> I personally think there are elements in *Ruth* which are totally Lennox and very beautiful. I think he wrestled a bit with the heroics [of *Nelson*]. *A Dinner Engagement* is probably the one which is consistently of the most exquisite quality . . . He writes most beautifully for the voice at all times . . . exploiting it with cunning, marvellously well . . . He had this quiet, kind character and disposition, things that don't immediately flourish in the artificial atmosphere of lights, footlights and the rest of it.[13]

And Michael Berkeley dealt with a central issue:

> I think my father's keenness to write opera meant that he sometimes allowed himself to be swayed into using a libretto that wasn't quite right . . . If you could have said to him 'What was the one thing you regret?' I think it would have been that he hadn't written an opera which through and through matched the quality of some of the other works – the Third Symphony, the Teresa of Avila songs, the Serenade, the Divertimento, the Piano Concerto.[14]

Finally the verdict remains open in the absence of evidence through productions and recordings.

Crozier recalled that he wrote the libretto of *Ruth* at 'almost the unhappiest period' of his life when he had a wrongly diagnosed illness and had great difficulty in working at all. In this context he found working with Berkeley, compared with his collaborations with Britten, a 'negative experience'. But he did have a role in determining the scale of *Ruth* as his letter of 6 December 1955 to his wife, the singer Nancy Evans, shows:

> I spent hours and hours on Sunday writing a letter to Lennox that should be unmistakeably firm and plain, yet kind. I posted it with trepidation, feeling that he would probably be overcome by my insistence on seventy-five minutes as the *total* length of our opera, including interval. I spent an uneasy night worrying about how miserable he would feel on reading it. I hesitated about answering the phone on Monday morning when it rang . . . Lo and behold! It *was* Lennox, as bright and gay as a spring morning, ringing to say that he *entirely* agreed with me and would begin that very day replanning scene 1! You can imagine my relief . . .

All the same, the duration given on the score is 'approximately 80 minutes' – without interval.

12 L. Berkeley, letter to Douglas Gibson, J. & W. Chester Ltd, 25 June 1957.

13 Interview with author, 27 November 1990.

14 Interview with author, 27 November 1990.

9. New directions

There are signs of a crisis in Berkeley's work around 1960. The high level of the previous two decades is not quite sustained and the demands of opera, as we have seen, were a severe test when set against the achievements of Britten. Finally, *A Dinner Engagement* seems completely successful, relaxed and amusing and *Ruth*, although perhaps over-extended, is particularly personal. However, Berkeley's letters show that Britten tried to get him to expand *Ruth*, especially by adding a longer prelude and some interludes, to make it suitable for a whole evening. Berkeley said he could not go back to the opera since he was obliged to continue with a film score. As we have seen, *Nelson* has not had a fair trial, but its scale may have been intimidating in spite of the excellent second act. With his lyrical gifts Berkeley ought to have reached the highest levels in opera and in the eighteenth or nineteenth century he might have done so. He tried again in *Castaway* in 1967 and yet again in *Faldon Park*, which he had to abandon in 1982 through illness. As early as 1976 Berkeley discussed the completed libretto in detail with Winton Dean and felt it was possible, especially since English National Opera had offered to put the new opera on.[1] Potential weaknesses in the operas, which can be compensated for in production, are usually identified as lack of dramatic and musical integration. There are signs of these problems even in instrumental works after the 1950s and also indications that the composer was becoming aware of them.

Under the impact of Britten, Berkeley's music had become more tonal but as the mood of the 1960s impinged he looked for new resources. In my article for *The New Grove*, I compared Berkeley's use of perfect fourths at the opening of his Trio for violin, horn and piano, Opus 44 (1954), with Schoenberg's Chamber Symphony No. 1 (1906) and felt that in both cases these intervals were pointing towards a kind of free atonality.[2] However, the perfect fourths which open the Horn Trio were in the air in British music of the period, notably with Tippett's Piano Concerto, completed in the following year although, unlike Tippett, Berkeley has not made them the basis of the whole work. The Horn Trio was commissioned by the pianist Colin Horsley and first performed and recorded by him with Dennis Brain and Manoug Parikian.[3] The opening

[1] L. Berkeley diary, 6 November 1976.

[2] P. Dickinson, 'Berkeley, Lennox', *New Grove Dictionary of Music and Musicians*, London, 2000, vol. 3, pp. 359–63.

[3] This first recording of the Horn Trio, initially on HMV CLP 1029, contains Berkeley's own

Allegro, permeated with fourths, is rich in themes and exploits the instruments, ventilating the texture by often using them in pairs rather than all together. The *Lento* is expertly gauged as a slow dirge with a more active central section. The last movement of the Trio is a set of variations on one of Berkeley's most obviously Mozartian themes in F major. In 1973 one of his pupils, John Tavener, recalled: 'Mozart is the composer I have always associated with Lennox. For him *Cosi fan tutte* is *le juste de la musique* and playing it with him on the piano is something I shall never forget.'[4] The sixteen-bar theme even has its second half repeated exactly. Berkeley then goes through a series of admirably planned variations much as in the last movements of the Violin and Piano Sonatina, Opus 17, or the Two-Piano Concerto. The sixth variation is a short waltz and the seventh turns the theme into a ground bass. Even the theme is varied in its final appearance. The Horn Trio has become one of the most frequently performed and recorded of Berkeley's chamber works.[5]

The Concertino, Opus 49 (1955) for recorder (or flute), violin, cello and harpsichord (or piano), commissioned by Carl Dolmetsch, came a year later.[6] The neo-baroque connotations of the scoring hark back to chamber pieces and harpsichord works from Berkeley's student days. There are ornaments and sequences which relate to Bach and the writing has a sparkle in the original scoring with recorder and harpsichord. Of the four movements, only the first and last are for the full ensemble. The central movements are two arias, one for flute and cello, the other for violin and harpsichord. This approach could have detracted from overall cohesion, although it has been no obstacle to the eventual establishment of Messiaen's much longer and even more diverse *Quatuor pour la fin du temps* as a classic. Early-music instruments are capable of redefinition in modern terms as in the Sonata for flute, oboe, cello and harpsichord (1952) or the Double Concerto (1961) by Elliott Carter, not to mention earlier harpsichord concertos by Poulenc and Falla. John Manduell was a pupil at the time when both the Sextet, Opus 47, and the Concertino were being composed and he found that Berkeley could be persuaded to discuss his work in progress. He seemed quite pleased with the idea of having the two inside movements of the Concertino as duos.[7]

notes and was made before the score was published. In a letter to Peter Craddock on 18 October 1967 Berkeley confirmed that the printed score is correct where it differed from the recording. Item 78, catalogue 199, May and May Ltd, March 1992.

[4] J. Tavener, 'Lennox Berkeley at 70', *Listener*, 10 May 1973, p. 625.

[5] The original recording with Brain, Parikian and Horsley (HMV CLP 1029) was available for many years but the most recent is with Pyatt, Chilingirian and Donohoe on Erato 8573–80217–2.

[6] For a recent recording of the Concertino, using flute and piano, with a rich crop of varied chamber works see: Berkeley Chamber Music, the Endymion Ensemble, Dutton Laboratories CDLX 7100 (1999). The first recording with Carl Dolmetsch used recorder and harpsichord (ORION ORS 73104) and is the original version of the work. By the time the score was printed in 1961 Berkeley had altered the endings of the first two movements and cut passages before figures 3 and 11 in the last movement.

[7] Interview with author, 27 November 1990.

One of the most interesting aspects of the Concertino is the second movement, Aria I, which uses elements of serial technique almost throughout. Only six years before, in the journal of the International Society for Contemporary Music, Berkeley made the following contribution about the future of music:

> I have never been able to derive much satisfaction from atonal music. The absence of key makes modulation an impossibility, and this, to my mind, causes monotony. I do not see how anything can replace the feeling of freshness which a really musically contrived change of tonality can produce. I am not, of course, in favour of rigidly adhering to the old key-system, but some sort of tonal centre seems to me a necessity. Much atonal music is, I suspect, worked out in the head without being actually heard by the composer, and although the intellectual element in music is an important one, the ear must come first. Thus tonal harmony is based on certain mathematical facts causing aural satisfaction, whereas the twelve-note system, for instance, is arbitrary. A correspondence in vibrations produces the relationship between tonic and dominant, but I cannot see that any reason in particular determines the order of notes in a 'row'. My ear may not be sensitive enough, but it does not feel a necessity for the initial note of a series, once all twelve tones have been sounded, nor does it desire the return of the original 'row' after the others have been used – all that it desires by that time is that the whole thing should cease![8]

That represented Berkeley's views in 1948 and they were widely shared in Britain, but his dismissive tone is surprising in view of what followed. In 1959 he felt differently:

> I'm not at all opposed to serial music; I've benefited from studying it – and I have sometimes found myself writing serial themes – though I don't elaborate them according to strict serial principles, because I'm quite definitely a tonal composer.[9]

Perhaps he never really changed his mind, but he was not going to leave the matter without trying out some aspects of twelve-note technique for himself. His approach is worth looking at in some detail in order to scrutinise what John Cage called the note-to-note procedure (Example 101, p. 162).

The row (A) is presented as a ground bass in the cello part, which is followed by four variations. All twelve notes are used in a set which emphasises the perfect fourth and where the second four notes are a transposition of the first four pitch classes. The recorder part (B) also opens with a chromatic melody – there are octave repetitions, but nine different notes are used rapidly and the others follow within the eight-bar phrase. In both cases Berkeley is thinking melodically. The recorder melody (B), marked *cantabile*, is an extension of the

[8] R. Myers, ed., *Music Today* I, London, 1949, p. 145. 'Open Forum: Variations on a Theme. Music's Future: Tonal or a-Tonal?' I have quoted Berkeley's contribution to this fascinating symposium complete. Other contributors range from Schoenberg and Berg to Berkeley's friend Francis Poulenc, who recognised the naturalness of twelve-note technique to the composers of the Second Viennese School but said 'Pour ma part je m'y refuse.'

[9] *The Times*, 2 April 1959.

Example 101. Concertino, Opus 49, Aria I

first two bars of the cello set (A): by interval expansion the perfect fourths become major sevenths. To accommodate the recorder melody at its first appearance, the cello's ground is extended by two bars, using octaves in bars 12 and 13, and strengthening the feeling of E as a tonal centre. The first variation of the recorder melody, bar 15, introduces a Mozartian turn which has the effect of making the melody sound more like Berkeley. In bars 20–22 the D sharp in the cello part is extended, it functions as a leading-note, but a run up to C at bar 23 starts a new process.

This is the point at which Berkeley might have become a serial composer. As a convert to a dogmatic religion he could have found doctrinal certainty attractive even in music, but he was too unsystematic. He exchanged the roles of recorder and cello by putting the recorder melody (B) into the bass and using the cello set (A) to provide the top part. He does this strictly, apart from a baroque trill and – almost blatantly – another Mozartian turn. Mozart is going to triumph over Schoenberg. The cello part follows the note-to-note procedure of the recorder melody until bar 29, which becomes free as it descends to the E, and resolves for the next variation. The crisis is over, roles are reassigned, although the material is varied to make the climax of the whole aria. From bar 31 four phrases, including a major seventh, reach upwards, each one higher. After bar 34 comes the descent and bar 38 onwards is a coda, with the cello outlining the tritone. So far this interval has hardly been noticed. Has the serial devil been exorcised? Not quite, as the future will show. This was only the beginning of Berkeley's disengaged engagement with serial techniques but his attitude to any dogmatic position is clearly demonstrated in this aria, if we ever had any doubt.

In his last decade Berkeley came back to the baroque connections of several of his early works and this Concertino. *Una and the Lion*, Opus 98, is described as a *Cantata concertante* for soprano voice, soprano recorder, viola da gamba and harpsichord. It is a setting of six poems from Edmund Spenser's *Fairie Queene* and, like the Recorder Sonatina and the Concertino, was commissioned by Carl Dolmetsch. With its purely instrumental sarabande, recitatives and arias, *Una and the Lion* is Berkeley's final reference to the musical styles of the baroque.

During the 1950s, serial techniques became a major professional issue. Stravinsky was edging his way in this direction, perhaps affected by the intellectual prestige attached to serialism in America, and even before that Copland, with the Piano Quartet (1950). Stravinsky's conversion was gradual, from the Cantata (1952) to *Threni* (1958), but it was as complete as Webern's thirty years earlier. It is notable that the public has not yet followed Stravinsky's late works with the enthusiasm it accords to his Russian and neo-classical masterpieces – neither did Berkeley. Copland operated an either-or situation depending on the nature of the composition – so did Schoenberg himself – and his late serial works came at a time of uncertainty which eventually led to his ceasing to compose. Both Copland and Berkeley had been obedient Boulanger students. For most composers of this background and generation, to become consistently twelve-note, in spite of the example of Stravinsky, would have been an extreme step, but Berkeley continued to play with the idea for at least fifteen years. Perhaps he realised that there were musical benefits to be gained from a discipline, such as Boulanger's studies in strict counterpoint, and he may have been encouraged by Britten's use of a twelve-note theme in *The Turn of the Screw* in 1954.

We have already noticed the change of mood in Boaz's recognition aria at the climax of *Ruth* (Example 98, p. 156). The introduction exposes the row in almost Webernian fashion with four groups of three notes in identical rhythm.

The chords below recur – four bars after figure 43 in the vocal score is a misprint – and the row itself is used as P4 and P2 before the whole process is loosened by sequence and varied repetition. This aria clearly indicates a greater freedom between melody and accompaniment than had become customary with Berkeley. Like Copland, who admitted this, Berkeley was being made to think of chords and relationships that might not otherwise have occurred to him. Systems can provide enchantment.

Meanwhile, the main instrumental work following the operas was the Second Symphony, Opus 59 (1958). It was commissioned by the Feeney Trust for the City of Birmingham Symphony Orchestra, an admirable series of commissions established in 1955 and still running, and the first performance was conducted by Andrzej Panufnik on 24 February 1959.[10] Berkeley himself conducted the first London performance with the BBC Symphony Orchestra the following autumn but after that the composer became uncertain about it and completed a considerably revised version in 1976 for the recording.[11] This symphony lacks the ebullience of the first one, with its colourful scoring and generous melodic writing, and is elusive at a first hearing.

Although the Second Symphony has a tonal centre of D, by this time Berkeley's music was becoming more dissonant, so that there is a perceptible difference between his tonal and more-or-less atonal styles. Both types coexist in the *Five Auden Poems*, Opus 53 (1958), commissioned by the American singer Alice Esty, where the second and fifth songs are clearly tonal but the third and fourth ones less so. Incidentally, Berkeley's setting of 'Carry her over the water' can be compared with Britten's in *Paul Bunyan* and, after Berkeley had seen my own *Four Auden Songs* (1956), he set three of the same poems in his own cycle.[12]

The climax – such as it was – of Berkeley's relationship with twelve-note technique came with the slow movement of the Violin Concerto, Opus 59 (1961).

[10] See P. Dickinson, ed., *Twenty British Composers*, London, 1975.

[11] The London Philharmonic Orchestra conducted by Nicholas Braithwaite, Lyrita LP SRCS 94 (1978). The composer's sleeve-note explained:

> My reasons for the revision were chiefly connected with scoring; I was much preoccupied at the time I wrote it with keeping the various orchestral colours distinct. Later, I felt that I had overdone this and that the work would gain from a freer and more robust treatment. I have introduced no new thematic material in the revised version, although certain passages have been somewhat extended . . . The slow movement which follows is the only part of the Symphony which remains entirely as it was in the earlier version.

[12] My own *Four W. H. Auden Songs* and Berkeley's *Five Auden Poems* were performed together by Meriel Dickinson and myself for BBC Radio 3 on 22 February 1977, in a programme for the seventieth anniversary of Auden's birth. For the recording of my *Four W. H. Auden Songs* see *Songcycles* on Albany TROY365. For Berkeley's *Five Poems by W. H. Auden* along with 'Night covers up the rigid land' and 'Lay your sleeping head my love' see Philip Langridge and Steuart Bedford on Collins Classics 1490–2 (1998). In 1988, as a tribute to Berkeley's eighty-fifth birthday, I wrote my *Auden Studies* for oboe and piano. I gave the first performance with Sarah Francis on 16 July 1988 at the Chester Festival and the London premiere was on 30 March 1989 at the Purcell Room. These are based on the music of the three poems that we both set.

Once again this was the second of a pair of works written close together, with the other being Five Pieces for Violin and Orchestra, Opus 56, written for Frederick Grinke: the Concerto, Opus 59, was commissioned by the Bath Festival Society for Yehudi Menuhin, who gave the first performance on 1 June 1961 in Bath Abbey with the composer conducting. Again Berkeley's approach to serial techniques is a free fusion of means, but the row is present in some form throughout the *Passacaglia: Lento* with the exception of the central *Allegro* portion, where the composer seems to cast off his serial shackles with some relief.

As in the Aria I from the Concertino, and the recognition aria from *Ruth*, the row starts as a ground bass:

Example 102. Violin Concertino, Opus 59

The oboe melody above is not serial, although it is connected to the row through the obsessive rising fourth. As in the Aria, Berkeley approaches the use of the row contrapuntally in a two-part context. When chords arrive, at figure 24, with the row in the bass, P10, they turn the texture into a Lydian F major soon varied through the chromatic bass line. In the next section, *Un poco piu vivo*, the row, P8, is a cantus firmus for the soloist against mostly triadic harmonies. For the *Meno vivo*, figure 28, the row, P4, appears only as the bass and then as the bass note of chords. At Tempo I, figure 30, the row is again a bass, P2, and then the last eight bars of the movement have PO in the violas, as when the movement began, and G is the tonal centre. This actually contradicts what the composer said in 1948 about his ear not 'desiring the return of the original row after many others have been used'.[13]

The difference between tonal and atonal elements in the Violin Concerto is so slight that the presence of the note-row in the *Lento* could go unnoticed. By not exploiting row techniques more fully at this stage, Berkeley expressed his dissatisfaction with something so rigorous, which he was to do again in the late 1960s. Had he continued, he might have tightened up what Redlich much earlier saw as a lack of relevance in his developments.[14] There are other ways in which the Violin Concerto is a far cry from the natural lyricism and colour of the Piano Concerto, for example. The scoring here, for two oboes, two horns and strings, seems grey and the command of harmony has less of the magical precision of the 1940s. By the following year, when Berkeley wrote his Sonatina, Opus 61, for oboe and piano, the note-row exposed in the piano's first three bars is soon lost in the oboe part, which uses the first nine notes, then changes the order of the tenth and eleventh before forgetting about it altogether (Example 103, p. 167).

There are more interesting aspects of this Sonatina than the abandoned row. It is a study in varied repetitions, with subtle passagework and it has a liveliness especially suited to the medium, which has a relatively small repertoire. The augmented triads at the opening of the finale might easily have come from Rawsthorne. In the later 1930s and in the 1940s, Berkeley and Rawsthorne were often mentioned together: they had both embraced continental influences, so it was said, and were then becoming known for instrumental rather than vocal works. Berkeley's operas and music to religious texts changed that, but he continued to have a high regard for Rawsthorne. In an obituary tribute for the BBC in 1971, he spoke generously about him:

> To say that by Alan Rawsthorne's death we have lost one of the most distinguished and highly talented composers the country has produced in this century is no exaggeration. His name is widely known, and yet his music is not as familiar as it deserves to be. As one looks through the list of his published works, as one studies his scores and listens to the many records of his music, one asks oneself why this should be so. The answer, I think, lies in great part in the character of the music

[13] R. Myers, ed., *Music Today* I, London, 1949, p. 145.

[14] H. F. Redlich, 'Lennox Berkeley', *Music Survey* 31, June 1951, pp. 245–9.

Example 103. Sonatina for Oboe and Piano, Opus 61

itself, in its avoidance both of the sensational and of any easy appeal to the senses. It is music that needs to be listened to with concentration and to be heard many times before it can be appreciated to the full. Combined with this, I have a feeling that he himself had a deep dislike of publicity . . . When I think about his music, the qualities that spring to mind are craftsmanship, imagination, logic, and yet a very personal kind of unpredictability. He had, too, the kind of originality that springs from the emergence of a distinctive personality, rather than the more superficial kind, so hectically pursued by so many today. Though his use of harmony evolved and changed a great deal, his music remained fundamentally tonal, and he preferred to perfect his own style rather than to experiment with newer and more fashionable trends.[15]

Almost every point Berkeley made about Rawsthorne related to his own position, including the dislike of publicity, and he went on to say that he particularly admired Rawsthorne's Third Symphony (1964). Direct comparisons can be made between their music at all stages. Rawsthorne's Symphonic Studies (1938), his first major orchestral work, is contemporary with Berkeley's Serenade or Symphony No. 1. Rawsthorne seems dry compared with Berkeley's attractive melodic qualities. Even a mature chamber piece like Rawsthorne's Quintet for Piano and Wind (1963) still shows derivations from Bartók and

[15] L. Berkeley, 'Alan Rawsthorne', *Composer* 42, Winter 1971–72, pp. 5–7. Based on BBC Radio 3 talk. The point that some music needs to be heard several times to be fully understood is one which I made about Berkeley in my *Musical Times* article of November 1968. The composer wrote to me on 3 November 1968: 'I was particularly glad that you pointed out that my music does not easily make an immediate impact. I've so often found that people get much more out of it when they've really got to know it.'

Hindemith, but it makes an interesting comparison with Berkeley's Quintet for the same resources, Opus 90 (1975), commissioned by the Chamber Music Society of Lincoln Center, New York. It is almost as if Berkeley's admiration for Rawsthorne has brought them closer together in Berkeley's later years into a terse neo-classicism comparable to the work of Walter Piston in America. Berkeley's Quintet took him 'the best part of six months' which he considered 'slow going'. He and Lady Berkeley made their first visit to New York for the premiere, and during rehearsals he wrote: 'I like the piece and think it has a certain toughness which was lacking in my earlier music.'[16] Both Berkeley and Rawsthorne wrote well for the piano in solo pieces, chamber music and concertos, and both admired Chopin, contributing substantial chapters to a book about his music.[17] Rawsthorne wrote a Ballade for the piano in 1967 and, as we have seen, Berkeley's tribute was *Three Mazurkas (Hommage à Chopin)*, written for the Chopin centenary. These attractive pieces with memorable tunes move deftly from Berkeley to Chopin and back in a technique which I have described as style-modulation.[18]

Emerging in the later 1930s, both Berkeley and Rawsthorne stood out against the English folk-song school led by Vaughan Williams; both wrote music for films; and in the later 1990s Rawsthorne's music had something of a revival, especially on CD.[19] Berkeley's admiration for him can partly be accounted for as respect for a colleague as capable as he himself was of sticking to his guns when fashion was against conservative composers of that generation. Tippett's opera *King Priam*, produced in 1962, and the works surrounding it showed his new departures, and both Berkeley and Rawsthorne were becoming more dissonant. Rawsthorne, like Berkeley, toyed with pitch-serialism, as the third movement of his Quintet for Piano and Wind shows. Britten continued to explore twelve-note successions in his pacifist opera *Owen Wingrave*, Opus 85 (1970). Only Walton took little notice of the new climate and has been criticised, even at his centenary in 2002, for what seemed to be his reactionary stance. In 1969 Freda and Lennox Berkeley visited the Waltons at Ischia and Berkeley was able to make some comparisons between the way the two composers lived:

> William took us to see his work room and I felt envious of the ideal conditions in which he can compose, so different from mine – and yet I thought I might easily do nothing in such perfect surroundings . . .[20]

[16] Berkeley, diary entries March 1975 and 28 January 1976.

[17] A. Walker, ed., *Frédéric Chopin: Profiles of the Man and the Musician*, London, 1966: Rawsthorne on 'Ballades, Fantasy and Scherzos', pp. 42–72; Berkeley on 'Nocturnes, Berceuse, Barcarolle', pp. 170–86.

[18] P. Dickinson, *Style-modulation as a Compositional Technique*, Goldsmiths College, University of London, 1996.

[19] The film scores were revived, some in arrangements by Philip Lane, CHAN 9749; new recordings of the concertos came out; an Alan Rawsthorne Society was formed; and the first full-length study appeared: J. McCabe, *Alan Rawsthorne: Portrait of a Composer*, Oxford, 1999.

[20] Berkeley diary entry, 12 May 1969.

Indeed it would have been difficult to imagine Berkeley working in Italy removed from his connections in London and his dedication to pupils and organisations such as the Performing Right Society, of which he was president from 1975 to 1983. The Berkeleys enjoyed social life in London and attended royal receptions before Berkeley received his knighthood from the Queen on 17 July 1974. These invitations continued and he lunched at Buckingham Palace in both 1982 and 1983. Berkeley gradually became an elder statesman of British music and his final connection with Britten was when he unveiled the memorial in Westminster Abbey on 21 November 1978.[21]

All these composers, to their credit, remained true to themselves. By the 1960s Berkeley was not following Britten in directions such as preaching against war or drawing on oriental music and had realised that serial techniques would not solve any problems – let alone indeterminacy and other fashions of the moment. So he embarked on a third period of impressive focus and cogency, including the Third Symphony (1969), which would not be his last, and the Guitar Concerto (1974).

[21] Berkeley received many honours both public and professional from this country and abroad. Apart from his knighthood, these included the CBE (1957); Ordre Nationale de Mérite Culturel de Monaco (1967); the Hon. D.Mus. from Oxford University (1970) and from City University (1984); the Papal Knighthood of St Gregory (1973); Master of the Worshipful Company of Musicians (1975); President of the Performing Right Society (1975); President of the Composers' Guild (1976); Foreign Honorary Member, American Academy and Institute of Arts and Letters (1980); Membre associé de l'academie royale des sciences, des lettres et des beaux-arts de Belgique (1983).

10. Final years

In a BBC Radio 3 interview at the time of Berkeley's seventy-fifth birthday in 1978, Julian Bream felt that his music evoked 'natural and pleasant things about life . . . a reflective feeling for landscape'. Moments of despair and irritation were rare, but one anecdote reveals something about Berkeley's interest in extending his range. Julian Bream was staying with friends in the country at the same time as Lennox and Freda Berkeley. The composer was obviously working on a piece, since he would go to the drawing room periodically and play the piano. At one point Berkeley was seen through the slightly open door with a pencil in his mouth playing extraordinarily dissonant chords and muttering, 'Not nasty enough, not nasty enough!'[1]

Perhaps this unusual story reflects some of the pressures of the 1960s. In a 65-birthday tribute to Berkeley, I tried to sum up the situation:

> In 1938 Berkeley belonged to new music. For some years after the war his work was too dissonant for British audiences, who had to wait until the early 1960s for the chance of coming to terms with Schoenberg and his school. By the time the post-Webern mania had gripped the young, composers of Berkeley's generation appeared ultra-conservative, clinging to traditional means in the face of onslaught; they sometimes seemed unable to develop beyond the early work which had established their reputation. Their music had also somehow to leave the 'new music' category and meet the average listener who can take in Elgar or Shostakovich.[2]

John Tavener, in a seventieth-birthday tribute, also set the scene: 'In a decade dominated by the figure of Stockhausen, when most artists work on large canvases, deal in big concepts and are given to gargantuan self-promotion, Lennox Berkeley is a stranger.'[3] More than thirty years later in a pop-dominated cultural environment the situation has deteriorated – for Stockhausen as well as Berkeley. Looking back to the 1960s, Michael Berkeley, who has since become one of the leading British composers and broadcasters of his generation, said in the ATV Network film made in 1980:

[1] In 'Music Now', ed. John Amis, BBC Radio 3, May 1978. Also in interview with author, 28 January 1991.

[2] P. Dickinson, 'Lennox Berkeley', *Musical Times* 109, November 1968, pp. 1013–14.

[3] J. Tavener, 'Lennox Berkeley at 70', *Listener*, 10 May 1973, p. 625.

> I remember there was a time when he felt, 'Oh dear, shouldn't I be more with-it perhaps?' He soon came to the conclusion – quite rightly in my opinion – that he had a very strong voice of his own and he should continue to cultivate that.[4]

Earlier, in an interview for Berkeley's seventy-fifth birthday, I asked him about the distinction between his dissonant and less dissonant manners, especially in the late 1960s:

> My music has always been fundamentally tonal, though it is true that I felt the need to explore more dissonant harmony around the period you mention, and still use it, though I think I have managed to incorporate it in my usual style in some of my later music . . . When the feeling I want to convey in a particular piece seems to demand it, I use traditional harmony – the *Canzonetta* from the Sinfonia Concertante, Opus 84, is a case in point – at the risk of being accused of eclecticism by the critics. I don't think this need destroy unity of style . . .[5]

The largest vocal work since *Ruth* (1956), and therefore something of a landmark, was the opera *Castaway.* It was designed to be a companion-piece to *A Dinner Engagement*, and the librettist was again Paul Dehn. As with *A Dinner Engagement* and *Ruth*, the English Opera Group gave the premiere – in the Jubilee Hall, Aldeburgh, on 3 June 1967 and on 12 July at Sadler's Wells – and the other half of the double-bill was Walton's *The Bear.* It was not until 1983 that *Castaway* was performed, as intended, along with *A Dinner Engagement* and the production by Trinity College of Music proved how successful the dual conception was, with *Castaway* as the first half.[6]

The musical language is varied, bearing out Berkeley's claim to have incorporated aspects of his more dissonant style with his older melodic characteristics. The story is based on the sixth book of Homer's *Odyssey*, where Odysseus has been shipwrecked on the Isle of Scheria (now Ischia). The opening, portraying a violent storm, gives Odysseus many phrases involving rising or falling major sevenths. Meanwhile, in the following scene at her father's palace, the lonely Princess Nausicaa is dreaming of finding a husband and sings an arioso starting in E flat major (Example 104, p. 172). That looks like the set number approach of the earlier operas but *Castaway* is through-composed and thus gains in continuity – and the piano is no longer merely continuo. Odysseus is discovered the next morning by Nausicaa and her handmaidens who have come to wash the royal laundry. He is dirty and unkempt but, when he is washed and robed, Nausicaa falls in love with him. He then has to find his own way to her father's palace since etiquette will not allow Nausicaa to ask who he is. The girls give him directions and Nausicaa concludes 'May the Gods guide

[4] ATV Network film, 'Composers', made in 1980 and shown on 14 May 1981. Director, Richie Stewart; Producer, J. B. J. Berrow.

[5] P. Dickinson, 'Berkeley at 75 talks to Peter Dickinson', *Musical Times* 119, May 1978, pp. 409–11.

[6] *Castaway* and *A Dinner Engagement* were produced by Trinity College of Music at the Bloomsbury Theatre, London, on 16, 17 and 18 June 1983. Conductors, Christopher Fifield and Meredith Davies; Producer, Richard Jones.

Example 104. *Castaway*, Opus 69, 2 bars before figure 8

you safely on your way'. Berkeley reflects her hopeful ardour orchestrally in a typical piece of melodic writing which reaches an ardent B flat major at times qualified by false relations (Example 105, p. 173). At dinner in the palace Odysseus hears the story of his own Trojan horse exploits sung by the blind minstrel, Demodocus. These are now part of history and it is assumed that Odysseus is dead. When he reveals his identity the romantic hopes of Nausicaa are dashed since she realises he must return to his long-lost wife, Penelope. There are touching moments in the score, especially when Odysseus sails off to find Penelope, leaving Nausicaa, and the whole subject is another naval

Example 105. *Castaway*, 7 bars before figure 42

connection in a Berkeley opera. There are several important places in the action where the published vocal score, as a result of revisions, is different from the version used at the first performance. The element of comedy, intruding occasionally, does not feel entirely natural in this serious and sometimes sentimental tale, but altogether *Castaway* is another work which deserves a better chance than it has had – married to *A Dinner Engagement*.

Berkeley's vocal output following *Castaway* included *Signs in the Dark*, Opus 69, for mixed chorus and strings to poems by Laurie Lee. It was commissioned for the 1967 Stroud Festival and Berkeley conducted it himself at the Proms in the following year. The *Magnificat*, Opus 71, for SATB, organ and orchestra, commissioned for the 1968 City of London Festival is a more substantial work which lost most of its detail in the excessively reverberant acoustic of St Paul's Cathedral. Berkeley's diary simply records a 'very unsatisfactory performance' – which he conducted himself. However, in a letter to me he said: 'I think the actual performance of the *Magnificat* was not too bad in the end – it certainly seemed to come over to some, but I would like to hear it in a building where one hears one bar at a time!'[7] Unusually Berkeley wrote an article in some detail about his setting of the *Magnificat* which appeared in the *Listener* four days before the premiere on 8 July. He describes the *Magnificat* as the central canticle of Vespers in the Catholic Church and then considers the traditional settings of this text by composers from Palestrina onwards. The idea of setting the *Magnificat* had been suggested to him and he welcomed it. Then he makes a point about the loss of Latin for the Roman Catholic rite: 'I chose the Latin because of its universality . . . and because permission to use the vernacular in the Catholic Church has been widely interpreted as a virtual proscription of Latin, to the great impoverishment of the liturgy.'[8]

In his *Listener* article Berkeley differentiates between liturgical music, such as the masses of Palestrina, and works written for the concert hall, such as Verdi's *Requiem*. He makes it clear that his own work is 'essentially a concert piece in which I have made no attempt to write liturgical music' and says he regarded the *Magnificat* as 'a text of remarkable directness, each verse going straight to the point. It attracted me particularly by qualities seldom found in the world we live in now – a joyful forgetfulness of self in the expression of faith in God and acceptance of his will.'

Once again the orchestral introduction provides a considerable build-up to the entry of the voices. The sopranos, entering on their own, sound close to plainsong but are soon contradicted by the harmonies for the full choir. The layout is spacious with eloquent orchestral interludes; unaccompanied double choir at 'Et misericordiae'; a beguiling *Lento* in G major for sopranos in three parts at 'Esurientes', perhaps the closest Berkeley ever came to César Franck; and a formal fugato at 'Suscepit Israel'. Throughout the 25-minute work the relationship between chorus and orchestra is carefully balanced. Choral and orchestral bass lines hardly ever overlap and there is no heavy doubling.

Unlike the first two symphonies, the Third is in a concentrated single movement lasting about a quarter of an hour. In 1969, Michael Berkeley discussed his father's use of note-rows in the Third Symphony.[9] At that time it seemed important to emphasise Berkeley's new cogency in terms of a personal use of serial techniques. Now it matters much less and, as always, the personality means more than the technique itself. The opening of the Oboe and Piano Sonatina looked like a calculated evaporation of the series after even one

[7] L. Berkeley, letter to author, 15 July 1968.

[8] L. Berkeley, 'Lennox Berkeley describes his setting of the *Magnificat*', *Listener*, 4 July 1968, p. 25.

[9] M. Berkeley, 'Lennox Berkeley's Third Symphony', *Listener*, 3 July 1969, p. 25.

appearance whereas the Third Symphony, for the first time, uses parts of a series harmonically. The first six notes come from two chords, D minor and B major, which dominate the opening *Allegretto moderato* and the second hexachord appears with the central *Lento*. There are many ingredients even in the first four bars:

Example 106. Symphony No. 3, Opus 74

The first chord, which also opens the final *Allegro*, is a kind of tonic substitute. It could be read as D major, underpinned by G sharp and containing D sharp, and it immediately characterises the restless mood. The first hexachord of the row is treated melodically in the second violins and varied repetition extends it. The bass line moves by tritones – G sharp, D, G sharp – and then imitates the second violins inexactly. The dotted rhythm is by now clearly integral to the main motif; it recurs some thirty times in the same number of bars; and is then evened out until a varied reprise after a section in 5/8, which has a kinship with other Berkeley movements dominated by this rhythm in similar mood. His use of this metre is tranquil rather than agitated, but the scoring is acute – at figure 5 three muted trumpets sustain the A minor triad whilst three flutes above weave a diatonic melody in parallel chords. Throughout the symphony the tritone, often connected with chords related to the dominant thirteenth, is used as a point of reference, a kind of punctuation. Tension reduces to the *Lento* where the second hexachord of the row appears in the solo flute, leading to regular crotchets in a bar-long sequence (Example 107, below and on p. 177).

Example 107. Symphony No. 3, figure 14

Example 107 (cont.)

The choice of a solo flute with its G sharp making an added sixth to the B major chord below is bound to bring French associations. Specifically, perhaps, with Debussy's *Prélude à l'après-midi d'un faune*, where the third appearance of the main theme is harmonised this way, but a perfect fourth higher, at figure 2. The second bar of Berkeley's *Lento* shows the flute completing and then repeating the second hexachord, but the clarinet deals with the first hexachord outlining the triads of B major and D minor. The bassoon part in the next bar is made up of these two triads so that for a few bars all twelve notes are in circulation, although ordering is unsystematic. The oboe solo brings the inversion of the six notes established in the flute's second bar – 10, 11, 6, 7, 8 and 9 – and in the horn solo too, but the accompaniment to the oboe becomes free. At figure 15 the divided choir of violins refers back to the bitonality of the 5/8 of figure 5 and much more use is made of the sequences from the row's second hexachord before the 6/8 *Allegro* arrives to act as finale, but the first violins' leap up of two consecutive octaves in the bar after figure 16 puts serial matters into perspective. The A–B flat–F comes from the second hexachord, but the patterns of descending fourths and thirds are free (Example 108, p. 178).

Example 108. Symphony No. 3, one bar after figure 16

The first chord of the *Allegro* refers back to the opening of the whole work and at figure 19 the first hexachord is employed in a repeated phrase typical of Berkeley at all periods. These articulations of the D minor and B major triads generate momentum leading to runs in the violins as a catalyst to some rhythmic heavy brass. Tritone references recur and Berkeley continues to invent, even at this stage in the work. At figure 30 the offbeat phrase from Example 109 lands on the beat and after a pause almost as pregnant as the first of those at the end of Sibelius' Fifth Symphony there is one more eruption of brass and a concentrated reminder of Example 109 in the timpani before the final chord – a D major triad with added sixth and major seventh.

Example 109. Symphony No. 3, figure 19

At this stage Michael Berkeley was closely aware of what his father was writing:

> I find the Third Symphony very powerful because it's muscular, it's taut, and at that time I was working a little bit with him. I can remember trying to tempt him to actually push out even further. I remember suggesting the rim shot on the last chord.[10]

The confident language of the Third Symphony prompts some comparison with the Roussel of the 1920s and 1930s – works such as the Suite in F and the Piano Concerto. But Roussel, who had absorbed some of Prokofiev's gawky melodic and rhythmic qualities, works in longer paragraphs. A tendency in late Berkeley, as in the Debussy of *Jeux*, is to work with short units freely related. But now his melodies are less memorable in themselves and the habitual attraction for constant development and inexact repetition is still at work.

Berkeley's next work, the *Windsor Variations*, Opus 75, continues with an almost tougher exterior. Commissioned by the Windsor Festival Society and conducted by Menuhin in its early performances, it shows an awareness of late Stravinsky, perhaps, with 6/8 passages in rapid tempo, such as the first variation,

[10] Interview with author, 29 January 1990.

as energetic as anything in Tippett. The Third String Quartet, Opus 76, written in the first half of 1970, showed no loss of this renewed vigour. The composer's programme-note is particularly revealing:

> The first movement begins, without any preamble, with a theme that in various guises reappears throughout the Quartet. Some of the reappearances seem to happen more or less accidentally, or at all events subconsciously, as I did not set out to write a monothematic piece . . .[11]

This is further confirmation of Berkeley's instinctive method, feeling his way towards relationships which only later become clear. What he says about the scherzo is equally interesting: 'There follows a scherzo, built on a phrase of six notes and its inversion.'[12] In fact the hexachord and its inversion together make up the twelve notes which Berkeley uses in various transpositions:

Example 110. String Quartet No. 3, Opus 76,

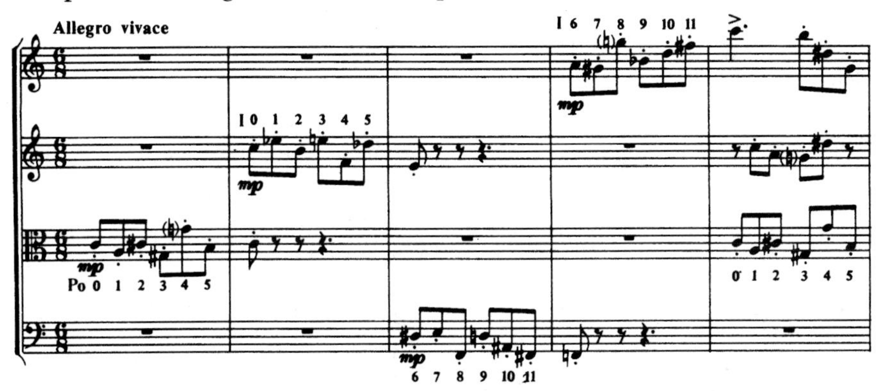

Free fragments are superimposed on the row, treated in two halves as in the Third Symphony, which Berkeley seems to have used, as in the Oboe and Piano Sonatina, to get himself going. Then, after writing the first two movements of the quartet, Berkeley wrote a simple unison setting of the hymn *Hail, Holy Queen* on 6 March. He then decided to base the slow movement on it, which resulted in almost Ivesian free associations, and felt that 'the tune I wrote for the Hymn is a descending sequence of notes not unlike the main theme of the Quartet'. It is easy to see how the opening theme of the *Lento* relates to the song, which starts with a version of Beethoven's *Lebewohl* motif from his Piano Sonata in E flat, Opus 81a (Example 111 and Example 112, p. 180). Two bars after figure 3 in the

[11] L. Berkeley, programme-note on String Quartet No. 3. See also Edmund Rubbra's review of the broadcast in the *Listener*, 9 September 1971, p. 345. The performance was followed by a talk in which the composer's 'statement of faith was echoed in music in which eloquence was always controlled, and which was as aphoristic as the points he made in his talk'.

[12] L. Berkeley, programme-note on String Quartet No. 3.

Example 111. Hail Holy Queen

Example 112. String Quartet No. 3

first movement the first violin has a related melody marked 'cantabile', and a version of the *Lento* recurs during the finale at figure 31. Part of the ostinato from the scherzo comes at figure 22 in the *Lento*, so there are many interconnections. The song itself, *Hail, Holy Queen*, owes something to plainsong and is an example of Berkeley's late technique at its simplest level. Archaic bare fifths and plain triads are found alongside discreet dissonances including three chords of the thirteenth, a harmony still possessing a magnetic fascination. In this quartet, Berkeley's relationship to the note-row and to his own song is of a highly individual nature justifying detailed study. Given his penchant for chamber music – a combination of the qualities and traditions of Fauré and Frank Bridge perhaps – this makes for a worthy successor to the outstanding Second Quartet twenty-eight years earlier.

There are other aspects about Berkeley's method of composition which emerged when he was introducing a performance of his Oboe Quartet, Opus 70, for a BBC Radio 3 broadcast in 1973:

> I find it often a mistake to adhere too strictly to a preconceived plan because this rules out things that may occur spontaneously, or even happen accidentally in the course of composition. An example of what I mean . . . is that I have sometimes, in playing a passage from my first rough sketch, misread a note and played something different, which turns out to be much better than what I had originally thought of and leads to something more significant in the material. This sounds so stupid and haphazard that I feel rather ashamed at having admitted it![13]

The achievements of Berkeley's late period can in some ways be compared with the 1940s. Then he became liberated from the confines of Boulanger's teaching through the example of Britten. When Berkeley, too, had explored opera he needed a new direction. In the sequence of religious poems, *Four Quartets*, T. S. Eliot wrote, 'Old men ought to be explorers.'[14] With great courage Berkeley set out to do this, like Copland, and to complement his early Parisian training with some recourse to Schoenberg's ideas emanating from the other centre which revitalised composition during the twentieth century – Vienna. Berkeley was never as rigorous as Copland, largely, one suspects, because he could not be bothered once a piece was going well. So a kind of dualism is maintained up to the end of Berkeley's composing career.

The *Chinese Songs*, Opus 78, written for Meriel Dickinson in late 1970, show the newer language in operation – and the two styles. They were commissioned by the Park Lane Group for a recital I devised of musical settings of E. E. Cummings, which was given at the Purcell Room on 22 March 1971, and broadcast on BBC Radio 3 on 26 July 1972.[15] Berkeley's new cycle was meant to fit this programme and he seemed interested after I gave him a volume of Cummings' poetry. At a late stage it turned out that he was setting Chinese

[13] L. Berkeley, BBC Radio 3, 16 May 1973.
[14] T. S. Eliot, *Four Quartets*, East Coker, p. 22.
[15] We recorded the *Chinese Songs* on Argo LP ZRG 788 (1975).

poems instead and my schemed collaboration between him and the American poet was not to be. However, the idea must have remained in Berkeley's mind since he made a setting of Cummings' 'I carry your heart with me' in July 1972 and dedicated it to the counter-tenor, Tay Cheng Jim.

In introducing a broadcast performance of the *Chinese Songs* Berkeley found another source for the characteristics of his style:

> I was attracted to these verses not only by their poetic quality but also by their brevity and almost epigrammatic style. Much is said in very few words and this is something that has always appealed to me. I have in music a dislike of over-emphasis and reiteration. My ideal would be to achieve as sparing a use of notes as the Chinese do of words. I hope that in these songs I have gone some little way towards this.[16]

Indeed the language of restraint does pay off in this atmospheric set of songs, beautifully imagined in every detail. The bleak octaves of the first song suggest an oriental scale, which can often be a cliché in Western composers, and Berkeley's second song provides another direct comparison with Britten – a setting of the same poem appeared as the third of his *Songs from the Chinese*, Opus 58 (1958) for tenor and guitar:

Example 113. Britten: *Songs from the Chinese*, Opus 58, No. 3

[16] L. Berkeley, interview, recital and discussion with Peter Dickinson, BBC Radio 3, 16 November 1974. The programme contained the *Chinese Songs*; three French songs – *D'un Vanneur de blé*, *Tant ques mes yeux* and *Automne*; and *Five Auden Poems*.

Britten's treatment is very quick, with a single guitar figuration broken only at the emotional moments when the poet remembers his absent lover. Britten marks these pangs with a rapid arpeggio, Berkeley with a held chord and silence. Once again, different methods create a comparable intensity. Britten's treatment is decorated monody with bass notes subtly hinted at whereas Berkeley also uses figuration but makes his points through harmony. In that sense Berkeley's allegiance to a bass-line links him to Ravel, but Britten's monodic approach derives from Debussy. Berkeley's song ends, like his first one, with a chord containing both major and minor thirds. The last song, 'The Riverside Village', makes a calm ending with sustained lyricism in D flat major, harking back to the tonal Berkeley of the middle-period operas, but finishing on a bare octave.[17] Berkeley's diary entry for 8 December 1970 indicates that the last of the *Chinese Songs* was something special:

> I've done more work on the Chinese Poems, and had the luck to hit on one ['The Riverside Village'] that I felt could have been made for me – I've seldom had so much pleasure in writing anything than this small song . . . I feel happy too about 'Dreaming of a dead lady'. It's very difficult to find a poem that will form a contrast to the mood of nostalgia and melancholy that pervades most of these . . .

Example 114. Berkeley: *Chinese Songs*, Opus 78, No. 2

[17] There are misprints in the printed score. Piano: p. 1, line 3, bar 3, second beat, l.h. B natural; p. 2, line 2, bar 2, beat 1, r.h. B not C; p. 2, line 2, bar 3, beat 2, r.h. C natural not D; p. 3, line 3, bar 4, r.h., C sharp; p. 6, line 2, bar 3, l.h. treble clef. Voice: p. 5, line 3, 'rowers' not 'sowers'; p. 12, line 1, bar 2, 'to' on last quaver, 'sleep' over both notes of following 3/2 bar.

If Berkeley's late work is a consolidation implied by what he achieved in the later sixties, then it proceeds in at least two channels and he is not always consistent. Sometimes he followed his own energetic lead in the Third Symphony and Third Quartet and at other times he looked back. Thus in 1971, in the same year, he could write the dissonant Duo for cello and piano, Opus 81, No. 1 – a cogent example of this style – and the *Palm Court Waltz*, Opus 81, No. 2a, which is almost exactly what its title suggests. Berkeley himself said: 'It's pure light music in which I could indulge my taste for sentimental harmony to the full.'[18] The principal melody is related to the expectation motif from Act I of *Nelson* with which it shares a blue note. The orchestral version is called *Diana and Actaeon Waltz* and was written for a charity concert which Richard Buckle put on at the Coliseum. This unpretentious piece is really in the tradition of Lord Berners' *Valses bourgeoises*, itself a parodistic glance at the Strausses and Ravel. About the totally different Duo, Berkeley wrote:

> I got to the end of the Duo after the usual struggles. It was more difficult to get the form right as I didn't want to follow any traditional pattern. Great difficulty too in finding the actual notes and timing of the ending, but I think I've got it right . . .[19]

He certainly did, with a final functioning dominant in the last six bars with dissonant chords superimposed. The Duo's motto is announced at the start with four chords in the piano which act as points of reference in an original way, avoiding any 'traditional pattern'. In the *Sinfonia Concertante*, Opus 84, for oboe and orchestra, as in the *Chinese Songs*, there is a mixing of styles from movement to movement which is convincing. In spite of his fears, Berkeley was not accused of eclecticism by the critics. Anthony Payne, reviewing the first performance of the Sinfonia Concertante, found that its simplest movement, the *Canzonetta*, provided 'one of the most elegant and adorable pieces of melodic writing you could wish for', and that as a whole the Sinfonia Concertante had 'hidden strength', suggesting 'more monumental feelings'.[20] It was the third work in which Berkeley showed a special affinity with the oboe, allied to a particular performer, Janet Craxton.

The Sinfonia Concertante was followed by a pair of almost liturgically introspective orchestral pieces, also from 1973. The two-movement *Antiphon*, Opus 85, commissioned by the Cheltenham Festival and dedicated to John Manduell, is for strings. Berkeley wrote:

> Its title refers to the theme on which the second movement is based – a plainsong melody from the *Antiphonale Romanum*. Although this is not heard in its entirety until the second movement, it is foreshadowed in various places earlier on, as, for example, in the slow introduction with which the work begins . . . The second movement is in the form of a theme and variations. The plainsong tune is a setting of the text 'Laetamini in Domino, et exultate justi'. It appears first played by the

[18] L. Berkeley diary, 2 December 1971.

[19] L. Berkeley diary, 10 November 1971. 24 November refers to revisions.

[20] A. E. Payne, 'Enchanting Sinfonia by Berkeley at 70', *Daily Telegraph*, 4 August 1973.

> violas . . . In the last variation almost the whole theme is played in the bass while the upper parts provide a descant to it.[21]

The second of these atmospheric pieces, *Voices of the Night*, Opus 86, is dedicated to an old friend, Charlotte Bonham Carter. It is interesting to observe that the more objective style of the liturgical music, with fewer individual characteristics, comes to dominate the works written for the concert hall in Berkeley's last period. After another work of similar length written in the same year, the four-movement Suite for Strings, Opus 87 – all these pieces begin and end slowly – Berkeley reached the Guitar Concerto, Opus 88, written for Julian Bream, with whom the composer worked closely in writing most of his guitar music.

Bream first met Berkeley in 1957 when he was about to write the Guitar Sonatina for him. He went to 8 Warwick Avenue in Little Venice, which had been the family home since June 1947:

> I remember going into this lovely house at Warwick Avenue and thinking how beautiful the whole place was. It had a certain spirit of aristocracy . . . After we'd worked together on the score we went into the drawing room which had some lovely pictures, wonderful furniture and vivid wallpaper – and also very nice, strong pink gins! It was always a lovely social occasion to visit Warwick Avenue. And then, of course, his children were around – they were quite lively . . . It was a real home, an artist's home.[22]

At this stage Bream knew the Serenade and the *Four Poems of St Teresa of Avila* and felt that Berkeley's lyrical style would be ideally adapted to the guitar. What Bream did not know and what Berkeley had obviously forgotten himself was that he had written a set of *Quatre pièces* for Segovia in Paris which the famous virtuoso never played. The manuscript was discovered in Andres Segovia's papers and it has been edited by Angelo Gilardino, for whom Berkeley composed his Theme and Variations, Opus 77, in 1970.[23] Segovia made his Paris debut in 1924, he quickly became famous, and two years later Schott started publishing his *Guitar Archive Series*, which included pieces by contemporary composers. Cyril Scott wrote a Sonatina for him in 1928 and Berkeley's *Quatre pièces* probably date from this period. In a 1931 report from Paris for the *Monthly Musical Record* Berkeley wrote:

> Another recital that aroused great enthusiasm was Segovia's concert at the Opéra. I think it is superfluous to praise Segovia's guitar playing – it will suffice to say that he was at the top of his form and amply justified his choice of the Opéra to perform in . . . the fact that one heard perfectly every sound bears witness not only to Segovia's power of tone-production but also to the acoustic properties of the Opéra.[24]

[21] L. Berkeley, programme-note for Park Lane Group Seventy-fifth Birthday Concert, Queen Elizabeth Hall, 12 May 1978.
[22] Interview with author, 28 January 1991: some clarifications, 17 July 2002.
[23] *Quatre pièces pour la guitare, à Senor Andres Segovia*, edited by Angelo Gilardino and Luigi Biscaldi, Berben Edizioni Musicali, 2002.
[24] L. Berkeley, 'Music in Paris', *Monthly Musical Record* 61, 1 July 1931, p. 210.

So Berkeley admired Segovia's success in the vast space of the Opéra and began his association with the guitar. After the Sonatina, Opus 52, Berkeley wrote for Bream again in *Songs of the Half-Light*, Opus 65, the second of his three cycles to poems by Walter de la Mare, who was the only poet Berkeley turned to three times for his song cycles. The Five Songs, Opus 26, were written for Pierre Bernac and Poulenc in 1946 and *Another Spring*, Opus 93, is a group of three poems commissioned to mark the retirement of Walter Hussey as Dean of Chichester Cathedral and performed there by Janet Baker and Geoffrey Pratley in 1977. Whereas the Five Songs are all charm and fantasy the last set is pensive and brooding. The last song, 'Afraid', is an epitaph for a seven-year-old girl and is marked 'very slow, in strict time throughout'. It is a pale reflection of 'The Riverside Village', which ended the *Five Chinese Songs* six years earlier, is in the same key and again has a demanding extended final phrase.

In 1983, Sheila MacCrindle described Berkeley as 'essentially a private person' and the restraint of his music has often been observed.[25] The musical qualities of the guitar fit such a temperament ideally, as Berkeley's solo music and song accompaniments for it had already shown, so it seems particularly fortunate that the composer's last concerto – originally entitled Concertino – should be the one for guitar, Opus 88. Julian Bream was engaged for the 1974 Festival of the City of London and had the opportunity to commission a concerto, so he decided to ask Berkeley:

> It's a very beautiful piece. I love the opening and the end of the first movement and also the slow movement, which has a most wonderful tune. What is interesting is that the notes are in the right part of the instrument. When some composers write guitar concertos they put their main thematic material high up on the instrument so that it carries. But the opening of this movement is in the tenor register and it has such a lovely sonority. I think it's a fine concerto and I was amazed how well he scored it.[26]

Bream said that for live performances of concertos, which were not frequent, he would use a discreet amount of amplification to avoid pressure on the orchestra, especially the strings.

The orchestra is limited to strings, single woodwind and two horns. The first movement opens with a duet for the two horns alone, which functions as an introduction anticipating the perfect fourths of the main theme. When the guitar comes in, it is in the humble role of accompanist to the flute. This is a beautiful melody in four-bar phrases, with the end of the first one just suggesting a blue note. The autumnal mood is typical as the guitar picks out and contributes to chords in the sustained strings (Example 115 on p. 187 and continued on p. 188). Berkeley's control of the difficult balance between guitar and orchestra is always careful, with a mixture of tutti, antiphonal treatments,

[25] S. MacCrindle, sleeve-note to *Sir Lennox Berkeley, an 80th birthday tribute*, Hyperion A66086 in association with the Performing Right Society, 1983. CD reissue, 2003.

[26] Interview with author, 28 January 1991.

Example 115. Guitar Concerto, Opus 88, 5 bars after figure 1

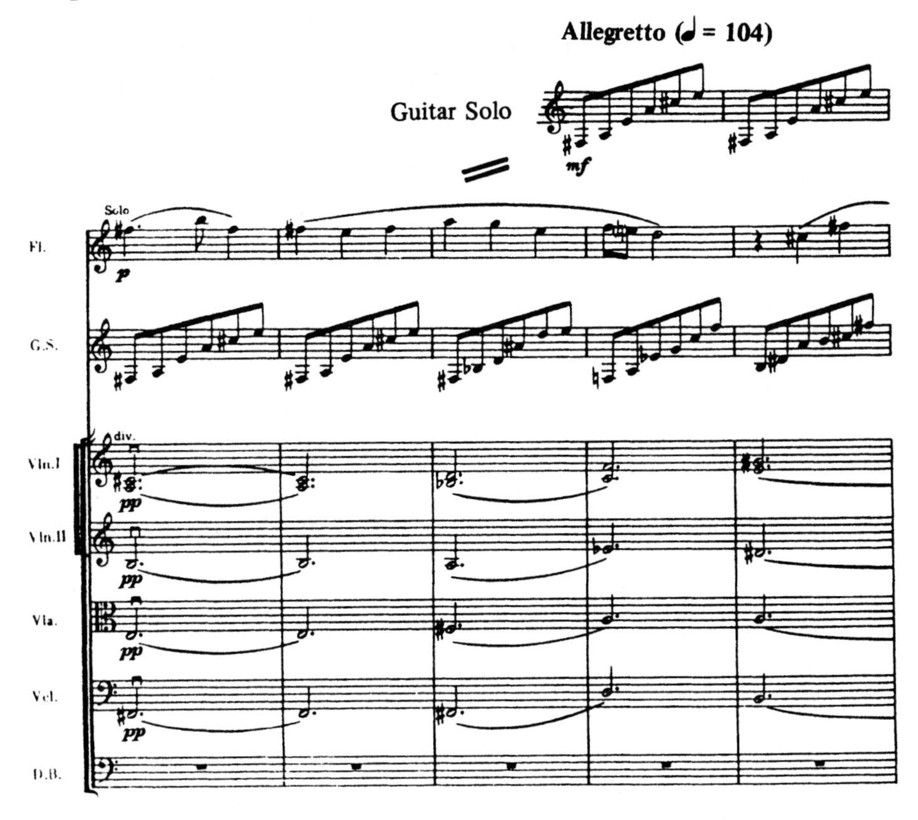

and very lightly scored accompaniments. A second theme emerges for guitar alone, *Meno vivo* – its quaver motif is shared with the first subject – and then the soloist is again accompanying the flute, this time doubled by bassoon two octaves apart (Example 116, pp. 189). This is followed, at figure 9, by a third melody – with barely disguised roots in Tchaikovsky – and the movement proceeds with veiled references to its themes in a delicate stream of consciousness, with a magical ending in guitar harmonics over sustained strings.

The second movement again has an introduction without strings. This time the four woodwind and two horns alternate, then the soloist enters in a trance-like E major context in 5/8, accompanied by lower strings. At the opening of the finale, *Allegro con brio*, the Flamenco personality of the instrument emerges for the first time with strummed chords. This settles the tonality of the finale as G major, whereas the first movement was ambiguous and the E major of much of the second movement turned to minor for the ending. The finale contains unobtrusive flashbacks to the previous movements. For example, the slow movement at figure 37 and the

Example 115 (cont.)

Example 116. Guitar Concerto, 5 bars after figure 7

third theme from the first movement in the cadenza before figure 39. Students of the concerto will need to study Bream's recording, which contains some differences of emphasis, and text, from the printed score.[27] Berkeley was accustomed to working closely with performers:

> Julian Bream came again to work with me on the Concerto. His suggestions have enormously improved it. The cadenza near the end of the third movement he has practically rewritten himself as I hoped he would, using what I had written merely as a guide to what I felt would be suitable.[28]

Four years after the Guitar Concerto, Berkeley completed his Fourth Symphony, Opus 94, in time for his seventy-fifth birthday in 1978. There were many

[27] RCA Red Seal, LP ARL 1–1181 (1975). In a interview with the author on 28 January 1991, Bream suggested that there may be details in the recording agreed with Berkeley which did not get into the printed score. On the other hand, Bream conceded, Berkeley might afterwards have preferred his original.

[28] L. Berkeley diary, May 1974. 28 December 1974 records: 'further revisions on a visit to Julian Bream'. 7 August 1976 states: 'to Julian Bream to check over proof of Guitar Concerto'. The miniature score was published in 1977 but it does not always reflect what Bream played, which could simply be a further revision. For example, in the finale, four bars after figure 42, Bream enters very broadly and he adds a further strum just before the final chord.

celebratory concerts and broadcast interviews to mark the occasion, including an appearance with Roy Plomley on his long-running series, *Desert Island Discs*, on BBC Radio 4. Here Berkeley admitted that his choice of records was more-or-less in order of priority. So Mozart came first with the *Andante* from Piano Concerto K467 in C – 'one of the most beautiful things in music'; then an aria from a Bach cantata; then late Beethoven. Bach cantatas and Beethoven quartets were features of Boulanger's analysis classes. Late Verdi followed, with an aria from *Falstaff*, and Debussy's *Prélude à l'après-midi d'un faune*, which Berkeley called, 'a masterpiece, a perfect expression of the music of that moment which had largely been invented by Debussy'. Berkeley then included part of the *Petite Symphonie concertante* (1945) for harp, harpsichord, piano and strings by the Swiss composer Frank Martin, whose neo-classical style has something in common with Berkeley. Next came a duet between Quint and young Miles from *The Turn of the Screw* (scene 8: At Night), which Berkeley called Britten's masterpiece. To finish his selection Berkeley chose the piano version of the third of Ravel's *Valses nobles et sentimentales*, which he felt had 'a great deal of Ravel's particular brand of nostalgia and charm'. When asked which single disc he would take with him Berkeley very surprisingly asked for the Frank Martin. I think he must have musunderstood the question since he would surely have preferred Bach or Mozart for extended desert island listening. His choice of a picture was a scene on the banks of the Marne by Renoir and, after hesitating over taking Proust, his book choice was the New Oxford Book of English verse.[29] His Anglo-French loyalties were finally settled on this side of the channel.

In an interview with Michael Oliver, Berkeley made some comparisons between the Third and Fourth Symphonies and introduced the new one.

> In my Third Symphony, which is in one movement . . . I felt that I had acquired a somewhat more forceful way of writing that I was able to put to the test. Then the RPO commissioned this [Fourth Symphony] through the Arts Council from me and I was particularly anxious to do it because I think it's a splendid thing if an orchestra commissions a contemporary composer to write something for it . . . I was also rather keen to see if I could do it on a bigger scale. This one has the complete three movements . . . and I hope I've managed to use this slightly more expansive manner . . .[30]

Berkeley also referred to his lifelong habit of varying his material:

> I think every composer feels that it's impossible to repeat note-for-note in the way the eighteenth-century composers did. Somehow it makes things move at too slow a pace for the way we feel and think today . . . I don't think people have

[29] *Desert Island Discs* with Roy Plomley on BBC Radio 4, 13 May 1978, BBC archives T 54060. Extracts were played from eight records Berkeley had chosen: *Andante*, Piano Concerto in C, K 467, Mozart; Duet (soprano and tenor) Cantata No. 42, Bach; *Lento Assai*, String Quartet in F, Op. 135, Beethoven; Duet (Fenton and Annetta), *Falstaff*, Verdi; *Prélude à l'après-midi d'un faune*, Debussy; *Petite Symphonie concertante*, Frank Martin; Duet (Miles and Quint), *The Turn of the Screw*, Britten; *Valses nobles et sentimentales*, No. 3, Ravel.

[30] L. Berkeley, interview with Michael Oliver, *Music Weekly*, BBC Radio 3, 28 May 1978.

> thought that out but it's instinctive. The musical language has reached a point at which exact repetition doesn't seem to be suitable.[31]

Berkeley went on to indicate the modified sonata form of the first movement, with a main theme and two subsidiary themes, and the second movement as a set of variations. To avoid what some composers have experienced as 'last movement problems', Berkeley said he often adopted a lighter tone for his finales. This time it is a kind of rondo.

Berkeley appreciated a 'good performance under Groves' at the Proms and – with no diminution of energy at the age of seventy-five – took overnight trains to Edinburgh both ways to hear a student performance under Harry Legge.[32] During the next two months he heard performances in Oslo and at the Royal Northern College of Music in Manchester, under Raymond Leppard, and at the Guildhall School of Music and Drama in London under Bernard Keefe.

By comparison with the Third Symphony, this one is spacious and partially retreats from what seemed to be the composer's new territory. The Sonata for Flute and Piano, Opus 97, the following year is a pale reflection of the Sonatina some forty years earlier, although James Galway premiered the Sonata at the Edinburgh Festival in 1978 and recorded both works along with the Flute Concerto, Opus 36, in 1982.[33] The harmony of the outer movements has lost its distinction, but the slow movement seems closely related to the last of the *Chinese Songs*. With such a large output, no composer can be at the top of his form all the time. Berkeley has been prolific and it seems to have been natural for him to write several pieces, as composers did in previous centuries when they were not competing with the entire history of music, rather than agonise over just one or two each year. In any case the onset of Alzheimer's disease was soon to make a difference to his work. It was in 1979 that he bravely set out on another opera, *Faldon Park*, for which Winton Dean had written the libretto as early as 1971. George Harewood, Director of the English National Opera company, offered to commission it and Berkeley confided to his diary: 'This is an offer which is really too good to refuse, but to begin something on this scale at the age of seventy-six is rather daunting – shall I live to complete it?'[34] In 1980 he wrote: 'I've made some progress with *Faldon Park*, going well half-way through the first act, starting to score.'[35] By the middle of that year there was a run-through of some of the first act, but soon afterwards his illness prevented him from continuing, although a number of friends tried to help.

There were still a few characteristic short pieces to come: a Mazurka, Opus 101, for piano, commissioned by the BBC to mark the 250th anniversary of

[31] Ibid.

[32] L. Berkeley diary, 18 and 24 August 1978.

[33] *James Galway plays Lennox Berkeley*, London Philharmonic Orchestra/Berkeley, Philip Moll (piano), LP RCA Red Seal RS 9011 (1983).

[34] L. Berkeley diary, 18 June 1979.

[35] L. Berkeley diary, 1980 (no date).

Haydn's birth, although this title makes the connection with Chopin again. The final song with piano is to a French text by Louise Labé, a poet who had earlier given rise to one of Berkeley's most perfect songs, *Tant que mes yeux. Sonnet*, Opus 102, was written in 1982 'for Hugues Cuenod with love and admiration' and is a setting of a poem addressed to Venus: the last stanza is a cry of despair especially poignant from a composer who would soon not be able to compose any more.[36] Many of Berkeley's fingerprints are still here at the end of his creative life. These include the blue-note false relations in bars 2 and 3; the dominant thirteenth in bar 5; and a favourite rhythm in a regular pattern, this one shared with the 'Libera me' in the same key from Fauré's *Requiem*.

The one completed work after this is the short carol *In Wintertime*, Opus 103, written for King's College, Cambridge, and first performed at the Festival of Nine Lessons and Carols on 24 December 1983. This is close to the style of the three hymn-tunes Berkeley wrote for the Cambridge Hymnal in 1967, and shows the reduction of Berkeley's idiom to its barest essentials. It is an intriguing coincidence that the memorable rising figure which opens the carol 'I sing of a maiden' permeates the opera *Mary of Egypt* (1991) by the Berkeley pupil John Tavener.

Example 117. Sonnet, Opus 102

[36] *Faldon Park*, the planned opera with a libretto by Winton Dean, breaks off before the end of the first act and exists only as a short score. However a tenor aria, 'You married couples are all the same', was sung by Edward Byles at an 85th-birthday concert given at St Mary's, Paddington Green, on 22 May 1988.

Finally it is possible to build up a picture of the man who wrote the music through recollections from his pupils, colleagues, friends and family largely in their own words. Berkeley has been influential as a teacher in ways which have barely been mentioned here. In a letter to me on 5 March 1978, in connection with one of his visits to the University of Keele, where he was an Honorary Professor, he wrote: 'I've found that private tutorials are the only thing I'm any good at – even then, one can only advise – composition being something one can't really teach!' Through his pupils such as Nicholas Maw, Richard Rodney Bennett, John Tavener, David Bedford and many more, including his own son Michael, some of Berkeley's ideals have continued. Even the sound of Berkeley can be traced in the music of all these composers at some stage in their careers. In an interview in 1978, Bennett remembered Berkeley as 'too kind to be a good teacher' and in 1990 Michael Berkeley looked back on his father as a teacher:

> He wasn't a very good teacher for me – I think it's very difficult for a father to teach a son anyway . . . When I went to him I needed a bit of the whip so I then went to Richard Rodney Bennett, who had studied with him, and he said: 'Lennox would never be able to give you what I'm going to give you'. Which was six of the best, technically speaking.[37]

This may not matter since many of his pupils have thought of him as a saintly figure passing on the love of music as a spiritual imperative in an increasingly foreign, material age.[38] Malcolm Williamson took work in progress to Berkeley and compared him with his other teachers:

> He was very gentle and very precise . . . he was able to see right through to the heart of things . . . Elisabeth Lutyens had a marvellous sense of orchestral colour: Erwin Stein had a judicious grasp of form. Lennox had both . . . The person who could see the sound, the shape and the tidiness of the piece was Lennox Berkeley.[39]

Nicholas Maw felt that the man fitted the music and found Berkeley an 'extraordinarily charming and kind person . . . capable of genuinely appreciating things which were very far removed from his own work'. Maw particularly admired the *Five W. H. Auden Songs*, especially the setting of 'O, lurcher-loving collier', the *Ronsard Sonnets*, the *Four Poems of St Teresa* and *Ruth*. With his pupils: 'He had the most wonderful way of encouraging you in your own imaginative enterprises, which I liked very much indeed. He was remarkably encouraging. He never said you should *do* something in a certain way . . .'[40] John Manduell was also a pupil:

> His way of teaching was in a very gentle way relaxed. He was quite clear what he felt he had to help us to acquire and, of course, a lot of that derived from his own

[37] Interview with author, 29 January 1990.
[38] R. R. Bennett, 'Music Now', BBC Radio 3, May 1978.
[39] Interview with author, 22 February 1991.
[40] Interview with author, 18 October 1990.

> studies with Nadia Boulanger and the way she had instilled all sorts of technical disciplines. But he was very hesitant about prescribing: he never did really.[41]

Nicholas Maw discovered, in an amusing incident, how loyal Berkeley remained to Boulanger and that he even wanted her pupils to feel the same way:

> At the time when she came over to this country to conduct a concert I had deliberately divorced myself from the Nadia camp – because one had to be right in it or right out of it . . . I found the people surrounding her very stifling . . . and he insisted that I accompany him to this concert (Stravinsky's Violin Concerto with Menuhin and the Fauré *Requiem*) . . . Afterwards everybody had to queue up and go behind to see her and Lennox insisted on dragging me off to see her. There was tremendous affectionate greeting from him to her . . . then he suddenly turned round as said, 'of course you remember Nicholas don't you?' There was a terrible silence which seemed to last for half-an-hour but must have lasted all of three seconds and she stretched out her arms to me and said, 'I forgive you everything!'[42]

Lady Berkeley thought her husband had a great sympathy for young people and always felt that older composers should help the younger ones: 'I think he got a lot from his teaching. He said he learnt a lot from his pupils.'[43]

What Berkeley said about his own sources in 1950 should, finally, put into perspective the impact of both Boulanger and Britten which has been of such concern in this study:

> Personally I've learnt more by studying the works of the great composers than any other way. Being consumed at a very early age by a passion for music, I studied the works of Bach, Mozart, Beethoven and the other great composers in order to find out how they were made. I took them to pieces just as a mechanically-minded boy will take a motor-bicycle to pieces in order to learn how to put them together again. People tend not to realise that musical composition is first and foremost construction. It is making something. And no good craftsman in any construction starts to make anything until he is thoroughly acquainted with the qualities and the limitations of the materials he proposes to make it out of. In music the expression of emotion must indeed be there but it is incidental. I feel strongly on this point. The composer who sets out with the idea of self-expression is generally a failure and always a bore! Individuality must be there in a composer but it must be unconscious. It must be perceptible to the listener but not to him.[44]

Roger Nichols saw this as a particularly French point of view that might have come from Ravel.[45]

41 Interview with author, 27 November 1990.
42 Interview with author, 18 October 1990.
43 Interview with author, 28 January 1991.
44 L. Berkeley, 'Techniques No. 8 – Musical Composition', BBC Radio 3, 9 May 1950, BBC archives T 15324.
45 BBC Radio 3 interval talk by Roger Nichols, Sir Lennox Berkeley Memorial Concert, Aldeburgh, 21 June 1990.

In the same year as that statement Berkeley wrote a programme-note for the first performance in England of Poulenc's Piano Concerto. Once again, in writing of a respected friend and colleague, Berkeley revealed much about himself:

> In looking back over Francis Poulenc's output during the thirty years in which he has been writing, one is struck by two things: the intensely individual flavour of his music, and the way in which he has been almost completely unaffected by the various musical fashions that have sprung up during that time. Indifferent to the frowns of those for whom an intellectual approach is all-important, he has gone his own way, developing those qualities that make him stand out so sharply from his contemporaries.[46]

This type of programme note was quite different from some, as Berkeley noticed:

> I am always slightly suspicious of music that requires a long programme-note if the audience is to understand it. I have even found sometimes, when listening to a new piece – perhaps by one of our more advanced composers – that I'm beginning to get the hang of it and not doing too badly. So I have a look at the programme note for reassurance – and then I find that I can't understand it at all![47]

It was not just fashionable intellectual pretensions that Berkeley wrily deflated with characteristic humour. Malcolm Williamson recalled that he was out of sympathy with British composers such as Bax, Vaughan Williams and Elgar. I discovered this for myself on one of my regular visits to Warwick Avenue to play some of Berkeley's favourite music for him on the piano in the last year or two of his life. I thought that the Roman Catholic content of *The Dream of Gerontius* would appeal to him so I started on the Prelude. He walked out of the room and went upstairs! On the other hand Berkeley confided to his diary in 1973, after a Royal Albert Hall performance: 'Elgar's First Symphony . . . is a fine work – expert and effective scoring, but the sound very thick and over-elaborate. One can't think of any other English composer of the time who could have achieved anything else even nearly as good.'[48]

Berkeley's attitude to Richard Strauss was similar, although he went to the operas: 'I can never really like Strauss, but can't help admiring the virtuosity of the scoring and his dramatic power.'[49] Berkeley was at the Three Choirs Festival for the first performance of his motet, 'Judica me', and then heard a fine performance of Mahler's Eighth Symphony but had to admit: 'I shall never really like Mahler whole-heartedly. Though I admire his obvious musicianship and his warmth and breadth of feeling, there is something about the quality of his music and his love of the grandiose that is to me unsympathetic.'[50]

[46] L. Berkeley, programme-note on Poulenc's Piano Concerto, BBC Symphony Concerts, 8 November 1950, pp. 11–12.
[47] BBC Radio 3 interval talk by Roger Nichols.
[48] L. Berkeley diary, 5 January 1973.
[49] L. Berkeley diary, 29 October 1973.
[50] L. Berkeley diary, 2 September 1938.

It was Berkeley's economy of means that Williamson greatly admired:

> I think he is the spire which will point towards the future . . . Lennox was the cleanser. It's very easy to write a piece with millions and millions of notes. It's very difficult to write a piece with very few notes. But to make sure that they are all the right notes – this Lennox Berkeley did.[51]

Berkeley recognised this himself when he said that he had learnt from Britten 'how freshness and intensity can be found with very few notes'.[52] This also brings us back to his veneration for Mozart. In 1966 he wrote in that particularly significant article, 'Truth in Music':

> One notices with the great masters, and especially with Mozart, that they often start a work with something that is not particularly memorable; it is what becomes of this material in the course of composition that makes it beautiful and significant. It may be because of this, the transformation of a phrase when in its place within the full design, or the merging of a part into the greater whole, that music can become another facet of religious truth.[53]

A kind of musical transubstantiation, in fact, with Mozart at the centre. In 1971 Berkeley wrote: 'The older I get the more I feel that it is Mozart I most love . . . The great works of his later period have about them an infallibility, a rightness in the choice and placing of every note that seems superhuman in its perfection and beauty.'[54] After attending *Cosi* at Covent Garden he wrote: 'I tend to lose my critical faculties in listening to the great Mozart operas because of my joy in just hearing the music.'[55] And after *Figaro*: 'I must have heard it many many times but can only marvel more each time at the endless melodic invention, the perfect form of each number, and in everything the unerring aim . . .'[56] Berkeley resented Peter Schaffer's portrayal of Mozart on stage and film:

> I have to confess I've not been able to bring myself to go to the play called *Amadeus* because it seems that the author portrays him as a loutish young man given to much scatalogical language. From the little one knows about him, this is totally unlike the impression he gave in public . . . I merely have such a great respect and love for him that I cannot bear to see him brought down to their own level by lesser men. The play is really about Salieri – a composer who was respected but has to admit to himself his lack of talent when brought face to face with his great contemporary.[57]

It is hardly surprising that with such high ideals in mind that Berkeley's normal posture was a kind of self-deprecation. In 1980 the ATV Network made a film about him. He had reservations about that:

[51] Interview with author, 22 February 1991.
[52] BBC Radio 3 interval talk by Roger Nichols.
[53] L. Berkeley, 'Truth in Music', *Times Literary Supplement*, 3 March 1966.
[54] L. Berkeley diary, 22–25 January 1971.
[55] L. Berkeley diary, 21 December 1972.
[56] L. Berkeley diary, 14 January 1975.
[57] L. Berkeley diary, 15 January 1982.

> Flattering as the idea might be, I felt rather dubious about it; a composer's life is bound to be somewhat uneventful as he has to spend so much time constructing his music, scoring it, copying it etc. that he has little time for anything else. Not only this, but music is very difficult to talk about, and not many composers are gifted writers – the great exception being Berlioz, who to me was a better writer than a composer . . .[58]

As we have seen, Berkeley inherited the ingredients of his musical style but for much of his life his sources were not yet sufficiently familiar for his skill in employing them to create his own kind of pure music to be recognised. In the film Michael Berkeley asked his father what he thought people in the future would think of his music. He cannot have enjoyed such a direct question so he replied in typical, slightly evasive fashion: 'I hope they would feel something from a personality that is new to them. In other words, I would hope my music would have enough individual character to make itself felt by people who are sufficiently interested to explore other music, new music.'[59] A year after the death of his father on 26 December 1989 Michael Berkeley looked back:

> He was always at peace with his own gifts. We live in an age when the quiet personality is not very fashionable. A big splash is much more important . . . He was somebody who was quite private and didn't like too demonstrative a show of emotion. The music is the work of an impeccable jeweller, a craftsman: he didn't like baring his soul . . . Perhaps his tragedy is that he was rather too happy for too long . . . But I think he was very much a classical man and that the standards and traditions that he espoused were very much classical standards . . . although there is that naughty Frenchness that he enjoyed – Poulenc and the orchestration of Debussy and Ravel. So it's a marriage – French classicism . . . and there was an element of English reserve.[60]

In spite of this reticence Berkeley was universally loved. Basil Douglas summed him up as 'a very lovable person – as simple as that. He had no sense of grandeur of his own achievements at all. He was a very modest person, very likeable, very good fun.'[61] Lady Berkeley recognised a certain historic inevitability:

> He always felt that he'd been lucky not to have been the Earl of Berkeley. He could never then have made his own life as a composer in the musical world. He'd have had to have run the estate. Then there's the Berkeley Hunt – Lennox could never have taken that on. All in all he really honestly felt that it was a good thing that things worked out the way they did.[62]

In 1975 Berkeley confirmed this himself when he went to the funeral of his aunt, Molly, Countess of Berkeley – at Berkeley Castle: 'I took the opportunity of wandering round the castle alone and thinking that it might have belonged to me,

[58] L. Berkeley diary, August 1981.
[59] ATV Network film, 'Composers'.
[60] Interview with author, 29 November 1990.
[61] Interview with author, 28 November 1990.
[62] Interview with author, 28 January 1991.

but I suspect that I'm better off, though not materially, as I am.'[63] Yehudi Menuhin contributed a characteristically fulsome tribute to one of the many anniversary concerts in 1978 and identified Berkeley firmly in terms of his music:

> Some men are thrust meteorically upon the public, some even thrust themselves, but there are others who seem to glow and sparkle quietly, hidden stars in the galaxy, awaiting discovery of their burning light. Such a man is Sir Lennox Berkeley, a great talent in our midst, a man who has enriched the musical life of this country, a human being whom we are fortunate in being able to recognise at the ripening age of seventy-five for the extraordinary contribution he has made to his country, his profession and his friends.
>
> Lennox IS his music.[64]

After Berkeley died there were many memorial concerts and obituary tributes. Malcolm Williamson wrote:

> He was a musical *entente cordiale*. Through his ancestry, his compositions and his teaching, Lennox Berkeley, while being the most British of composers, gave us a deeper understanding and love for the greatness of our French neighbours. All of which, whilst significant, matters less to the music of our time than that he was a genius. A tiger for work with technique to burn, Lennox was able to realise his inspired intentions more than most composers. If quality means more than fame, and it ought, we must place him as a composer in a position of the highest eminence.[65]

Forty years ago, having known Berkeley's music then for more than ten years, I wrote a tribute to him for his sixtieth birthday. What I said at that time, like the best of Berkeley's music, has stood the test of time. My conclusions today, even in another century, are little different – but now I hope to have provided more evidence and from a wider range of sources:

> Berkeley is a stylist and a craftsman whose music is personal rather than humanitarian. Sometimes, as in his slow movements or songs, he creates a rare world of restrained beauty which is best revealed on its own terms: as with the music of Delius, the listener may overhear but is not compelled. His faster movements, abundant in artifice, show an external elegance comparable to Ravel . . . In an age suspicious of melody, Berkeley has asserted the primacy of song. Twentieth-century English music would be seriously incomplete without his cultivated and imaginative art.[66]

The climax of the obituary tributes to Sir Lennox Berkeley came with the Memorial Requiem Mass at Westminster Cathedral on 20 March 1990, which

[63] L. Berkeley diary, 24 August 1975.

[64] Y. Menuhin, in the programme of *A 75th Birthday Homage: Sir Lennox Berkeley CBE*, Wigmore Hall, London, 14 May 1978.

[65] M. Williamson, 'Sir Lennox Berkeley', *Independent*, 29 December 1989.

[66] P. Dickinson, 'The Music of Lennox Berkeley', *Musical Times* 104, May 1963, pp. 327–30.

was broadcast on BBC Radio 3. On that occasion Sir John Manduell's Tribute summed up Berkeley's legacy:

> Our great blessing is that no factor of human mortality can take from us the hundred and more works which, in their rich diversity, collectively represent his life's work. That diversity is – perhaps typically – exemplified in Lennox's four operas which offer through the heroic in *Nelson*, the comic in *A Dinner Engagement*, the pastoral in *Ruth*, and the classical in *Castaway* a range to satisfy any opera enthusiast. Richly complementary are the four symphonies. No less satisfying is the refreshing variety of Lennox's chamber music. No British composer has written more sensitively for the human voice or has left us songs more beautifully moulded. No British composer has written more distinctively for the piano. Of such richness and diversity is Lennox's bequest to us and to posterity. It is, moreover, all cast in a style and language unmistakably his with characteristics which we instantly identify as his and his alone – above all, perhaps, his great natural gifts as a melodist.[67]

[67] Memorial Requiem Mass for Lennox Randal Francis Berkeley 1903–89. Before the service on BBC Radio 3: Duo for cello and piano, Op. 81, No. 1 (recording by Julian Lloyd Webber and John McCabe, Oiseau-Lyre DSLO 7100). Fr. Cormac Rigby introduced the service live from Westminster Cathedral (organ – Bach: *Herzlich thut mich verlangen* and then the second of Berkeley's Three Pieces for Organ, Op. 72, No. 1). Celebrant His Eminence the Cardinal Hume, Archbishop of Westminster. Address by Bishop Gordon Wheeler; readings by Tony Scotland; and Tribute by Sir John Manduell. Lennox Berkeley: Mass for Five Voices, Op. 64; *Ubi caritas*, Op. 96, No. 2. Michael Berkeley: *Qui me dignatus est.* Lennox Berkeley: 'O that I once past changing were' (from *A Festival Anthem*, Op. 21, No. 2); Toccata for organ (from Three Pieces, Op. 72). Master of the Music: James O'Donnell. Organist: Iain Simcock. BBC Radio 3, 20 March 1990.

Appendix 1: List of works

Dramatic

Opera

Nelson, op. 41, 1949–54 (3 acts, Alan Pryce-Jones), soloists, Sadler's Wells Chorus and Orchestra/Vilem Tausky, London, Sadler's Wells, 22 September 1954

A Dinner Engagement, op. 45, 1954 (1 act, Paul Dehn), soloists, English Opera Group Chamber Orchestra/Vilem Tausky, Aldeburgh, Jubilee Hall, 17 June 1954

Ruth, op. 50, 1955–56 (3 scenes, Eric Crozier), English Opera Group Chorus and Orchestra/Charles Mackerras, London, Scala Theatre, 2 October 1956

Castaway, op. 68, 1966 (1 act, Paul Dehn), soloists, English Opera Group Chorus and Orchestra/Meredith Davies, Aldeburgh, Jubilee Hall, 3 June 1967

Faldon Park, incomplete, op. 100 (Winton Dean), 1979–83

Ballet

Ballet (untitled), 1932

The Judgement of Paris, 1938, The Vic-Wells Orchestra/Constant Lambert, London, Sadler's Wells, 10 May 1938 [Boosey & Hawkes]

Incidental music

Puppet Play and Farce: *The Seven Ages of Man/The Station Master* (Montague Slater), vc, cl, vn/dulcitone, pf, 1938, London, Mercury Theatre, 22 June 1938

The Tempest (Shakespeare), Stratford, Shakespeare Memorial Theatre, BBC Singers, National Symphony Chamber Orchestra, 20 April 1946

Jig-Saw, 1948, and *Venus Anadyomene*, 1945, 2 pf, perc, in revue *Oranges and Lemons*, London, Globe Theatre, 29 January 1949

A Winter's Tale, Stratford, Shakespeare Memorial Theatre, Shakespeare Memorial Theatre Wind Band/Brian Priestman, 30 August 1960

Film scores

Sword of the Spirit, December 1942

Out of Chaos, January 1944, London Symphony Orchestra

Hotel Reservé, June 1944, BBC Northern Orchestra/Muir Mathieson

The First Gentleman, April 1948, Royal Philharmonic Orchestra/Thomas Beecham, April 1948

Youth in Britain, April 1958

[dates are months of review]

Radio scores

Westminster Abbey (Louis MacNeice), 1941, section of BBC Northern Orchestra, London, BBC, 7 September 1941

Yesterday and Today (Phillipa Stewart Craig), 1943, Wireless Singers/Father J. B. McElligott, Evesham, BBC, 19 April 1942
A Glutton for Life (Audrey Lucas), c. 1946, ad hoc orchestra/Walter Goehr, London, BBC, 15 February 1946
The Wall of Troy (Homer/Patric Dickinson), 1946, ad hoc orchestra/Lennox Berkeley, London, BBC, 21 November 1946
Iphigenia in Taurus (Goethe), c. 1954, Welbeck Orchestra/Lennox Berkeley, London, BBC, 3 October 1954
The Seraphina (George Barker), 1956, Sinfonia of London/Lennox Berkeley, London, BBC, 4 October 1956
Look Back to Lyttletoun (Carl Brahms), 1957, English Opera Group Orchestra, Ambrosian Singers/Norman del Mar, London, BBC, 8 July 1957

Orchestral

Suite, 1927, Straram Orchestra/Walter Straram, Paris, 12 September 1929 [Novello]
Overture, op. 8, 1934, BBC Symphony Orchestra/Lennox Berkeley, London, 1 October 1935
Mont Juic, op. 9, suite of Catalan dances, 1937, collab. Benjamin Britten (op. 12), BBC Orchestra/Joseph Lewis, London, BBC, 8 January 1938 [Boosey & Hawkes]
Symphony No. 1, op. 16, 1940, London Philharmonic Orchestra/Lennox Berkeley, London, 8 July 1943
Divertimento in B flat, op. 18, 1943, BBC Orchestra/Clarence Raybould, Bedford, 1 October 1943
Nocturne, op. 25, 1946, BBC Symphony Orchestra/Adrian Boult, London, 28 August 1946
Overture, 1947, London Chamber Orchestra/Anthony Bernard, Canterbury, 27 June 1947
Sinfonietta, op. 34, 1950, London Chamber Orchestra/Anthony Bernard, London, 1 December 1950
Suite, 1953, BBC Symphony Orchestra/Malcolm Sargent, London, BBC, 6 June 1953
Suite from *Nelson*, op. 42, 1955, Cheltenham, Hallé Orchestra/John Barbirolli, 29 July 1955
Interlude from *Nelson*, c. 1955
Symphony No. 2, op. 51, 1958, City of Birmingham Symphony Orchestra/Andrzej Panufnik, Birmingham, 24 February 1959; rev. for recording, 1976
Overture, 1959, BBC Concert Orchestra/Vilem Tausky, London, 4 July 1959
Suite from *A Winter's Tale*, op. 54, 1960, BBC Symphony Orchestra/Rudolf Schwarz, Norwich, 27 May 1961
Partita, op. 66, chmb orch, 1965, Frensham Heights School Orchestra/Edward Rice, Farnham, 17 May 1965
Symphony No. 3, op. 74, 1969, L'Orchestre national de l'office de radiodiffusion télévision Française/Jean Martinon, Cheltenham, 3 August 1969
Windsor Variations, op. 75, chmb orch, 1969, Menuhin Festival Orchestra/Yehudi Menuhin, Windsor, 18 September 1969
Diana and Actaeon Waltz (*Palm Court Waltz*), op. 81/2, 1971, Welsh Philharmonia Orchestra/Lennox Berkeley, London, 22 June 1971

Voices of the Night, op. 86, 1973, City of Birmingham Symphony Orchestra/Lennox Berkeley, Hereford, 22 August 1973
Symphony No. 4, op. 94, 1978, Royal Philharmonic Orchestra/Charles Groves, London, 30 May 1978

Orchestrations

Sarawak National Anthem, orch/military band, 1941, BBC Scottish Military Band, London, BBC, 18 September 1941
Ballet: *La Fête étrange* (Gabriel Fauré), 1947, Sadlers Wells Ballet Orchestra/Constant Lambert (?), London, Sadlers Wells Theatre, 25 March 1947
Air and recitative from *Ruth* (George Tolhurst), soloists, First Orchestra and Chorus of the Royal Academy of Music/Anthony Lewis, London, 6 March 1973
Flute Sonata (Francis Poulenc), op. 93/2, c. 1976, James Galway, Royal Philharmonic Orchestra/Charles Dutoit, London, 24 March 1977

String orchestra

Serenade, op. 12, 1939, Boyd Neel Orchestra/Boyd Neel, London, 30 January 1940
Variation on an Elizabethan Theme – *Sellinger's Round* (No. 3 of collaboration), 1953, Aldeburgh Festival Orchestra/Benjamin Britten, Aldeburgh, 20 June 1953, unpubd
Antiphon, op. 85, 1973, Academy of St Martin's in the Fields/Neville Marriner, Cheltenham, 7 July 1973
Suite, op. 87, 1974, Westminster Cathedral String Orchestra/Colin Mawby, London, 1 June 1974
Elegy, op. 33/2b, 1978, arr. of Elegy, op. 33/2a, St John's Smith Square Orchestra/John Lubbock, London, 26 April 1978

Solo instrument(s) and orchestra

Introduction and Allegro, op. 11, 2 pf, orch, 1938, Lennox Berkeley, William Glock, London Symphony Orchestra/Henry Wood, London, 6 September 1940
Concerto for Cello, 1939, Moray Welsh, Hallé Orchestra/James Loughran, Cheltenham, 17 July 1983
Concerto for Piano, op. 29, 1947, Colin Horsley, London Symphony Orchestra/Basil Cameron, London, 31 August 1948
Concerto for Two Pianos, op. 30, 1948, Phyllis Sellick, Cyril Smith, London Symphony Orchestra/Malcolm Sargent, London, 13 December 1948
Concerto for Flute, op. 36, 1952, John Francis, BBC Symphony Orchestra/Malcolm Sargent, London 29 July 1953
Concerto for Piano and Double String Orchestra, op. 46, 1958, Colin Horsley, BBC Symphony Orchestra/Lennox Berkeley, London, 11 February 1959
Five Pieces for Violin and Orchestra, op. 56, 1961, Frederick Grinke, BBC Symphony Orchestra/Lennox Berkeley, London, 31 July 1962

Concerto for Violin and Chamber Orchestra, op. 59, 1961, Yehudi Menuhin, Festival Chamber Orchestra/Lennox Berkeley, Bath, 1 June 1961

Dialogue, op. 79, vc, chmb orch, 1970, Maurice Gendron, English Chamber Orchestra/ Raymond Leppard, King's Lynn, 30 July 1971

Sinfonia Concertante, op. 84, ob, orch, 1973, Janet Craxton, BBC Northern Symphony Orchestra/Raymond Leppard, London, 3 August 1973

Concerto for Guitar, op. 88, gtr, orch, 1974, Julian Bream, English Chamber Orchestra/ Andrew Davis, 4 July 1974

Choral

Choir with orchestra

Ode, SATB, tpt, str, c. 1932

Jonah, op. 3, oratorio, T, B, Tr, SATB, orch, 1935, Joan Cross, Jan van der Gucht, William Parsons, BBC Chorus and Orchestra/Clarence Raybould, BBC Broadcasting House, London, 19 June 1936

Deux poèmes de Pindare, SATB, orch, c. 1936, Oriana Madrigal Society Choir and A Capella Singers, London Symphony Orchestra/Nadia Boulanger, London, 24 November 1936

Domini est terra, op. 10, SATB, orch, 1937, London Select Choir, BBC Orchestra/Arnold Fulton, London, 17 June 1938

Colonus' Praise, op. 31 (W. B. Yeats), SATB, orch, 1948, BBC Choral Society, BBC Symphony Orchestra/Leslie Woodgate, 13 September 1949

Variations on a Hymn by Orlando Gibbons, op. 35, T, SATB, str, org, 1951, Peter Pears, Ralph Downes, Aldeburgh Festival Choir and Orchestra/Lennox Berkeley, 21 June 1952

Batter my Heart, Three Person'd God, op. 60/1 (J. Donne), S, SATB, ob, hn, vcs, dbs, org, 1962, Riverside Church Choir of New York/Richard Weagley

Signs in the Dark, op. 69 (L. Lee), SATB, str, 1967, The Festival Choir and Orchestra/Eric Saunders, Stroud, 22 October 1967

Magnificat, op. 71, SATB, orch, org, 1968, choirs of St Paul's Cathedral, Westminster Abbey and Westminster Cathedral, London Symphony Orchestra/Lennox Berkeley, London, 8 July 1968

Choir with organ

Lord, when the Sense of Thy sweet Grace, op. 21/1 (R. Crashaw), SATB, org, 1944

A Festival Anthem, op. 21/2 (G. Herbert/H. Vaughan), SATB, org, 1945, Northampton Parish Church Choir, Charles Barker/Lennox Berkeley, Northampton, 21 September 1945

Look up sweet Babe, op. 43/2 (R. Crashaw), Tr, SATB, org, 1954, Westminster Abbey Choir/William McKie, London, December 1954

Salve Regina, op. 48/1, vv, org, 1955

Sweet was the Song, op. 43/3 (W. Ballet), SATB, org, c. 1957

Thou hast made me, op. 55/1 (J. Donne), SATB, org, 1960, combined choirs/John Dykes Bower, London, 22 November 1960

Missa brevis, op. 57, SATB, org, 1960, Westminster Cathedral Choir/Francis Cameron, 12 March 1960 (also Anglican version)

Hail Holy Queen, vv, org, 1970
Adeste fideles, arr. Tr, SATB, org/pf, c. 1964
Hymn for Shakespeare's Birthday, op. 83/2 (C. Day Lewis), SATB, org, 1972, Exsultate Singers/Garrett O'Brien, London, 23 April 1972
The Lord is my Shepherd, op. 91/1, Tr, SATB, org, 1975, Choir of Chichester Cathedral, Ian Fox/John Birch
Magnificat and Nunc dimittis, op. 99, SATB, org, 1980, choirs of Chichester, Salisbury and Winchester Cathedrals/John Birch, Chichester, 26 July 1980

Unaccompanied choir
The Midnight Murk (Sagittarius), SATB, 1942, unpubd, BBC Singers/Trevor Harvey, Bedford, BBC, 20 June 1942
Legacie (J. Donne), SSATBB, unpubd
There was neither Grass nor Corn (Francis Cornford), SATB, 1944, BBC Singers/Leslie Woodgate, Bedford, BBC, 5 December 1944
Ask me no more, op. 37/1 (T. Carew), TTBB, c. 1952
Spring at this Hour, op. 37/2 (P. Dehn), SSATBB, 1953 (No. 5, *A Garland for the Queen*), Cambridge University Madrigal Society and the Golden Age Singers/Boris Ord, London, 1 June 1953
Crux fidelis, op. 43/1, T, SATB, 1955, Peter Pears, Purcell Singers/Imogen Holst, London, 6 March 1955
Justorum animae, op. 60/2, SATB, 1963
Mass for Five Voices, op. 64, SSATB, 1964, Westminster Cathedral Choir/Colin Mawby, London
Three Songs for Four Male Voices, op. 67/1 (R. Herrick/R. Bridges), TTBB, 1965, the Schubertians/Carl Zytowski, Santa Barbara, 15 March 1966
The Windhover, op. 72/2 (G. M. Hopkins), SATB, 1968, BBC Northern Singers/Stephen Wilkinson, Stonyhurst, 13 December 1971 [Novello]
Ubi caritas et amor, ATBB, 1969
Grace, SATB, 1971, Linden Singers, London, 8 July 1971, unpubd
Three Latin Motets, op. 83/1, SSATB, 1972, Choir of St John's College, Cambridge/George Guest, St Asaph, 28 April 1972
The Hill of the Graces, op. 91/2 (E. Spenser), SSAATTBB, 1975, BBC Singers/John Poole, London, 20 October 1975
Judica me, op. 96/1, SSATBB, 1978, Festival Chorus/Donald Hunt, Worcester, 2 September 1978
Ubi caritas et amor, op. 96/2, SSATB, 1980, Westminster Cathedral Choir, London, 11 July 1980
In Wintertime, op. 103 (B. Askwith), SATB, 1983, Choir of King's College/Stephen Cleobury, Cambridge, 24 December 1983

Other works
La Poulette grise, 2 children's chs, tpt, 2 pf, c. 1931, unpubd
Hymn tunes: 'Christ is the World's Redeemer' (St Columba), 1963, local choirs, Britannia Band of Derry/Lennox Berkeley, Gartan, Co. Donegal, 2 June 1963 [Novello]
'Hail Gladdening Light', c. 1963, unpubd; 'Hear'st Thou, My Soul' (R. Crashaw), 1967, Cambridge Hymnal, No. 40; 'I Sing of a Maiden' (15th cent.), 1967, Cambridge

Hymnal, No. 152; 'Lord, By Whose Breath' (A. Young), 1967, Cambridge Hymnal, No. 61

Solo vocal

Songs with orchestra

Four Poems of St Teresa of Avila, op. 27 (trans. A. Symons), A, str, 1947, Kathleen Ferrier, Goldsborough String Orchestra/Arnold Goldsborough, London, BBC Broadcasting House, 4 April 1948

Stabat Mater, op. 28, solo SSATBB, fl, ob, cl, bn, hn, hp, perc, str qt, 1947 (orch. M. Berkeley, op. 28a, 1978), English Opera Group/Lennox Berkeley, Zurich, 19 August 1947

Four Ronsard Sonnets, Set 2, op. 62, T, orch, 1963, Peter Pears, BBC Symphony Orchestra/Lennox Berkeley, 9 August 1963; arr. chmb orch

Songs with one voice and piano

Three Early Songs (J. du Bellay/13th cent. anon./C. d'Orléans), 1: *D'un vanneur de blé aux vents* (1st version) 2: *Pastourelle* 3: *Rondeau*, S/T, pf, 1924–25; *D'un vanneur de blé aux vents/The Thresher* (J. du Bellay, trans. M. D. Calvocoressi), Mez/Bar, pf, 1925 (2nd version) [OUP/Chester] 1: C. Day Lewis, Lennox Berkeley, Oxford, 12 March 1925; 2: Oxford, 16 June 1924

Tombeaux (J. Cocteau), S/T, pf, 1926, Charles Sautelet, Lennox Berkeley, Paris, 1 June 1927

Trois Poèmes de Vildrac (C. Vildrac), Mez/Bar, pf, 1929

How Love came in (R. Herrick), S/T, pf, c. 1935 [Boosey & Hawkes]

Night covers up the rigid Land, op. 14/2 (W. H. Auden), S/T, pf, 1937 [Boosey & Hawkes]

Lay your sleeping Head, my Love, op. 14/2 (W. H. Auden), S/T, pf, c. 1937, unpubd

Beacon Barn, op. 14/2 (P. O'Malley), Mez/Bar, pf, 1938

Eleven-fifty, op. 14/2 (P. O'Malley), Mez/Bar, pf, 1938, unpubd

Bells of Cordoba, op. 14/2 (F. Garcia Lorca, trans. S. Richardson), S/T, pf, 1938

Ode du première jour de mai, op. 14/2 (J. Passerat), Mez/Bar, pf, 1940

Tant que mes yeux/A Memory, op. 14/2 (L. Labé/trans. M. D. Calvocoressi), S/T, pf, 1940, Sophie Wyss, Lennox Berkeley, London, 20 February 1945 [OUP/Chester]

Five Housman Songs, op. 14/3 (A. E. Housman), S/T, pf, 1940

The Ecstatic (C. Day Lewis), S/T, pf, 1943, unpubd

Lullaby (W. B. Yeats), S/T, pf, 1943, unpubd

Five Songs, op. 26 (W. de la Mare), Mez/Bar, pf, 1946, Pierre Bernac, Francis Poulenc, London, 9 February 1947

The Low Lands of Holland (anon., ed. J. Hayward), arr. Mez/Bar, pf, 1947, Sophie Wyss, Lennox Berkeley, London BBC Broadcasting House, 12 July 1947

Three Greek Songs, op. 38 (Sappho/Antipater/Plato, trans. F. A. Wright), Mez/Bar, pf, 1951, Iris Kells, John Gardner, London, 15 March 1951

Four Ronsard Sonnets, Set 1, op. 40 (P. de Ronsard), 2T, pf, c. 1952, Peter Pears, Hugues Cuenod, George Malcolm, London, 8 March 1953; rev. 1977, Peter Pears, Ian Partridge, Stuart Bedford, Snape, 14 June 1978

Five Poems, op. 53 (W. H. Auden), S/T, pf, 1958, Alice Esty, New York, March 1959

So sweet Love seemed (R. Bridges), Mez/Bar, pf, c. 1959, Meriel and Peter Dickinson, Manchester, 30 October 1975, unpubd

Autumn's Legacy, op. 58 (T. L. Beddoes, L. Durrell, A. Tennyson, G. M. Hopkins, W. H. Davies, H. Coleridge), S/T, pf, 1962, Richard Lewis, Geoffrey Parsons, Cheltenham, 6 July 1962

Automne, op. 60/3 (G. Apollinaire), Mez/Bar, pf, 1963

Counting the Beats, op. 60/4 (R. Graves), S/T, pf, 1963, Gerald English, John Constable, London, 16 July 1963; rev. 1971 [Thames]

Five Chinese Songs, op. 78 (trans. A. Waley/R. Kotewell/N. L. Smith), Mez, pf, 1971, Meriel and Peter Dickinson, London, 22 March 1971

i carry your heart with me (e. e. cummings), Mez, pf, 1972, unpubd

Another Spring, op. 93/1 (W. de la Mare), Mez/Bar, pf, 1977, Janet Baker, Geoffrey Pratley, Chichester Cathedral, 20 July 1977

Four Score Years and Ten (V. Ellis), v, pf, 1977, unpubd

Sonnet, op. 102 (Louise Labé), S/T, pf, 1982, Janet Watson, London, 26 June 1990

Other songs

Songs of the Half-Light, op. 65 (W. de la Mare), S/T, gui, 1964, Peter Pears, Julian Bream, Aldeburgh, 22 June 1965

Five Herrick Poems, op. 89 (R. Herrick), S/T, hp, 1973, Peter Pears, Ossian Ellis, Snape, 19 June 1974

Una and the Lion, op. 98 (E. Spenser), S, srec, gamba, hpd, 1979, Elizabeth Harwood, Jeanne and Marguerite Dolmetsch, Joseph Saxby, London, 22 March 1979, unpubd

Chamber and instrumental

Three to eight instruments

Prelude-Intermezzo-Finale, fl, vn, va, pf, 1927, Aeolian Players, Gordon Bryan, October 1927, unpubd

Serenade, fl, ob, vn, va, vc, c. 1929, unpubd

Piece, fl, cl, bn, 1929, unpubd

Suite, fl/pic, ob, vn, va, vc, c. 1930, unpubd

Polka, op. 5/1, 2 pf, tpt, cym, tambour de Basque, triangle, c. 1934, unpubd arr. Polka op. 5

Trio, fl, ob, pf, 1935, Sylvan Trio, 1935, unpubd

String Quartet No. 1, op. 6, 1935, Pro Arte String Quartet, London, November 1935 [Boosey & Hawkes]

String Quartet No. 2, op. 15, 1940, Stratton Quartet, London, 5 June 1941

String Trio, op. 19, 1943, Frederick Grinke, Watson Forbes, James Phillips, London, August 1944

Trio, op. 44, hn, vn, pf, 1953, Denis Brain, Manoug Parikian, Colin Horsley, London, 28 March 1954

Sextet, op. 47, cl, hn, str qt, 1955, Melos Ensemble, Cheltenham, 11 July 1955

Concertino, op. 49, rec/fl, vn, vc, hpd/pf, 1955, Carl Dolmetsch, Jean Pougnet, Arnold Ashby, Joseph Saxby, London, BBC, 24 January 1956

Diversions for 8 instruments, op. 63, ob, cl, bn, hn, pf, vn, va, vc, 1964, Delphos Ensemble, Cheltenham, 13 July 1964

Oboe Quartet, op. 70, ob, vn, va, vc, 1967, London Oboe Quartet, London, 22 May 1968
String Quartet No. 3, op. 76, 1970, Dartington String Quartet, Dartington, 28 November 1970
In Memoriam Igor Stravinsky, str qt, 1971, John Tunnell, Peter Carter, Brian Hawkins, Charles Tunnell, London, BBC, 8 April 1972 [Boosey & Hawkes]
Canon, str tr, 1971 (contrib. to *Greetings to Sir Arthur Bliss*)
Fanfare for the Royal Academy of Music Banquet, 7 tpt, timp, 1972, Trumpeters of the Band of the Royal Marines/Paul Neville, London, 14 July 1972
Quintet, op. 90, ob, cl, hn, bn, pf, 1975, Members of the Chamber Music Society of Lincoln Centre, New York, 30 January 1976

Two instruments
Minuet, 2 rec, c. 1924, unpubd
Petite Suite, ob, vc, 1927, London, 1928
Sonatine, cl, pf, 1928, unpubd
Sonata No. 1, vn, pf, 1931, Yvonne Astruc, Madeleine Grovlez, Paris, 4 May 1932, unpubd
Sonata No. 2, op. 1, vn, pf, c. 1928
Suite, ob, vc, c. 1930, Paris, 31 May 1930
Sonatina, op. 13, rec/fl, pf, 1939, Carl Dolmetsch, Christopher Wood, London, 18 November 1939 [Schott]
Sonatina, op. 17, vn, pf, 1942, Max Rostal, Lennox Berkeley, London, 25 September 1944
Sonata in D minor, op. 22, va, pf, 1945, Watson Forbes, Denise Lassimonne, London, 3 May 1946
Elegy and Toccata, op. 33/2–3, vn, pf, 1950, Frederick Grinke, Ernest Lush, London, BBC, 27 September 1950
Allegro, 2 tr rec, 1955; arr. 2 ob, 1981 [Boosey & Hawkes]
Andantino, op. 21/2A, vc, pf, 1955, arr. *A Festival Anthem*, op. 21/2, 1945
Sonatina, op. 61, ob, pf, 1962
Introduction and Allegro, op. 80, db, pf, 1971, Rodney Slatford, Clifford Lee, 1971 [Yorke]
Duo, op. 81/1, vc, pf, 1971, Elizabeth Wilson, Kathleen Sturrock, London, 11 January 1972
Canzonetta, ob, pf, c. 1973, arr. Sinfonia concertante op. 84
Sonata, op. 97, fl, pf, 1978, James Galway, Phillip Moll, Edinburgh, 30 August 1978

One instrument
Quatre pièces, gui, c. 1928
Three Pieces, cl, 1939
Introduction and Allegro, op. 24, vn, 1946, Ivry Gitlis, London, June 1947
Theme and Variations, op. 33/1, vn, 1950, Frederick Grinke, Zurich, 8 September 1950
Sonatina, op. 52/1, gui, 1957, Julian Bream, London, 9 March 1958
Nocturne, op. 67/2, hp, 1967 [Stainer & Bell]
Theme and Variations, op. 77, gui, 1970, Angelo Gilardino, Tronzano-Vercelli, Italy, 19 December 1971 [Berben/Chester]

Keyboard

Piano

March, pf, 1924, unpubd
Mr Pilkington's Toye, hpd/pf, 1925, unpubd
Toccata, 1925, J. F. Waterhouse?, Oxford, 6 March 1926
For Vere, pf, 1927, unpubd
Piano Pieces, 1927, Jan Smeterlin, London, 1929, unpubd
Les Amoureux, Andante (Blues), Java, arr. from Ballet, 1932, unpubd
Polka, op. 5/1a, 1934, arr. Polka op. 5
Three Pieces, op. 2, 1935 [Augener/Stainer & Bell]
Three Impromptus, op. 7, 1935 [Boosey & Hawkes]
Five Short Pieces, op. 4, 1936
Four Concert Studies, op. 14/1, 1940 [Schott]
Paysage, 1944, Lennox Berkeley, London, 20 February 1945
Sonata for Piano, op. 20, 1945, Clifford Curzon, London, 28 July 1946
Six Preludes, op. 23, 1945
Three Mazurkas (Hommage à Chopin), op. 32/1, 1949, Colin Horsley, London, BBC, 23 March 1950
Scherzo, op. 32/2, 1949, Colin Horsley, Australia, 1950
Concert Study in E flat, op. 48/2, 1955, Colin Horsley, London, BBC, 20 January 1955
Improvisation on a Theme of Manuel de Falla, op. 55/2, 1960
Four Piano Studies, op. 82, 1972, Margaret Bruce, London, 9 December 1975
Prelude and Capriccio, op. 95, 1978, Roger Woodward, Cardiff, 24 February 1978
Mazurka, op. 101/2, 1982 (contrib. to Homage to Haydn), John McCabe, London, BBC, 18 March 1982

Piano four hands

Sonatina, op. 39, 1954, Michael Lindsay, Sybil Jones, Stoke on Trent, 8 July 1954
Theme and Variations, op. 73, 1968, unpubd
Palm Court Waltz, op. 81/2a, arr. 1971

Two pianos

Polka, Nocturne and Capriccio, op. 5, 1934–38
Sonatina, op. 52/2, 1959, Ashley Clarke, Nini Straneo, Rome, 26 May 1959
Bagatelle, op. 101/1, 1981, Margaret Bruce, Jennifer Bowring, London, 1 May 1983

Organ

Impromptu, 1941, unpubd
Three Pieces, op. 72/1, 1966–68, Simon Preston, Cheltenham, 5 July 1968
Fantasia, op. 92, 1976, Nicholas Kynaston, London, 1 December 1976
Andantino, op. 21/2a, org, arr. J. Bate, 1981, from *A Festival Anthem*, op. 21/2, 1945

Other

Suite for Harpsichord, 1930
Prelude and Fugue, op. 55/3, clvd, 1960

Lost works

La belle dame sans merci (J. Keats), v, pf, Oxford, 16 June 1924
Two songs: *Sonette de Ronsard* and *Les Dimanches* (anon.) v, pf, Oxford, 4 December 1924
Two Dances, pf duet, Oxford, 12 March 1925
Four Pieces for Organ, 1925
Four Pieces for Flute, Oboe and Piano, 1925
Two Songs (W. H. Auden), v, pf, C. Day Lewis, Lennox Berkeley, Oxford, 1926
Introduction & Dance, chmb orch, London Chamber Orchestra/Anthony Bernard, London, 26 April 1926
Four Pieces, chmb orch, 1926
Sinfonietta, chmb orch, 1926
Concertino, chmb orch, London Chamber Orchestra/Anthony Bernard, London, 6 April 1927
Two Pieces for String Quartet, Paris, 2 May 1930
Sonatina, vn, 1927
Symphony, str orch, London Chamber Orchestra/Anthony Bernard, 14 December 1931
Three Poems by Mary Webb, v, pf, 1938

Principal publisher: Chester Music Ltd

This list of works is based on my own catalogues brought up to date by Joan Redding for the Lennox Berkeley article in the *New Grove Dictionary of Music and Musicians: Second Edition*, 2000, and on valuable information from her and Stewart Craggs contained in his *Lennox Berkeley: a Source Book*, Ashgate Publishing, 2000, Aldershot, Hants, and Burlington, Vermont, USA. See also S. R. Craggs, *Lennox Berkeley: a Bio-bibliography*, Greenwood Press, New York, forthcoming.

Appendix 2: Writings by Lennox Berkeley

Chronological list:

Regular reports 'Music in Paris' in the *Monthly Musical Record*:
June 1929, p. 174; August 1929, p. 242; December 1929, p. 370; May 1930, p. 143; August 1930, p. 242; January 1931, p. 4; March 1931, p. 82; May 1931, p. 146; July 1931, p. 210; December 1931, p. 360; February 1932, p. 37; March–April 1932, p. 63; June 1932, p. 112; September 1932, p. 159; December 1932, p. 365; March–April 1932, p. 63; June 1933, p. 112; December 1933, p. 231; June 1934, pp. 110–11

'Britten and his String Quartet', *Listener*, 27 May 1943, p. 641

Letter in *Maurice Ravel*, N. Demuth, London, 1947, p. 177

'Open Forum: Variations on a Theme – Tonal or Atonal?' in *Music Today* 1 (Journal of the ISCM), ed. R. Myers, London, 1949, p. 145

'The Composer looks at the Opera', *Philharmonic Post* 5, March/April 1950, pp. 12–13

'Britten's Spring Symphony', *Music and Letters* 31, July 1950, pp. 216–19

'Poulenc's Piano Concerto', programme note, BBC Symphony Orchestra, 8 November 1950, pp. 11–12

'The Light Music', in *Benjamin Britten: a Commentary on his Works from a Group of Specialists*, ed. D. Mitchell and H. Keller, London, 1952, pp. 278–94

M. Cooper, 'Lennox Berkeley and his new Symphony', *Listener*, 19 February 1959

Special Correspondent, 'Mr. Lennox Berkeley on the Composer's Need to hear his own Works', *The Times*, 12 April 1959

Review of *More than Music* by A. Robertson, *Tablet*, 9 December 1961, p. 1178

'The Sound of Words', *The Times*, 28 June 1962, p. 15

'Concert-going in 1963', *Sunday Times*, 30 December 1962, p. 28

'Francis Poulenc', obituary, *Musical Times* 104, March 1963, p. 205

'Britten's Characters', *About the House* 1, no. 5, 1963, p. 14

'Boulanger the Dedicated', *Piano Teacher* 8, no. 2, 1965, pp. 6–7

'Nocturnes, Berceuse, Barcarolle', in *Frédéric Chopin: Profiles of the Man and Musician*, ed. A. Walker, London, 1966, pp. 170–86

'Truth in Music', *Times Literary Supplement*, 3 March 1966, p. 158

'Berkeley describes his Setting of the Magnificat', *Listener*, 4 July 1968, p. 25

'Lili Boulanger', *Listener*, 21 November 1968, p. 692

'Last Week's Broadcast Music', *Listener*, 13 February 1969, p. 218

'Last Week's Broadcast Music', *Listener*, 23 February 1969, p. 579

'Charles Burney's Tour', *Listener*, 5 March 1970, p. 321

'Lennox Berkeley writes about Alan Rawsthorne', *Listener*, 30 December 1971, p. 913

'Alan Rawsthorne – 1', *Composer* 42, Winter 1971–72, pp. 5–7

'A Composer Speaks – 2', *Composer* 43, Spring 1972, pp. 17–19

'Walton – yesterday', *Performing Right* 57, May 1972, pp. 18–19

Tribute to A. Robertson, in *Dear Alec – a Tribute for his 80th Birthday from his Friends known and unknown*, Worcester, 1972, p. 11

'Views from Mont Juic', *Tempo* 106, September 1973, pp. 6–7
Comments on each Prom in *Radio Times*, July 19–25 to September 20–6, 1975
'Foreword', in *Francis Poulenc, the Man and his Songs*, P. Bernac, London, 1977, pp. 11–12
'A Composer looks back', in *250 Years of the Three Choirs Festival*, ed. B. Still, Three-Choirs Festival Association, 1977, p. 45
'Maurice Ravel', *Adam International Review* 404–6, 1978, pp. 13–17
Introduction, in *Britten*, C. Headington, London, 1981
Remarks in *Bid the World Goodnight* ed. R. Ricketts, London, 1981, pp. 19–21
'Igor Stravinsky: a Centenary Tribute', *Musical Times* 123, June 1982, p. 395
Tribute in *Mademoiselle: Conversations with Nadia Boulanger*, B. Monsaingeon (trans. R. Marsack), Manchester, 1985, p. 120
Tribute in *Michael Tippett – a Celebration*, ed. G. Lewis, Tunbridge Wells, 1985, p. 21

Appendix 3: Selected writings about Lennox Berkeley

Chronological list:

G. Bryan, 'The younger English Composers – Lennox Berkeley', *Monthly Musical Record* 59, June 1929, pp. 161–2
B. Falk, *The Berkeleys of Berkeley Square and some of their Kinsfolk*, London, 1944
D. Brook, *Composers' Gallery*, London, 1946, pp. 20–2
E. Lockspeiser, 'The Music of Lennox Berkeley', *Listener*, 10 July 1947, p. 76
R. Hull, 'The Music of Lennox Berkeley', *Chesterian* 23, January 1948, pp. 61–4
M. Flothius, *Modern British Composers*, Stockholm/London, 1949, pp. 31–5
R. Hull, 'The Style of Lennox Berkeley', *Chesterian* 24, April 1950, pp. 84–7
H. F. Redlich, 'Lennox Berkeley', *Music Survey* 31, June 1951, 245–9
V. Drewery, 'Lennox Berkeley – some recent compositions', *Chesterian* 26, October 1951, pp. 1–4
A. Frank, *Modern British Composers*, London, 1953, pp. 64–68
I. Holst, 'Lennox Berkeley's Stabat Mater', *Chesterian* 28, April 1954, 115–18
W. Mellers, 'The Music of Lennox Berkeley', *Listener*, 24 June 1954, p. 1113
A. Pryce-Jones, 'Some Notes on the Text of Nelson', *Opera* 5, October 1954, pp. 595–8
W. Dean, 'Lennox Berkeley's Orchestral Music', *Listener*, 7 April 1955, p. 637
C. Mason, 'The Progress of Lennox Berkeley', *Listener*, 27 September 1956, p. 485
C. Headington, 'The Instrumental Music of Lennox Berkeley', *Chesterian* 32, Winter 1958, 82–5
H. Costley-White, *Mary Cole, Countess of Berkeley*, London, 1961
M. Schafer, *British Composers in Interview*, London, 1963, pp. 83–91
P. Dickinson, 'Berkeley on the Keyboard', *Music and Musicians*, April 1963, pp. 10–11, 58
P. Dickinson, 'The Music of Lennox Berkeley', *Musical Times* 104, May 1963, pp. 327–30
P. Dickinson, 'Lennox Berkeley', *Music and Musicians*, August 1965, pp. 20–3, 54
F. S. Howes, *The English Musical Renaissance*, London, 1966, pp. 274–7
P. Dickinson, 'Berkeley's Music Today', *Musical Times* 109, November 1968, pp. 1013–14
M. Berkeley, 'Lennox Berkeley's Third Symphony', *Listener*, 3 July 1969, p. 25
J. Tavener, 'Lennox Berkeley at 70', *Listener*, 10 May 1973, p. 625
P. Dickinson, 'Interview with Sir Lennox Berkeley', in *Twenty British Composers: the Feeney Commissions*, London, 1975, pp. 23–9
P. Dickinson, 'Berkeley at 75 talks to Peter Dickinson', *Musical Times* 119, May 1978, 409–11
D. Mitchell, J. Evans, *Benjamin Britten: Pictures from a Life 1913–1976*, London/Boston, 1978
E. Hughes, T. Day, 'Discographies of British Composers 1. Sir Lennox Berkeley', British Institute of Recorded Sound, London, 1979
P. Dickinson, 'Lennox Berkeley', *New Grove Dictionary of Music and Musicians*, London, 1980, vol. 2, pp. 560–3
E. Levi, 'Music by Lennox Berkeley – 1: Chamber Music', *WH-News* 1, 1983, pp. 2–6

W. Dean, 'Heroic Stature', *Listener*, 20 October 1983, p. 32
R. H. Hansen, 'The Songs of Lennox Berkeley', DMA dissertation, North Texas State University, 1987
J. Redding, 'A Descriptive List of the Musical Manuscripts of Sir Lennox Berkeley', MSc. (Library Science), University of North Carolina at Chapel Hill, 1988
P. Dickinson, *The Music of Lennox Berkeley*, London, 1988
R. H. Hansen, 'Lennox Berkeley: his Influence and his Songs', *NATS Journal* 46, March/April 1990, pp. 4–11, 50
M. Williamson, 'Sir Lennox Berkeley (1903–1989)', *Musical Times* 131, April 1990, pp. 197–9
P. Dickinson, 'An Unobtrusive Man: Sir Lennox Berkeley's wide-ranging achievement', *Listener*, 14 June 1990, pp. 44–5
D. Mitchell, P. Reed, eds, *Letters from a Life: Selected Letters and Diaries of Benjamin Britten*, London, 1991, passim
P. Dickinson, J. Redding, 'Lennox Berkeley', *New Grove Dictionary of Music and Musicians: Second Edition*, 2000, vol. 3, pp. 359–63
S. R. Craggs, *Lennox Berkeley: a Source Book*, Aldershot/Burlington VA, 2000 [consult this reference book for a more detailed bibliography]
S. R. Craggs, *Lennox Berkeley: a Bio-bibliography*, Greenwood Press, New York, forthcoming

Index of Works by Lennox Berkeley

Andante Blues) 1932) 20 n54, 22–4, 70
Andantino cello & piano/organ), op. 21/2 93, 93 n11
Another Spring de la Mare), op. 93 186
Antiphon, op. 85 185
Auden songs [see *Five Auden Poems*]
Automne Apollinaire) op. 60/3 182 n16

Ballet untitled) 1932) 21–3
Batter my Heart, op. 60/1 102–3
Beacon Barn, The O'Malley), op. 14/2 88
Belle dame sans merci, La Keats) 1924) 4
Bells of Cordoba Lorca), op. 14/2 87–8

Castaway, op. 68 129, 159, 171–3, 199
Chinese Songs, op. 78 181–6, 191
Concertino 1927) 12, 13 n33
Concertino, op. 49 140–1, 160–3, 165
Concerto for Cello 1939) 33, 42
Concerto for Flute, op. 36 191
Concerto for Guitar, op. 88 169, 185–9
Concerto for Piano, op. 29 70–1, 73, 76–85, 113, 158, 166
Concerto for Piano and Double String Orchestra, op. 46 78 n30, 85
Concerto for Two Pianos, op. 30 42, 73, 76, 84–5, 113, 126, 160
Concerto for Violin, op. 56 113, 164–6
Crux fidelis, op. 43/1 124

Deux Poèmes de Pindar c.1936) 35
Dianah and Actaeon Waltz [see *Palm Court Waltz*]
Dimanches, Les anon) 1924) 5
Dinner Engagement, A, op. 45 113, 128–9, 139, 142–9, 159, 171, 199
Divertimento, op. 18 8, 43 n1, 61–2, 76, 102, 113, 158
Domini est terra, op. 10 40–1, 46, 91
Duo cello & piano), op. 81/1 184

Ecstatic, The Day Lewis) 91, 100
Eleven-fifty O'Malley) 87 n3

Faldon Park, op. 100 159, 191
Fantasia organ), op. 92 85, 86 n45
Festival Anthem, A, op. 21 41, 85, 92, 93 n11, 95–8, 126, 199 n67
First Gentleman, The 1948) 61
Five Herrick Poems, op. 89 100
Five Housman Songs, op. 14/3 88–91, 99
Five Pieces for Violin and Orchestra, op. 56 113, 165
Five Poems W. H. Auden), op. 53 87, 164, 182 n16, 193
Five Short Pieces, op. 4 vii, 20 n54, 33–4, 44, 73
Five Songs de la Mare), op. 26 51, 93, 186
For Vere 1927) 8, 20 n54
Four Concert Studies, op. 14/1 63–4
Four Poems of St Teresa of Avila, op. 27 45, 76, 100–15, 118, 126, 132, 149, 158, 185, 193
Four Ronsard Sonnets, op. 40 96, 100
Four Ronsard Sonnets, op. 62 96, 100, 193

Hail, Holy Queen 1970) 179–81
How Love came in Herrick) 20, 87, 100

'i carry your heart with me' e.e.cummings) 1972) 181–2
Impromptu organ) 1941) 91
In Wintertime, op. 103 192
Introduction and Allegro two pianos & orchestra), op. 11 39, 42, 63
Introduction and Dance 1926) 8

Java 1932) 21
Jonah, op. 3 28–36, 46, 91, 129, 139
Judgement of Paris, The 1938) 41, 142
Judica me, op. 96/1 195

'Lay your sleeping head my love' Auden) c.1937) 20 n54, 39, 87 n3
Look up sweet Babe Crashaw), op. 43/2 124
Lord is my Shepherd, The, op. 91/1 126
Lord when the Sense of Thy sweet Grace Crashaw), op. 21/1 91–2
Lullaby Yeats) 91, 100

Magnificat, op. 71 41, 126, 173–4
Magnificat and Nunc dimittis, op. 99 126

Mass for Five Voices, op. 64 123 n23, 123, 199 n67
Mazurka [see Three Mazurkas]
Mazurka, op. 101 191–2
Minuet for two recorders c.1924) 8
Missa brevis, op. 57 123–5
Mont Juic, op. 9 35
Mr. Pilkington's Toy 1925) 8

Nelson, op. 41 26, 71, 100, 128–40, 149, 157, 159, 184, 199
'Night covers up the rigid land' Auden) 1937) 20 n54, 39–40
Nocturne, op. 25 89

Oboe Quartet, op. 70 181
Ode c.1932) 35
Ode du premier jour de mai Passerat), op. 14/2 85, 88, 100
Overture, op. 8 32–3, 35

Palm Court Waltz, op. 81 17, 184
Partita, op. 66 43 n1
Pastourelle [see *Three Early Songs*]
Paysage 1944) 9 n24, 76 n23, 85
Petite Suite oboe & cello) 1927) 10, 20 n54
Piano Sonata vii, 7, 60, 64–6, 73–6, 80, 91
Piece flute, clarinet & bassoon) 1929) 15
Polka [see Three Pieces two pianos)]
Prelude, Intermezzo Blues), and Finale 1927) 8 n17, 23

Quatre pièces guitar) c.1927) 185–6
Quintet, op. 90 168

Rondeau [see *Three Early Songs*]
Ruth, op. 50 104, 126, 127, 129, 139, 148–59, 163–4, 165, 171, 193, 199

Salve Regina, op. 48/1 124
Scherzo piano), op. 32/2 78 n30
Serenade for Strings, op. 12 42–7, 52, 56, 60, 63, 88, 102, 119, 158, 167, 185
Sextet, op. 47 140–1, 160
Signs in the Dark Lee), op. 69 173
Sinfonia Concertante oboe & orchestra), op. 84 43, 171, 184
Six Preludes piano) op. 23 vii, 64–74
Sonata flute & piano), op. 97 191
Sonatina guitar), op. 52/1 185–6
Sonatina oboe & piano), op. 61 166, 174, 179
Sonatina piano duet), op. 39 85
Sonatina recorder/flute & harpsichord/ piano), op. 13 50–2, 163
Sonatina two pianos), op. 52/2 85
Sonatina violin solo) 1927) 23
Sonette de Ronsard 1924) 5, 96
Songs of the Half-Light de la Mare), op. 65 100, 186
Sonnet Labe´), op. 102 192
Stabat Mater, op. 28 48–9, 76, 100, 102, 113, 115–23, 126
String Quartet No. 1, op. 6 32
String Quartet No. 2, op. 15 52–3, 180
String Quartet No. 3, op. 76 53, 179–81, 184
String Trio, op. 19 51
Suite for Strings, op. 87 185
Suite flute, oboe, violin, viola & cello) c.1930) 20–21
Suite for orchestra 1927) 2–14
Sweet was the Song Ballet), op. 43/3 124
Symphony for strings c.1931) 14, 21
Symphony No. 1, op. 16 42, 54–62, 71, 76, 88, 102, 113, 167
Symphony No. 2, op. 51 57, 73, 74 n19, 115 n15, 164
Symphony No. 3, op. 74 73, 78, 158, 169, 174–9, 184, 191
Symphony No. 4, op. 94 73, 189–91

Tant que mes yeux Labe´), op. 14/2 85, 88, 100, 182 n16, 192
Teresa of Avila Poems [see Four Poems]
Theme and Variations guitar), op. 77 185
Thou hast made me, op. 55/1 124
Three Early Songs 1924/5) 4–5, 12, 20 n54, 87–8, 182 n16
Three Impromptus, op. 7 20 n54
Three Latin Motets, op. 81/1 125
Three Mazurkas, op. 32/1 vii, 63–4, 168
Three Piano Pieces 1927) 14
Three Pieces clarinet) 20 n54, 21
Three Pieces organ), op. 72/1 86, 199 n67
Three Pieces piano), op. 2 8 n16, 28
Three Pieces two pianos), op. 5 20 n54, 26–28, 33, 64
Toccata 1925) 6–7, 20 n54, 26
Tombeaux Cocteau) 1926) 10–12, 20 n54, 88, 100, 116
Trio flute, oboe & piano) 1935) 20 n54, 21, 24, 88
Trio horn, violin & piano), op. 44 42, 78 n30, 140, 159–60
Trois Poèmes de Vildrac 1929) 15, 20 n54
Two Dances 5

Ubi caritas et amor, op. 96/2 199 n67
Una and the Lion Spenser), op. 98 163

Vanneur de blé aux vents, D'un *The Thresher*) [see *Three Early Songs*]
Variations on a Hymn by Orlando Gibbons, op. 35 100, 148
Viola and Piano Sonata, op. 22 66, 76, 91
Violin and Piano Sonata No. 1 1931) 25
Violin and Piano Sonata No. 2, op. 1 20 n54, 25–6, 51
Violin and Piano Sonatina, op. 17 51, 54, 160
Voices of the Night, op. 86 185

Windhover, The Hopkins), op. 72/2 153
Windsor Variations, op. 75 178–9

General Index

Acton, Sir Harold 7, 9
Aldeburgh Festival 74 n17, 96, 100, 115, 128, 140, 142, 147–8, 158, 171–2, 194 n45
Apollinaire, Guillaume 69
Ashton, Sir Frederick 41
Auden, W. H. 1–2, 4–5, 5 n13, 36–38, 66, 87–8, 164
  'Carry her over the water' 164
  Letters from Iceland 38
  'Lay your sleeping head' 39, 66
  'Night covers up the rigid land' 37–40, 96
  'Underneath the abject willow' 37–8
  'What's in your mind' 51, 164 n12
Augustine, St 112

Bach, J. S. 16, 30, 160, 190, 194
  Mass in B minor 12
  Brandenburg Concerto No. 3 43
Baker, Dame Janet 186
Ballet, W. 124
Banfield, Stephen 100, 139
Barbirolli, Sir John 78
Bartlett, Ethel 26
Bartók, Béla 51, 95, 167
  Mikrokosmos 73
  Music for Strings, Percussion and Celesta 73
Bate, Jennifer 86 n45, 93
Bax, Sir Arnold 195
BBC 9 n21, 10, 17, 20 n54, 29–30, 36, 52, 53 n18, 63–4, 77, 86–7, 89, 96, 115, 130, 140, 170, 181–2, 190, 191, 199
Bedford, David 99, 193
Beecham, Sir Thomas 60, 61, 64 n5
Beethoven, Ludwig van 16, 190, 194
  Piano Sonata, op. 81a 179
Bell, Clive 9
Bennett, Sir Richard Rodney 193
Berg, Alban
  Violin Concerto 33
  Wozzeck 132
Berkeley, Lady Elizabeth Freda wife) 16, 47, 76, 77, 123, 138–9, 154, 168, 170, 194, 197
Berkeley, George Lennox Rawden Seventh Earl of Berkeley paternal grandfather) 2
Berkeley, Geraldine sister) 3
Berkeley, Captain Hastings George FitzHardinge RN father) 2, 63
Berkeley, Julian second son) 125
Berkeley, Sir Lennox Randal Francis [see separate index of works by Berkeley]
  on Britten 47–50, 128
  choral works compared with Britten 92–9
  on later Britten 139–40
  friendship with Britten 29–30, 33–6
  setting same poems as Britten 36–41, 87, 182–3
  Boulanger's teaching 16–18
  compositional technique 161, 171, 182, 190–1, 194
  as conductor 78
  Desert Island Discs 190
  family 2–3, 63, 76–7, 131 n17, 185
  French influences 16, 52–3, 153, 176, 197–8
  Lennox Berkeley Society xi, 76 n24
  Monthly Musical Record reports 16, 18, 27, 185
  on Mozart 123 n21, 160, 190, 196
  Oxford 4–8, 169 n2 1
  Paris 9–15, 18, 22–4, 50
  as pianist 63, 85
  on Poulenc 69, 123, 195
  Radio Times comments 12 n32, 46 n3
  on Ravel 19, 23
  on Rawsthorne 166–8
  on recordings 74
  religious sources 16, 93, 101–2, 122–6, 174, 185

Berkeley, Sir Lennox Randal Francis *cont.*)
reputation vii–viii, 102, 115, 127–8, 170, 198–9
on Stravinsky 18–20
as teacher 193–4
temperament 155, 197
Berkeley, Michael eldest son) 2, 49–50, 61 n23, 78, 85, 101, 117 n18, 125, 138, 154–5, 158, 170, 174, 193, 197, 199 n67
Coronach 61 n23
Horn Concerto 61 n23
Qui me dignitatus est 199 n67
Berkeley, Molly Countess of 197
Berlioz, Hector 82, 197
Nuits d'été, Les 88
Bernard, Anthony x, 8, 10, 14
Bernard, Mary x, 8
Berners, Lord 1 3, 44–5, 47
Valses bourgeoises 184
Bernac, Pierre 186
Bernini, Gianlorenzo 112
Bernstein, Freda [see Berkeley, Elizabeth Freda]
Birch, John 126
Bizet, Georges
Carmen 69
Bliss, Sir Arthur 61
Bliss 22–3
The Rout Trot 22–3
Blom, Eric 129 n8, 130
Bonham Carter, Charlotte 185
Boulanger, Lili 15, 17 n39, 18, 19
Boulanger, Nadia vii, 1, 6, 8, 10, 15–17, 19, 20, 34, 36, 40, 43–4, 50, 52, 61–2, 66, 77, 127–8, 163, 181, 190, 194
Boulez, Pierre 79
Le Marteau sans maître 124
Boult, Sir Adrian 77
Bowden, Pamela 102, 106 n8
Bradshaw, Susan 76 n22
Brahms, Johannes 74
Eleven Chorale Preludes 66
Rhapsody in G minor 68
Vier ernste Gesänge 66
Brain, Dennis 159
Braithwaite, Nicholas 78 n30, 164 n11
Bream, Julian 49, 141, 170, 185–9
Bridge, Frank 1, 13, 181
Britten, Benjamin Lord vii–viii, 1–2, 4, 10, 13, 15, 29–31, 34–5, 41–2, 45, 48, 50–2, 54, 60, 63, 73, 77, 85, 87–8, 100, 115, 118, 123, 127–8, 136, 148, 153–5, 159, 169, 182–3
Albert Herring 39, 41, 49, 96, 128, 134, 147, 149
Ballad of Heroes, The 37
Beggar's Opera, The 128
Billy Budd 96, 99, 128, 139, 147
Boy was born, A 36
Curlew River 140
Death in Venice 139
Gloriana 128
Holiday Diary 67
Holy Sonnets of John Donne, The 51, 93 n10, 102
Les Illuminations 47, 50–1
Little Sweep, The 28, 149
Mont Juic 35
Missa brevis 125
'Night covers up the rigid land' 37–9
Night Mail 87
On this Island 37, 39, 88
Our Hunting Fathers 34, 36–7, 66
Owen Wingrave 168
Paul Bunyan 24, 154, 164
Peter Grimes 128, 132, 139, 140
Piano Concerto 24, 39, 47
Prince of the Pagodas, The 129
Rape of Lucretia, The 49, 114, 128, 154
Rejoice in the Lamb 92–6
Seven Sonnets of Michaelangelo 51
Sinfonia da Requiem 104–5
Sinfonietta 37
Songs from the Chinese 182–3
Spring Symphony 30
St Nicholas 31
Suite for Violin and Piano 33
Te Deum in C 95
Tit for Tat 93
Turn of the Screw, The 128, 130, 140, 163, 190
'Underneath the abject willow' 37–8
Variations on a Theme of Frank Bridge 40, 43, 84
Variations on a Theme of Purcell 35
War Requiem 38
'What's in your mind' 51
Britten, Beth 1
Britten, Edith 50
Brosa, Antonio 33
Brown, Timothy 93 n10, 126 n30
Bruckner, Anton 101
Bryan, Gordon 8, 9, 14
Buckle, Richard 184
Bucknell, Katherine 5 n13
Burra, Peter 35–6

Bush, Alan 127
Byles, Edward 192 n36

Cage, John 161
Calvocoressi, M. D. 29
Cameron, Basil 12, 78
Cardus, Neville 29
Carpenter, Humphrey 7 n15, 37, 50 n12
Carter, Elliott 17, 160
Chappell, William 142
Chardin, Teillard de 112
Chester, J. & W. [Chester Music] x, xi, 7, 26, 44, 61 n24, 93 n10, 115, 118 19, 158 n12
Chopin, Frédéric 14, 28, 64, 74, 84, 168
  Ballade No. 2 68
Cocteau, Jean 10, 116
Cohen, Harriet 28
Cole, Mary Countess of Berkeley 2
Collis, Peter 4
Cooper, Martin 74, 115, 129 n7
Copland, Aaron 15, 17–18, 79, 118, 163–4, 181
  Piano Quartet 163
  Piano Variations 84
  Symphony for Organ and Orchestra 17
Cortot, Alfred 10
Craft, Robert 19
Crashaw, Richard 91–2, 112, 124
Craxton, Janet 184
Crozier, Eric 1 49, 157 n11
Cuenod, Hugues 96, 192
Cummings, E. E. 87
  'I carry your heart with me' 182
Cunard, Nancy 9
Curzon, Sir Clifford 74

Davis, Sir Colin 79
Dean, Winton ix, 136, 159, 192 n36
Debussy, Claude 6, 16, 51, 53, 183, 190, 197
  Jeux 178
  Prélude à l'après-midi d'un faune 177
  Pelléas et Mélisande 8
de la Mare, Walter 93, 186
Dehn, Paul 142, 171
del Mar, Norman 35, 48, 60–1
Delius, Frederick 6, 60, 76, 198
  Sea Drift 73
Demuth, Norman 12
Diaghilev, Sergei 13
Dickinson, Francis 93 n11
Dickinson, Meriel vii, 10 n29, 87 n2, 164 n12, 181
Dickinson, Peter
  Auden Studies 164 n12
  Four W. H. Auden Songs 164
Dolmetsch, Carl 50–1, 160, 163
Donne, John 51, 93 n10, 102, 124–5
Douglas, Basil 29, 49, 52, 77, 89, 128, 142, 197
Drewry, Val 64 n6, 77
Drummond, Cecile Countess of Berkeley maternal grandmother)
Duchamp, Marcel 7
Dukas, Paul 10
Dusseau, Jeanne 10

Eisenberg, Maurice 42
Elgar, Sir Edward 9, 170
  Cello Concerto 42
  Dream of Gerontius, The 46, 195
  Symphony No. 1 195
Eliot, T. S. 9, 181
English National Opera 159, 191
English Opera Group 48–9, 100, 114, 128, 140, 142, 147–9, 171
Esty, Alice 164
Evans, Nancy 157 n11

Falla, Manuel de 160
Fauré, Gabriel 9, 52–3, 116, 181
  Requiem 16, 34, 194
  Pénélope 52
Feeney Trust 9 n21, 164
Ferrier, Kathleen 102, 106, 114
Finch, Hilary 130
Françaix, Jean 34
Francis, John x, 23
Francis, Sarah 164 n12
Franck, César 66, 93, 153, 174
Frank, Alan 61
Fraser, Peter 89, 92

Galway, James 50, 191
Gershwin, George 79
  Rhapsody in Blue 23
Gilardino, Angelo 186
Gill, Rev Colin 86
Glock, Sir William x, 36, 63
Goddard, Scott 1 29 n9
Goldberg, Albert 47
Goossens, Sir Eugene 78
Gounod, Charles 93, 153
GPO Film Unit 36
Green, Julian 16 n37, 112 n10
Greenfield, Edward 31, 130 n15
Greenidge, John 5
Grinke, Frederick 165
Groves, Sir Charles 78, 191

Hamburger, Paul 73
Handel, George Frideric
Zadok the Priest 41
Harewood, George 191
Harris, Aline Carla mother) 3, 131 n17
Harris, Sir James father-in-law) 131 n17
Harris, Nellie aunt) 63
Harris, Roy 17
Harris, Sir W. H. 6, 66, 86
Harvey, Trevor 92
Hawkes, Ralph 45, 88
Haydn, Joseph 58, 192
Headington, Christopher 36 n26, 76, 100 n14, 117 n18
Heenan, His Eminence the Cardinal 125, 199 n67
Herbert, George 92–3
Herrick, Robert 100
Hickox, Richard 60
Hill, Ralph 116 n16
Hindemith, Paul 168
Holst, Gustav
The Perfect Fool 95
Holst, Imogen 116–17, 121, 124
Homer
Odyssey 171
Honneger, Arthur 10, 20
Rugby 18
Cello Concerto 18
Hopkins, Anthony 115
Hopkins, Gerard Manley 153
Horsley, Colin x, 64, 69–70, 74, 77–8, 85, 136, 159
Housman, A. E. 88
Howells, Herbert 47, 116, 124
Howes, Frank 13 n34
Hügel, von 112
Hull, Robin 28, 115
Hussey, Rev Walter 92, 126, 186
Huxley, Aldous 9

International Society for Contemporary Music 32–3, 35, 40, 78, 117, 161
Isherwood, Christopher 2
Ives, Charles 60

Jackson, Sybil cousin and godmother) 3, 63
Jazz 23

Keefe, Bernard 191
King, Thea 21
Koechlin, Charles 10
Kynaston, Nicholas 85

Labé, Louise 88, 192
Lambe, Admiral Sir Charles 131
Lambert, Constant 24, 27, 78
Elegiac Blues 23
Music for Orchestra 13
Rio Grande 22–3
Lee, Laurie 173
Legge, Harry 1 91
Lennox Berkeley Society xi, 76 n24
Leppard, Raymond 191
Levi, Erik 52
Lewis, C. Day 5, 91, 100
Lewis, C. S. 112
Lewis, Sean 5
Liszt, Franz 111
Llewellyn, Grant 130
Lockspeiser, Edward 66
Lorca, Frederico Garcia 87
Loughran, James 42
Lutoslawski, Witold
Paroles tissés 99
Cello Concerto 105
Lutyens, Elisabeth 193

MacCrindle, Sheila xi, 126, 186
Mackerras, Sir Charles 149
Mahler, Gustave 60, 79, 106
Symphony No. 8 195
Manduell, Sir John 63–4, 158, 160, 184, 193–4, 199
Manuel, Roland 20
Markevitch, Igor 18
Martin, Frank
Pétite Symphonie concertante 190
Martinu, Bohuslav 18, 20
Mason, Colin 115, 139, 149
Maughan, Somerset 28
Maw, Nicholas 61, 73, 101, 193–4
McCabe, John 168 n19, 199 n67
Mellers, Wilfrid 31, 33, 44, 130
Mendelssohn, Felix 66
Menuhin, Yehudi Lord 165, 178, 194, 198
Messiaen, Olivier 106
Quatuor pour la fin du temps 121, 156, 160
Milhaud, Darius 10, 20–1
Milnes, Rodney 130 n15
Mitchell, Donald x, 130, 135, 147, 149
Mitford, Nancy 112 n10, 142
Moore, Henry 37
Morris, R. O. 1
Mortimer, Raymond 9, 76, 85
Mozart, Wolfgang Amadeus vii, 43, 46, 62, 76–7, 82, 84, 123 n21, 131–2, 141, 162–3, 190, 194
Cosi fan tutte 160, 196

Le nozze di Figaro 196
Piano Concerto K467 190

Nettleship, Ursula 40
Nichol, Jim xi, 76 n24
Nichols, R. 5 n11, 6, 101 n1, 194
Noble, Jeremy 116
Northcott, Bayan 42

Oliver, Michael 190
O'Malley, Patrick 88
Oman, Carola 139
Orr, Robin 62

Palestrina, Giovanni Pierluigi da 101, 116, 174
Panufnik, Sir Andrzej 164
Parikian, Manoug 159
Partridge, Ian 89, 96
Partridge, Jennifer 89
Payne, Anthony 184
Pears, Sir Peter x, 1, 2, 34–5, 37, 39, 45, 88–9, 91, 96, 99, 100, 140
Philipp, Isidore 10
Pierson, Henry Hugo 9
Pilkington, Vere 8
Piston, Walter 168
Plomley, Roy 8 n19, 190
Porter, Andrew 102
Poulenc, Francis 20–1, 53, 61, 68–9, 96, 116, 147, 161 n8, 186, 195, 197
Aubade 18
Gloria 68
Harpsichord Concerto 160
Le Bal masqué 20
Le Bestiaire 1 0
Nocturnes 16 n37, 68
Piano Concerto 195
Quatre motets pour un temps de pénitence 124
Sonata for clarinet and piano 151
Sonata for piano duet 13–14
Trois Pièces 67
Powell, Anthony 112 n10
Pratley, Geoffrey 186
Preston, Simon 86
Prokofiev, Sergei 82, 180
Proust, Marcel 190
Pryce-Jones, Alan 7, 26, 131 n18, 137 n24
Puccini, Giacomo
Gianni Schicchi 134
Pudney, John 4
Purcell, Henry 51, 120, 156

Radcliffe, Philip 41
Raffalli, José 33, 34, 45
Ravel, Maurice 8–9, 16, 53, 64, 76, 112, 183, 194, 197
Boléro 1 9, 23
Daphnis et Chloé 20
Habanera 93
La Valse 19
Left-hand Piano Concerto 23
L'Enfant et les sortilèges 23
Pavane pour une infante défunte 84–5
Sonatine 7
Valses nobles et sentimentales 190
Violin and Piano Sonata 23
Rawsthorne, Alan 61, 127, 166–8
Symphony No. 3 167
Symphonic Studies 167
Quintet for piano and wind 167
Redding, Joan x, 18 n47
Redlich, Hans 82, 136
Reinhardt, Django 24
Rennert, Jonathan 30
Renoir, Pierre Auguste 190
Rigby, Fr Cormac 199 n67
Robertson, Alec 25
Robertson, Rae 26
Ronsard, Pierre de 96
Rossini, Gioachino 116, 118
Roussel, Albert 12, 61
Suite in F 178
Piano Concerto 178
Rubbra, Edmund 127, 179 n11

Salieri, Antonio 196
Sampson, Anthony 2
Sargeant, Malcolm 84
Satie, Erik
Socrate 12, 115–16
Sautelet, Charles 1 0
Scarlatti, Domenico 8
Schaffer, Peter
Amadeus 196
Schoenberg, Arnold 66, 163, 170
Chamber Symphony No. 1 159
Schubert, Franz 3, 43, 72, 131
Erlkönig 91
Scotland, Tony 16 n37, 76, 131 n16–n17, 139 n28, 199 n67
Scott, Cyril
Sonatina for guitar 185
Searle, Alan 28
Segovia, Andrés 185
Sellick, Phyllis 84

Shawe-Taylor, Desmond ix, 16, 48, 85, 89, 102, 157
Shostakovich, Dimitri 49, 82, 143 n4, 170
Sibelius, Jean
  Symphony No. 5 178
Sitwells 1, 9
  Edith, Dame 27, 86
Six, Les 10, 12–13, 26
Smart, Christopher 92–3
Smeterlin, Jan 14
Smith, Cyril 84
Spenser, Edmund 163
Stein, Erwin 193
Steiner, George 1
Stevens, Denis 130
Stockhausen, Karlheinz 170
Straram, Walter 12
Strauss, Richard 54, 84, 184, 195
Stravinsky, Igor viii, 12–13, 15, 18–20, 30, 39, 41, 43, 46, 53, 66, 78, 84, 95, 127, 135, 178
  Apollon musagète 19
  Capriccio for piano and orchestra 28
  Cantata 163
  Duo concertant 19, 20, 25
  Firebird 19
  Les Noces 16
  L'Histoire du soldat 20
  Octet 18
  Oedipus Rex 29
  Perséphone 20
  Petroushka 19
  Rake's Progress, The 30
  Rite of Spring, The 19
  Serenade in A 68, 76 n22
  Symphonies of Wind Instruments 83
  Symphony in C 145
  Symphony of Psalms 18–19, 30, 118, 151
  Threni 163
  Three Pieces for clarinet 21
  Two-Piano Sonata 19
  Violin Concerto 20, 194
Stravinsky, Soulima 19
Sullivan, Sir Arthur 147
Symonds, Arthur 112
Szymanowski, Karol 117

Tavener, Sir John 101, 160, 170
  Mary of Egypt 192
Tay, Cheng Jim 182
Tchaikovsky, Pyotr Ilych 187
  Eugene Onegin 111
Temperley, Nicholas 9
Teresa of Avila 102, 112
Terroni, Raphael 76
Thomson, Virgil 17
Tippett, Sir Michael 1, 24, 67, 79, 118, 127, 179
  Child of our Time, A 31
  Concerto for Double String Orchestra 43
  King Priam 168
  Midsummer Marriage, A 128, 153
  Windhover, The 153

UNESCO 64

Vaughan, Henry 92
Verdi, Guiseppe 116, 119
  Requiem 174

Wagner, Richard 84, 137, 149
Walker, Kathleen xi, 76 n24
Walton, Sir William 1, 24, 61, 118, 127, 168–9
  Bear, The 171
  Belshazzar's Feast 30, 31, 154
  Cello Concerto 2
  Façade 18, 22, 27
  Magnificat and Nunc dimittis 126
  Symphony No. 1 34
  Troilus and Cressida 128
Waterhouse, J. F. 7
Waugh, Evelyn 112 n10
  Brideshead revisited 7
Weagley, Richard 103
Webern, Anton 163, 170
Weill, Kurt 22
  Der Jasager 23
  Die Dreigroschenoper 23
  Mahagonny 23
Wellesz, Egon 19
Welsh, Moray 42
White, Michael John 130
Whitman, Walt 92
Wilde, David 78 n30, 84
Williams, Ralph Vaughan 8, 12, 61, 92, 124, 169, 195
  Symphony No. 4 34, 46
Williamson, Malcolm 19, 73, 101, 193, 195, 198
  Hammarskjold Portrait 50
  Happy Prince, The 44
Wolf, Hugo 91
Wyss, Sophie 47, 85, 100, 115

Yeats, W. B. 91, 100